BRITISH DEMOCRACY

By ROBERT M. RAYNER, B.A.

A SHORT HISTORY OF BRITAIN. Complete in
   One Volume. With many Illustrations, and in
   parts :
             To 1485.   1714–1938.
          1485–1714.

A CONCISE HISTORY OF MODERN EUROPE,
   1789–1914. With an Epilogue 1914–1938. With
   Maps and Charts.

A CONCISE HISTORY OF BRITAIN TO 1939.
   With Maps.
             To 1603.   1714–1939.
          1485–1714.
       And Complete in One Volume.
       A short School Certificate History of Britain.

A CONCISE HISTORY OF BRITAIN TO 1934.
   With a Supplement on Great Britain in World
   Affairs, 1789–1936, by W. T. G. AIREY, M.A.

NINETEENTH CENTURY ENGLAND. A Political and Social History of the British Commonwealth, 1815–1914. With 9 Maps and 3 Folding
   Charts.

THE TWENTY YEARS' TRUCE, 1919–1939.
   With Maps.

ENGLAND IN TUDOR AND STUART TIMES,
   1485–1714. With 6 Maps and 9 Date Charts.

ENGLAND IN MODERN TIMES, 1714–1939.
   With 12 Maps and 7 Date Charts.

   Published by LONGMANS, GREEN AND CO. LTD.

───────────

A MIDDLE SCHOOL HISTORY OF ENGLAND
   (In Three Volumes).
   Vol. I., To 1485 ; Vol. II., 1485-1714 ; Vol. III., From 1714.
       Published by JOHN MURRAY.

───────────

A PUBLIC SCHOOL MANUAL OF RUGBY
   FOOTBALL.
       Published by ANDREW MELROSE, LTD.

BRITISH DEMOCRACY

AN INTRODUCTION TO CITIZENSHIP

BY

ROBERT M. RAYNER

AUTHOR OF 'ENGLAND IN MODERN TIMES,'
'THE TWENTY YEARS' TRUCE,' ETC.

LONGMANS, GREEN AND CO.
LONDON · NEW YORK · TORONTO

LONGMANS, GREEN AND CO. LTD.
OF PATERNOSTER ROW

43 ALBERT DRIVE, LONDON, S.W.19
NICOL ROAD, BOMBAY
17 CHITTARANJAN AVENUE, CALCUTTA
36A MOUNT ROAD, MADRAS

LONGMANS, GREEN AND CO.

55 FIFTH AVENUE, NEW YORK 3

LONGMANS, GREEN AND CO.

215 VICTORIA STREET, TORONTO 1

First published 1946

CODE NUMBER : 62972

Printed in England at THE BALLANTYNE PRESS
SPOTTISWOODE, BALLANTYNE & CO. LTD.
Colchester, London & Eton

CONTENTS

Whence did this happy organisation first come? Was it a tree transplanted from Paradise, with all its branches in full fruitage? . . . Let History answer. With blood it was planted; it was rocked in tempests; the goat, the ass and the stag gnawed it; the wild boar has whetted his tusks on its bark. . . . The whirlwind has more than once forced its stately top to touch the ground; it has been bent like a bow and sprang back like a shaft. Mightier powers were at work than expediency ever yet called up: yea, mightier than the mere understanding can comprehend.

COLERIDGE.

When we contemplate our institutions in their monumental dignity, and the world-wide span of our Empire— it would be a mean thing to take stock of our inheritance without asking how we came by it. But it is not possible to do so. . . .

ANSON.

BRITISH DEMOCRACY

PREAMBLE

AN APOLOGY FOR THE STUDY OF CITIZENSHIP

MEN and women are by nature citizens. They cannot bring out the best that is in them except in association with others, under a government.

Until man learned to live in society his life was ' solitary, poore, nasty, brutish and short.' He could raise himself from this condition only by learning to co-operate with his kind. The commodities and services which make up civilisation are social products.

But full citizenship is possible only in a democracy—a state governed by the majority-votes of its subjects. ' Democracy ' was once an expression of disgust, synonymous with mob-rule, the end of everything noble and orderly and good; and it became so again in Fascist Italy and Nazi Germany. It is true that Parliamentary government has its seamy side and requires a long political apprenticeship ; but no form of government has yet been devised which gives so many people so much scope for the good life.

' It is by words that men are ruled,' wrote Disraeli ; but in this book we shall try to see what words really stand for. When we say with Abraham Lincoln that democracy is rule for and by the people, do we imply that certain of the United States of America and of the Provinces of South Africa are not democratic because they exclude from full citizenship the races that form the majority of their population ? Or that France under the Third Republic was no democracy because it denied the vote to women—also a majority ? Some of our American friends dispute our claim to have democratic government because we have a King and a House of Lords. But is democracy identifiable with republicanism ? That would make the disguised dictatorship of swarthy generals in Latin America truer democracies than Norway or Holland. Which is, of course, absurd.

B

Democracy, then, is a machine by which nations govern themselves. But if they will not take the trouble to understand how it works, to apply the power that drives it and to keep it in running order, it falls into decay and becomes positively dangerous. This is a responsibility we all have to share. It is sometimes irksome, but if we shirk it we sell the pass to the enemies of liberty, as the wretched Italians and Germans did when they wearied of the effort to make their democracies work. Their excuse must be that they lacked the long traditions of 'freedom slowly broadening down.' The national qualities required for self-government are not created in a decade, or in a century.

The working of our own governmental machine is more difficult to understand (and therefore more interesting) than that of any other form of democracy. For all other constitutions have been designed in accord with the teachings of political science (based largely on the experience of Britain). But ours has gone on growing and developing, with an inward life of its own, ever since the Anglo-Saxon invasions. It has grown up with our nationhood into forms which suit our circumstances and national character. It is full of bits and pieces which have been added or put to new uses as need arose ; for it is a deeply ingrained trait in British human nature to try to 'make do and mend' rather than start afresh. That is why to understand the present working of our institutions we have to inquire into their past. The constitutions of the French and Swiss Republics, of the United States, or our own Dominions, of the Scandinavian monarchies and of the U.S.S.R. can each be printed in a neat little pamphlet. But ours could not be contained within the covers of any book, or put into any tangible form. For it consists in a mass of customs and traditions and statutes, always in process of transformation and development. It behoves us all to do our part in keeping the process going on the right lines. We shall be failing in our duty to our ancestors and our descendants if because we are lazy or uninterested or cynical we neglect or ignore it. And we have been warned : we have seen what happens to other nations who do so.

It is in this spirit that we embark on the study of Citizenship. Since our institutions arose spontaneously we must give at least a glance to their origin and early stages. Then we must investigate their present working, always bearing in mind that things are not always what they seem. We must also know something of other institutions which powerfully affect our lives as citizens—Trade Unions, the Social Services, and the administration of the Law. Thereafter our survey will turn to the Empire for which we are responsible and the Dominions which people of our race have set up overseas—not averting our eyes from the difficult problems set by Ireland and India. Finally, since we can no longer suppose that we, or the Commonwealth, or any other nation or group of nations can live in isolation, we must have some notion of other forms of democracy, totally unlike our own, which have arisen in America and Russia ; the more so because the future of the human race depends upon our co-operation with them.

CHAPTER I

THE ROOTS OF DEMOCRACY

HOW THEY GERMINATED AND SPREAD UNDERGROUND

OUR democracy is little more than a century old. This does not contradict its claim to ancient origin : it is like a coral reef that builds itself up for centuries before it shows above the surface. Down to 1832 the government of these islands was in the hands of land-owners. There was a property-qualification for the Members of Parliament who controlled national affairs and for the Justices of the Peace who controlled local affairs ; and whatever such a system may be it is not democratic.

Thus our present regime has grown up since the first Reform Act ; but the shape it has taken has been pre-determined by forces at work for ten centuries.

FEUDALISM.—The association of land with power arose from what was once a physical fact. To till the soil, or have it tilled for one by others, was the first essential of life. In feudal times this took the form of ' land for service.' The expression ' feudal system ' was invented by historians, and they have had much disputation as to how it worked, for it left very scanty written records. But we shall be safe in assuming that, broadly speaking, the unit of feudal holding among the warrior class was a self-contained, self-supplying ' manor,' coinciding more or less with what we now call a village (though an ugly squalid ill-kept one, by modern standards), and with what we now call a parish—an area served by a priest and his church. And (leaving out of account local variations) it will be true to say that the King granted estates to tenants in return for military service ; that some of the greater tenants (we will call them ' Barons ' for short) sub-let individual manors to ' Knights ' (a generalised term for one-manor men), also in return for military service ; and that Barons and Knights granted strips of their manor-lands to ' villeins ' for agricultural service. Thus everyone's place in society depended on the land he held.

As every baron had a military following it was easy for him to make war on his neighbours, or to join with them against the King. This feudal anarchy was the bane of the Middle Ages ; it checked all progress in material prosperity and civilisation. England was better off than other countries, in having a number of strong and able kings, who, whatever their failings in other directions, had the will and the character to be masters of the realm. And a strong king was a good king. If he ruled with a rod of iron, it kept in order local magnates who in those days of slow and difficult communications were in general far worse tyrants than any king could be.

One of the most highly-prized feudal privileges (*libertates* as they were called in Magna Carta) was the right to hold courts of law ; for this not only raised the holder's power and importance, but enriched him with fines and fees. ' Knights ' held petty sessions on their own manors, and once a quarter attended a County Court where they were presided over by some great noble.

But the King soon contrived to build up the idea that *he* was the fountain of justice, and that evil-doers had broken *his* peace. As early as the reign of Henry I royal officials began to go round three or four times a year to the county-towns to deal with crimes and disputes brought before them by the sheriff (the King's special representative among the landowners of the shire). And about the middle of the fourteenth century Edward III appointed one-manor ' Justices of the Peace ' to do justice in his name in their own villages.

THE DECAY OF MEDIEVAL CIVILISATION.—This growth of royal power weakened the feudal system, but what finally shattered it was the increasing use of money. In pure feudalism money was scarcely required, but developing civilisation created needs quite beyond the range of ' land for service.' As time went on men devoted themselves more and more to making things to sell ; and this could be done to advantage only in the towns which now began to grow up at cross-roads and river-fords and hill-gaps. Some of these towns were on the lands of the Church or of great nobles, but the King got as many as he could into his own hands. And he had the great advantage that he could grant them what they most wanted—

a royal charter of ' incorporation ' as boroughs. It was troublesome for the landlord's steward to have to collect dues from individual burghers and equally troublesome for the burghers to have the steward poking his nose into their workshops and warehouses. But the King could give them permission to elect a mayor and corporation to act for them collectively and to do justice among the citizens.

As town-life and trade grew in complexity, those engaged in each industry formed ' gilds,' to prevent undue competition, to ensure that their trade should not be overcrowded, and to keep up proper standards of measure and quality. The leading officers of these gilds were often the members of the corporation ; but nobody designed borough government—it grew up according to local needs and circumstances.

Of course government, local and national, was a much simpler business then than now. The Church did something in a desultory and haphazard way for the relief of the poor and sick, and a few children were taught their letters in monastery cloisters with a view to becoming clergymen. But the care of roads and bridges and housing and sanitation was nobody's business ; there was no army or navy or diplomatic service. The ' Government ' consisted of half-a-dozen ministers—all clerics, for laymen could not read or write.

But as civilisation advanced the duties and expenses of government grew. It was the essence of feudalism that the King should ' live of his own,' *i.e.* on the produce of his own manors and the feudal dues paid by his tenants. This now became impossible. Kings began to need *money*—more and more of it, especially in war-time. Yet it was impossible to collect taxes unless the tax-payers agreed to them after hearing about the King's needs and purposes.

This was the origin of Parliament. Kings had from Anglo-Saxon times summoned assemblies of magnates two or three times a year to consult them on affairs of the realm (and perhaps to keep an eye on them) ; and during the thirteenth century other classes were sometimes invited to send representatives. But in 1295 Edward I found himself in exceptional difficulties, with a French war and a Scottish rebellion on at the same time. So he held the largest and most representative parliament ever seen. He summoned the great tenants-in-chief—the earls and barons and abbots and bishops—by name, and he gave instructions to the Lord Chancellor to see that two knights should be chosen in each shire-court and two burghers in each borough. The importance of this famous Parliament was not what it was or did in itself, but the fact that men afterwards looked back to it as a ' Model.'

Much the same is true of the Great Charter. Actually it merely limited the feudal rights and payments which King John was entitled to demand from his tenants ; but to later generations, who did not realise that the *libertates* it guaranteed were licences to the nobles to do pretty much what they liked on their own domains, it seemed a guarantee for all time of the foundations of civil liberty— No Taxation without Representation, Trial by Jury, and the existence of fundamental laws which no king can override.

Still, such historical illusions can, by swaying the thoughts and actions of men, be more important than truths—*e.g.* the ' Aryan ' myth in Hitler's Germany.

The scene at these medieval parliaments was something like the Opening of Parliament to-day. The King was on his throne, his ministers at hand, his clerks at the table in front, the nobles ranged on one side, the bishops on the other, the commons standing bare-headed at the end of the hall. The King explained his situation, his intentions and his needs ; the several ' estates ' then drew off the confer separately. The first thing the Commons did was to elect a Speaker to preside over them and act as their spokesman.

One vital characteristic of later parliaments did not take shape until fifty or sixty years after the ' Model.' At that assembly there had been three Estates—Clergy, Nobles, Commons—like the French States-General. It was not until the time of Edward III that the ' Knights of the Shire ' ceased to hang on to the Nobility and joined the Burghers. They were certainly more like Nobles than Burghers in social position ; but on the other hand they resembled the Burghers in the fact that they did not attend as individuals but as the representatives of communities—' communes.' The two elements of the later House of Commons were now conjoined, though right down to the days of Pitt and Fox the ' County Members ' preserved their distinction from mere ' Borough Members ' by appearing in the House in top-boots.

THE TUDOR ' JUSTICES.'—In the fifteenth century a disputed succession and the rivalry of the Roses let the nobles get out of hand, and the resultant chaos made the nation welcome the despotism of the Tudors. The growth of commerce and the use of money were rapidly dissolving the remnants of feudalism, but the power and prestige associated with land-owning remained. Indeed it grew stronger than ever ; for men who had made fortunes in trade bought up estates thrown on the market by the dissolution of the monasteries, and thus injected fresh blood and energy into ' the landed classes.'

But the bugbear of the sixteenth century was the bad times resulting from the general rise in prices due to the influx of American gold and silver, and the unemployment caused by the turning of arable into pasture. There was destitution on a scale unknown in the Middle Ages, when every man had his place, however lowly, in the community ; and there were now no monasteries to relieve the sick and needy. The Council issued edicts and Parliament passed acts by the score, but the Government lacked money to pay officials to carry them out. All the work had to be piled on to the unpaid Justices of the Peace. They were made responsible for local roads and bridges and gaols ; for seeing that people went to church ; for binding boys apprentice to craftsmen (now that the old gilds were decaying) ; for the relief of the poor, and the punishment of sturdy vagabonds. Minor offences the Justice of the Peace tried in Petty Sessions, usually in his own manor-house, without a jury, aided by his lawyer-clerk who generally acted as man-of-business for the estate. Four times a year he travelled to the county-town and met his brother Justices at Quarter Sessions, to try more serious cases and to form a Grand Jury to ' present ' persons charged with felony at the Assizes. And all these manifold duties he performed gratis, merely from public spirit and for the honour of belonging to the ruling class.

The climax came in the closing years of Elizabeth, with the famous ' Elizabethan Poor Law.' Hitherto attempts to tackle the problems of poverty had been only piecemeal. It was felt to be not only un-Christian, but unsafe, to let people starve ; but there was as yet little regular taxation, and the revenue was too small for the poor to be relieved from the Treasury. So private charity had to be organised and made compulsory. The Justices were now ordered to collect a rate from all holders or owners of land in the parish, and to appoint ' overseers ' to administer the fund so raised.

The facts that the parish was made the unit for Poor Relief is the reason why to this day paupers are said to ' go on the parish,' although the parish has long ceased to have anything to do with the matter.

PARLIAMENT WINS SOVEREIGN POWER.—By the time James I became King internal order was secure, external dangers had receded, and the parliamentary classes were beginning to resent the royal dictatorship which their ancestors had welcomed. But the new King was bent on continuing and extending it, not as a mere expedient but on a theory that monarchy was the divinely appointed government for mankind. His challenge was taken up.

In every state there must be a sovereign-power—a power whose decisions no one, in the last resort, can gainsay. The seventeenth century was to see Parliament establishing itself in this position, in fact if not in theory, not so much through thought-out principles and planned events as through a succession of disputes about practical issues. The bases of the constitution had been laid during the thirteenth and fourteenth centuries, and in the struggles which now ensued each party maintained that it was merely maintaining ancient rights. There was no historical precedent for a legislature exercising sovereign power, but Parliament had the advantage of a price-revolution which made it impossible for the King to carry on the government without the taxes which it alone could grant. Its resistance to the Stuart kings consisted largely in preventing them from collecting revenue not so authorised.

These disputes coupled with religious questions into which we cannot enter here, led to a civil war ending in a Republic. The King's trial on a charge of treason laid bare the real significance of the quarrel, for treason is action against sovereign power. In his speech on the scaffold Charles put the case for monarchy in a nutshell :

' For the people, their liberty . . . consists in having government by which their lives and goods are most their own. It is not their having a share in the government ; that is nothing pertaining to them. A subject and a sovereign are clear different things.'

Those who cut off his head thought otherwise.

The nation—or those strata of it that were articulate—longed to return to its traditional government by King, Lords and Commons ; but the Restoration could not obliterate the effects of the past twenty years. It was a compromise though nobody said so and very few even realised it. Henceforth though the outward signs of sovereignty were still held by the monarchy the reality was held by Parliament.

This situation was advanced a long stage further when James II united the whole nation against him by attacking the privileges of the Church of England and such cherished guarantees of liberty as *Habeas Corpus* and the independence of the judges.

Habeas Corpus, finally defined in an Act of 1679, prevents the Government from keeping prisoners in gaol without public trial by the law of the land. But no legal safeguards are any use if the King can control the law-courts.

The result was the Revolution of 1688, when Parliament imported a foreign King on terms that would ensure its own supremacy. The formal contract was the famous Bill of Rights ; but, characteristically, the statute made no mention of principles ; it merely forbade certain unlawful practices—the suspension of laws, the collection of taxes without parliamentary sanction, and so on. The British mind instinctively feels that to affirm abstract rights achieves nothing ; it relies on the power to enforce particular rights and avert particular wrongs. (For instance, the regular summoning of Parliament was ensured by making the existence of the army depend on an annual Mutiny Act.) Thus the Revolution attempted no clean cut with the past ; it merely cleared obstacles from a road the nation had long been travelling.

This is not to say that *nobody* saw the principles underlying the Revolution. The publication of Locke's Treatise on Civil Government (1690) drafted many years earlier, was designed to justify the Revolution after the event. It dominated the political thinking of Europe for a hundred years, and the American colonies and France put into practice its basic doctrines—the sovereignty of the people and the dependence of government on the consent of the governed.

THE RISE OF ' RESPONSIBLE GOVERNMENT.'—The next problem to be solved by this trial-and-error fumbling was to find a way for Parliament to control the ministers in the day-by-day business of government. The solution, gradually evolved in the course of the next century, was for executive power to be held by a Cabinet collectively responsible to (*i.e.* dismissible by) the House of Commons.

It is now that the Cabinet, in the modern sense of the word, began to take shape. Charles II and William III had paid little regard to Parliament in the matter. The Privy Council had grown too unwieldy to conduct public affairs. Committees of it had been given charge of specific business—*e.g.* the Board of Trade ; but ministers were chosen by the King from it at his own will. They came together to discuss policy under his chairmanship more often after than before the Civil War, but there was no bond of union among them.

Under Queen Anne there was a new development. In 1703 the Queen dismissed the anti-war Tories to please the Marlboroughs, and in 1710 she dismissed the pro-war Whigs to make peace. In each case her action was endorsed at the next general election ; and by the end of her reign it was beginning to be assumed that the Cabinet was a coherent body of one mind about public policy. But it remained the Sovereign's Cabinet ; its relationship to Parliament was still very hazy.

The haze gradually cleared—again from the force of circumstance—in the course of the next half-century. The link between Parliament and Ministry, between Legislature and Executive, was found in the emergence of a Prime Minister, and in the hardening of Cabinet solidarity. These processes were stimulated by the accession in 1714 of the House of Hanover. For George I, and to a lesser degree George II, being accustomed to very different conditions in their German home-state, found the complications of British politics incomprehensible and disgusting, and were glad to leave them in the hands of their English ministers. And these ministers were necessarily Whigs, for the Tories had been reluctant to accept the Hanoverian Succession. Furthermore George I, being unable to follow the Cabinet's discussions, stayed away from its meetings ; which meant that one of the ministers had to take the chair and act as intermediary between Cabinet and King. And another stroke of fate put into this position a statesman most able and eager to build up his personal authority. Walpole got rid of colleagues who ventured to disagree with him ; and in 1733 he dismissed from office all who had opposed his Excise Bill. The idea of a ' Prime Minister' still aroused great jealousy in the House, and Walpole always denied that this was his position ; but it was a *fact* ; and so was the Cabinet-unity by which he kept himself in office. Other signs of a changing outlook were that, avid as Walpole was for power, he resigned at once when defeated in the Commons, that the King could not keep him (or, later Carteret) in office against the will of the House and that he was the first English statesman to remain a member of the Commons all his active political life.

The terms ' Whig ' and ' Tory' indicate the gradual shaping of the two-party system which was now becoming another feature of British governmental machinery. It is essential to that system that there should be a coherent party out of office, with a policy which it is trying to persuade the nation to adopt —a party which keeps a searching light playing on everything done by the party in office.

In these formative years, 1714–1743, the Whig ascendancy was maintained by great landlords who were members of the House of Lords and controlled the elections to the Commons in the boroughs on their estates. In many constituencies it was easy for the local magnate to bribe or bully the electors (often only a dozen or so) into voting as he told them. There was always a number of these landed aristocrats in the Cabinet, and their ministerial power enabled them to keep their supporters in good humour by Government jobs and pensions. It was the golden age of landed property.

THE BIRTH OF DEMOCRACY.—By 1760 Cabinet responsibility had taken such firm hold that when it was at last put to the test of determined opposition its roots had gone deep enough to withstand the strain. But perhaps it was fortunate that the resistance came from a King who though very determined was not very intelligent. George III set himself to restore the royal control over the Executive which his grandfather and great-grandfather had let slip from their grasp. But he allowed himself to be drawn into a quarrel with the American Colonies. This was *his* policy, it led to *his* war, and he obstinately pursued them despite the misgivings of the ministers he put into office to carry them through. If the American Rebellion had been suppressed the development of the British Constitution would have been deflected if not checked. (That was one reason why the Whig Opposition in Parliament rejoiced at its successes.) But the loss of the Colonies took the wind out of the King's sails, and he was glad to save what he could from the wreck of his designs by the compromise personified by young Mr. Pitt. Pitt was a new kind of Tory. He refused to be another Lord North, kept in office by royal power against public feeling ; his position was always that of head of a Cabinet dependant for its authority on Parliament. Though now and again he found it expedient to give way to royal whims, it was he and his colleagues who ruled the country. And King George clung to him lest worse things—e.g. Charles James Fox— should befall.

The next thirty years, lit up in the military field by the deeds of Nelson and Wellington, were a stagnant interlude in constitutional history. Little further progress could be made so long as Parliament and Government were monopolised by a landed oligarchy. The idea of making them democratic by reforming the electoral system was ' in the air ' ; Pitt himself had thoughts of it. But the classes in possession would not easily be ousted from their privileges ; and all hope of this was put back indefinitely by the outbreak of the French Revolution, especially when it began to spread its doctrines into other lands by force of arms and actually declared war on Britain (1793). Any move towards increasing the power, or even improving the lot, of the working-class could now be made to look like playing with fire. ' Democracy' became a word of mingled contempt and horror, like ' Bolshevism ' was to western Europe after the first World War. Only Fox and a handful of his friends kept the torch of liberalism alight. And the immediate effect of the Industrial Revolution was in the same direction. Mass-production, which could be expanded indefinitely when steam-power was applied to it, created a new rich class and a new middle-class determined to keep ' the mob ' from becoming dangerous.

Yet in the end these two revolutions made parliamentary reform inevitable. For the doctrines of Liberty, Equality and Brotherhood brought inspiration, and hope, and a demand for a democratic Parliament as the first step towards better times for the poor and humble. And men who were making money out of the new industries resented being shut out of political power merely because they did not belong to the " landed classes."

At last the waters piling up behind the dam swept it away. In 1830 a Whig Ministry pledged to Reform gained office ; sheer weight of public feeling enabled it to force the Reform Bill of 1832 through the House of Commons by a general election, and through the House of Lords by the threat of creating enough new peers to vote the opposition down.

Thus we have reached the great day towards which all the events of this chapter have been tending. British democracy was now born. It was as yet but a weakly infant. The Act deprived very small boroughs of their members and gave them to large ones created by the Industrial Revolution ; and it gave the vote to all householders who paid £10 or more a year rent. This was a sad disappointment to the working-people whose efforts had done so much to force it through ; for very few of them paid as much as £10 a year rent. Its main effect was to compel the landed classes to share their power with the employers and the professional men who were living, directly or indirectly, on the new industries. Still, it was the first step, and the first step is always the hardest in such matters.

CHAPTER II

EARLY STAGES IN LOCAL GOVERNMENT

HOW IT GREW, STEP BY STEP, WITH PARLIAMENTARY GOVERNMENT

THE agitation that carried through the Reform Bill quickened the feeling that it is the duty of government to make life livable for the governed. This philanthropic spirit had survived the ' anti-Jacobin ' dread of Revolution, and it was now outliving *laissez faire*, the doctrine that the less the Government interferes with ' the natural law of supply and demand ' the better.[1] Thus the first reformed Parliament put through a whole series of overdue social reforms. The Government now had to get into closer touch with the nation. Hitherto its chief contact with the common people had been to punish them for misdeeds by means of judges, magistrates and hangmen. But to apply the new laws it had to develop elected bodies working in conjunction with paid officials. It is with the beginnings of this evolution that we are concerned in this chapter.

BOROUGH COUNCILS.—The first step was to make Town Councils represent the ratepayers, as Parliament now represented (more or less) the taxpayers. Many towns had old charters vesting the civic property (which often included endowments for schools and hospitals and almshouses) in a corporation which co-opted new members whenever a vacancy occurred, and took care to keep membership within the circle of a few families. For, being responsible to nobody, they often neglected the interests of the town and spent its revenues on feasting (hence the euphemism ' corporation ' for a well-lined

---

[1] One characteristic form of this doctrine was taught by Malthus in his *Essay on Population* (1803)—that people will always increase and multiply up to the limit of the subsistence available for them, and that the poor are therefore condemned to be for ever on the brink of starvation, except in so far as famine, pestilence and war check the increase of population. The only flaw in this argument (which was used by the well-to-do as an excuse for doing nothing to improve conditions for the poor) is that the assertion is not true. It is not the very poor, but people who are doing pretty well and are hopeful of doing better, who restrict their families.

waistcoat), or on sinecures for themselves and their dependants. But the new spirit disregarded a system (or lack of system, for no two boroughs were exactly alike) whose only justification was that 'it was always thus,' and the *Municipal Corporations Act* (1835) created the framework of town-government as it is to-day. The rate-payers were to elect Town Councillors to hold office for three years, while the Council was to elect aldermen (not more than a third of their number) to serve for six years and a Mayor to serve for one year.

The immediate effect was not so startling as might have been expected. Almost the only actual obligation laid on the new corporations was to employ a police force on the model which Peel had just adopted for London. The other powers given to the Councils by later Acts were mostly permissive : they *could* provide water, lighting, sewers and so on, but it took time for public spirit and civic pride to reach the level of paying for these amenities by increased rates. Still, all this followed in the course of the next half-century, and it was the Act of 1835 that made it possible. It has been said that indirectly it did more to improve the daily lives of common people (like us) than any other measure ever passed.

THE NEW POOR LAW.—The boroughs might have gone unreformed a little longer, but in another matter the need for reform was urgent and immediate. The old Elizabethan Poor Law had fallen to pieces. In the last years of the eighteenth century rural destitution (mainly due to the large-scale farming which had accompanied the concentration of industry in towns) seemed likely to lead to a 'Jacobin' revolution. In dread of this the Berkshire magistrates meeting in an inn at Speenhamland, just outside Newbury, adopted a scheme to make up wages out of the Poor Rate to subsistence level, according to the size of families and the price of bread ; and their example was quickly followed over a great part of the country. The results were dire. Farmers no longer had to pay a living wage—those who tried to do so could not compete with those who did not. Wages fell until no labourer, however hard-working and thrifty, could live without ' parish relief.' It meant the death of independence and self-respect for millions of English men and women. And the farmers and their landlords did not really benefit by the system, for the Poor Rate soared until in some districts it was higher than the annual value of the land.

By 1830 the situation had become impossible, and a Royal Commission was set up to consider what was to be done.

A Royal Commission is the means by which the Government often inquires into a subject on which it proposes to legislate. It consists of a small body (from three to a dozen or more) of Members of Parliament and others, representing all political groups, who are interested in the matter in hand. Sitting usually in a room in the Houses of Parliament, it calls before it people who know the facts and have suggestions to make. Then, after discussion, it draws up a Report, reviewing the evidence and making recommendations. (If some members disagree with the recommendations they can make a ' Minority Report.') All this, together with the evidence *verbatim* (often running into tens of thousands of questions and answers) is printed in a ' Blue Book,' which is circulated among Members of Parliament and can be bought very cheaply by the public. The Report—whether the Government acts upon it or not —is bound to have an important influence on the ministers, on Parliament, and on public opinion generally.

This Commission was dominated by Edwin Chadwick (1800–1890), a man of vigorous personality who, as a disciple of Jeremy Bentham, was convinced that all human ills could be cured by legislation designed to promote ' the greatest good of the greatest number.' The Report—really the work of Chadwick—proposed to cure the disease by the most drastic surgery : to stop all ' outdoor relief' completely and immediately, and to send the destitute into ' workhouses ' to be maintained by ' unions ' of neighbouring parishes. In these workhouses, conditions were deliberately to be made more unpleasant than the worst conditions outside—families were to be separated, for one thing. Then employers would *have* to pay a living wage, and labourers would *have* to find work to make life worth while. The new system was to be administered, not like the old Poor Law by magistrates, but by ' Guardians of the Poor ' elected by the ratepayers, who were to appoint overseers and workhouse officials, and were to act under the supervision of a central ' Poor Law Commission ' sitting in London.

A *Poor Law Amendment Act* on these lines was passed in 1834, Chadwick himself becoming paid Secretary to the central

c

Commission. Some such reform was doubtless necessary, and after a time matters adjusted themselves, as Chadwick prophesied ; but meanwhile the Act caused terrible suffering. Seas of bitter tears were shed, and curses both loud and deep fell upon Chadwick and his ' Bastilles.' Chadwick did not care. He drove relentlessly on, impatient of opposition. But he made enemies of everybody with whom he came into contact ; and this failing crippled his life's work. It had been a weakness of his scheme that the Commission was not responsible to Parliament ; and in 1846 the Government replaced it by a ' Poor Law Board ' with a President in the House of Commons, and took good care that the domineering Chadwick should have nothing to do with it.

There the story of Poor Relief ends, for the time being. The elected Guardians were at any rate another step towards democratic local government.

THE FACTORY ACT.—Soon the Justices lost another function. The nation was harrowed by the Cry of the Children, worked and starved to death to build up the industrial strength of Britain. Several well-intentioned Acts had been worked through the un-reformed Parliament, but they had all failed of effect because their enforcement had to be entrusted to local magistrates, who felt a common interest with employers when the latter complained that shorter hours or higher pay would ruin their trade. But the cause was now taken up by Lord Ashley (who later became Lord Shaftesbury). He was a very different type from Chadwick, being an austere, evangelical Tory aristocrat. His first attempt at a Factory Act was defeated by *laissez faire* indignation at ' interference between master and man '—even when the ' men ' were six or eight years old. But the Government carried a bill of their own, which forbade the employment of children under nine, and limited the hours of those under thirteen to eight a day. Above all it required the Home Secretary to employ full-time inspectors to go round and see that it was carried out. A few years later another Act dealt with the employment of women and children in mines ; and legislation to improve working conditions for employed persons has gone on from that day to this.

With the Factory Act of 1834 officialdom began to spread its tentacles over the country ; but it was officialdom responsible to a Government Department, which was responsible to Parliament, which was responsible to the electorate.

FIRST STEPS IN NATIONAL EDUCATION.—Another emanation of the philanthropic spirit of the age was a new interest in education. Hitherto this had been left to chance, and chance had done very little. In some places persons too decrepit for any other kind of work ' taught ' their neighbours' children for a few coppers a week ; and most of the old towns had grammar-schools founded by former burgesses, but the funds of many of these had been perverted—some had become boarding-schools for the rich. Recently two voluntary societies had been formed to raise funds to establish schools with religious aims : the Nonconformists had founded ' The British and Foreign Schools Society ' in 1808, and the Anglicans had reacted in 1814 with a ' National Society for Promoting the Education of the Poor in the Principles of the Church of England.' Enlightened individuals tried from time to time to get the Government to bestir itself in the matter, but these efforts were all defeated by such arguments as ' To give the poor ideas above their station in life would merely make them discontented ' ; ' Why should we pay taxes to educate the children of others ? ' ' If people want education they will find a way to get it.'

But after 1832 the spirit of reform began to overcome this obscurantism. In the very next year Parliament voted an annual appropriation of £20,000 to help the voluntary societies to build more schools ; and in 1839 the grant was raised to £30,000, some of which might be spent on books and desks and teachers. But if public money was to be poured out on this scale (half as much as was spent in this same year on new stables for Buckingham Palace !) the Government had to see that it was well used. So inspectors were appointed, and the Lord President of the Council was called on to act as Minister of Education without being so called. (The post of Lord President had hitherto been a sinecure, but the holder now had to do something for his money.) The amount paid by the Government, and the number of inspectors sent out, gradually increased during the next thirty years.

So here again we see a growing sense of responsibility for the well-being of the people, and a further development of bureaucracy.

THE BEGINNING OF 'PUBLIC HEALTH.'—When Edwin Chadwick was engaged on his New Poor Law he saw the close connection between poverty and disease. In an interim report which he wrote for the Home Secretary in 1834 he pointed out that

'Labourers are thrown suddenly, by infectious disease, into a state of destitution ; and in the case of death their widows and children are thrown as paupers on the parish. . . . Thus the lack of health provision puts an impossible burden on the funds available for relief.'

The wonder was that in the prevailing conditions any townsfolk lived at all. It was *laissez faire* gone mad. Very few towns had any drains. West-end residences in London were built over cess-pits. In poor neighbourhoods people threw garbage of every description (of *every* description) into the street, where the gutters ran with filthy liquid which collected into stagnant pools. Drainage from burial-grounds polluted the wells which were the only source of water. Slum-dwellings in industrial areas were run up over open ditches to save digging out basements ; back-to-back houses, with no through-current of air, may still be seen in some of our cities. It never seemed to occur to anybody to do anything about all this. There were no experts on drains and sewers ; nobody had ever heard or thought of ' preventive medicine ' ; it was nobody's business, and likely to make trouble for anyone who tried to interfere.

But this is where ' interfering busybodies ' like Chadwick come in useful. As his grip on the Poor Law Commission weakened he took up the cause of public health with his accustomed vigour and pugnacity ; and in fighting the vested interests who opposed every attempt at improvement he had strong support from lovers of humanity like Dickens, and apostles of Christian Socialism like Charles Kingsley. But the most compelling arguments of all were the repeated epidemics of cholera, which frightened people into a conviction that ' something must be done about it.' By the time Chadwick's Poor Law Commission came to its untimely end he had got a Public Health Commission set up. Its Report (450 pages, written almost entirely by Chadwick) was even more striking than that on the Poor Laws, and the weight of it was sufficient to drive a *Health of Towns Act*, after terrific struggles, through both Houses of Parliament. This set up a General Board of Health including Chadwick and Shaftesbury (an ill-assorted pair !) and later Dr. Southwood Smith. But the Act fell far short of Chadwick's desires, for it contained no compulsory powers. At the request of the ratepayers of a Borough or a Poor Law Union, the Central Board could appoint a local Board, and if the death-rate of a district was abnormally high it could insist on this being done ; but even when the local Board had been set up there was no way to compel it to do anything. The central authority had not even the power to make grants-in-aid to help in building hospitals or making sewers. And Chadwick soon made his Health Board as obnoxious as he had made his Poor Law Commission. It had only been set up for an experimental period of five years ; in 1858 it was quietly dropped in all but name. As *The Times* said, ' We as a nation prefer to take our chance of cholera and the rest rather than be bullied into health.'

This hatred of being organised by the Government, even for our own good, is still a leading trait—in some ways an unfortunate one—in our national make-up. We can see it at work in the matter of vaccination. Before this prophylaxis was discovered only a minority of the population escaped smallpox, and of those attacked by it a large proportion died. Compulsory vaccination (in a series of Acts passed between 1840 and 1854) banished it almost completely. But compulsion has been whittled away to spare ' conscientious scruples,' until to-day only about 40 per cent. of babies are vac-cinated. (It is rigidly compulsory in most other civilised countries.) And a large proportion of parents let their children run the risk of suffocation by diphtheria rather than have them immunised at the public expense.

So Chadwick passed out of public life ; but by the time he died in 1890 he had seen his principles triumph. He and his colleagues, Dr. Southwood Smith and Dr. Simon (the first Medical Officer of Health for London), had between them created the ' Sanitary Idea,' to which millions of us owe the fact that we are alive to-day.

ANOTHER ERA OF REFORM.—After this spate of reforms the waters subsided for a couple of decades ; but the industrial prosperity of the country increased by leaps and bounds. Some of it percolated down to the working-classes, and by the

1860's discontent at the limited degree of democracy granted by the Act of 1832 forced through the Reform Act of 1867, which enfranchised respectable artisans while still leaving the lowest strata of society (especially farm-workers) out in the cold. It was a Conservative Government that carried the Bill, but it owed much to amendments forced through by the Liberals under Gladstone, and it was they who reaped the benefit at the ensuing General Election.

And now the tide of reforms began to flow again. Some, such as those that concerned Ireland (always one of Gladstone's main preoccupations) and the Army, are outside our present scope, but others have deeply affected the social and political life of the nation from that day to this.

First came nation-wide elementary education. The extension of the franchise made it necessary to ' educate our masters.' The Act of 1870, framed by W. E. Forster, was a typical British reform, in that it did not plan but patched. It took over the ' voluntary ' schools, which were to remain under their old managers, and merely filled the gaps with Government schools under ' School Boards ' elected by ratepayers. The schools were supported partly out of local rates, partly by Government grants dependent on reports made by Inspectors.

The maintenance of the old schools with public money started religious squabbles which have gone on intermittently every since. Nonconformists said ' Why should we have to pay rates to support schools controlled by Anglican parsons ? ' The teaching of religion in the new Board schools was to be ' undenominational,' but this was equally offensive to Churchmen. ' What ? ' they said (and still say), ' Are our children to be brought up without the definite doctrines contained in the Catechism and the Thirty-nine Articles ? '

An interesting experiment was tried in the School Board elections. Each voter had as many votes as there were members of the Board, and could plump them all for one candidate or distribute them in any way he thought fit. The object was to give representation to minorities such as Quakers and Catholics ; but the scheme was not a success. It filled the Board meetings with wrangling and was eventually dropped.

Colleges were started for the training of teachers, and by 1876 there were enough schools to make elementary education compulsory, the corollary of which was the abolition of all school-fees some years later. Standards and methods of teaching were gradually raised by successive ' Codes ' issued by the Department.

Here we see once more the growth of local representation *plus* (but sometimes *versus*) Whitehall bureaucracy.

An important advance in electoral democracy was made by the *Ballot Act* (1872), which made voting secret, and thus freed electors from the fear of offending influential patrons and employers and landlords.

The machinery of government was further improved by new methods of selecting the members of the Civil Service who carry on the day-to-day business of the Departments. Hitherto they had been recruited by ' patronage '—*i.e.* on the recommendation of ministers, who found themselves obliged to gratify friends and supporters by procuring safe jobs for the latters' relatives and dependants. The result has been made for ever ridiculous by Dickens in *Little Dorrit.* Gladstone, always a stickler for efficiency and economy in Government business, tried in 1854 to substitute a competitive examination ; but the old oligarchy was as yet too strong to be driven out of this, its chief remaining stronghold. So he had to be content with a qualifying examination which at least excluded congenital idiots. But when the Government of India was overhauled after the Mutiny (1858), the administrative posts under it were thrown open to competition ; and in 1871 Gladstone got the system applied, permissively, to other Government Departments. Within a few years nearly all had adopted it. It is not perfect ; sometimes it excludes men who would become first-rate administrators but do not shine in examinations. But nobody has yet devised anything better.

The Gladstone Government also took up the question of Public Health again. The connection between sickness and poverty which Chadwick had seen in 1834 was now recognised : the two evils were to be combated by a single Department It was to be called ' The Local Government Board ' ; fo. conditions varied so much in different parts of the country that they had to be dealt with on the spot, and the main function of the new ministry was to stimulate and guide local authorities. The country was divided into Urban and Rural Sanitary Districts. In Urban Districts the local authority was to be the Borough Council ; in Rural Districts it was to be the Board of Guardians. But the new Department was as yet too weak for its work. Local authorities *could* take various precautions and appoint various officials ; there was nothing to compel them to do so, and in a low state of public spirit it was not very likely that they would incur much expense, even when stimulated by the offer of grants-in-aid from the Board.

DISRAELIAN SOCIAL SERVICE.—By 1874 the Gladstone Government had outrun its mandate. The actions of every Government offend more people than they gratify ; and this Government had been very active indeed. So in 1874 a General Election turned them out and installed the Conservatives under Disraeli. Disraeli, the cleverest politician of the Victorian era, was always more aware of social problems than Gladstone. He had one great stroke of luck (or was it judgment ?) in his Home Secretary, a hitherto unknown Liverpool man named Richard Cross. For the reforms which Cross fathered were among the best achievements of the Ministry.

One of them was a Factory Act consolidating into one comprehensive statute all the piecemeal legislation on the subject passed since 1833. Another was the *Employers and Workmen Act* (1875), which put British Trade Unions fifty years ahead of those of any other country in the world, as we shall see later. Another was the *Artisans' Dwelling Act* (1875), the first serious attempt to grapple with housing problems. This gave boroughs power to buy up slum-property, pull it down and substitute model dwellings. It was only permissive, but it was a tacit admission that the Government had a duty in the matter.

What is commonly called the *Plimsoll Act* (1876) set up sound standards of ship-construction, to prevent merchant seamen being sent to sea in ' coffin-ships,' that owners might draw insurance-money. In future all ships were to be inspected and registered by the Board of Trade, and marked with a ' Plimsoll Mark ' below which they must not be laden.

Lastly, a new *Public Health Act* (1875) made it compulsory for all the new Sanitary Districts to appoint Medical Officers of Health and Inspectors of Nuisances, the Local Government Board paying half their salaries provided they were duly qualified for the work. The Prime Minister's chief contribution to the measure was his famous quip ' *Sanitas, sanitas, omnia sanitas.*' But, as he himself remarked, it is by words (and phrases) that men are governed.

CHAPTER III

LOCAL GOVERNMENT TO-DAY

COUNTY, DISTRICT AND PARISH COUNCILS :
WHAT THEY ARE AND DO

IN 1884 the *County Franchise Act* gave all householders the vote, irrespective of the value of their dwellings. This third Reform Act doubled the electorate created by the second (1867), just as the second had doubled that created by the first (1832). And as before, the extension of parliamentary democracy was followed by a corresponding development of Local Government.

REVIVAL OF ' SHIRE,' ' HUNDRED ' AND ' TOWNSHIP.' Since 1832 spasmodic twinges of social conscience had impelled Parliament to set up all manner of local bodies—Health Boards, Boards of Guardians, Burial Boards, Highway Boards, School Boards, District Sanitary Boards—with overlapping areas and conflicting powers. By about 1880 eighteen different ' rates ' were collected to pay for these services. Some broader and more inclusive organisation of local government was required. The central government in London was too remote and too busy with national affairs to be able to apply regulations to individual circumstances, but these one-job committees had the opposite weakness—they were too close to the people with whom they had to deal to be free from personal prejudices and influences. And it was impossible to keep them up to the mark in economy and efficiency.

The area which offered the happy medium was the County. As a governmental unit it was older than the country itself—there had been earldormen of Kent and Gloucester before there were Kings of England ; the Lord Lieutenant still commanded the ' County Militia,' the County Sheriff still ' presented ' prisoners to the judges at Assizes ; deep-dyed county loyalties are kept alive in games.

So in 1888 the County Councils Act set up Councils elected by the ratepayers of each county, to meet at least four times a year at the county-town. But the larger towns, some of them with age-old charters, hotly resented the loss of the autonomy confirmed to them by the *Municipal Corporations Act,* and in response to their protests the biggest of them were made ' County Boroughs,' outside the authority of the new Councils.

Thus towns fell into two classes, ' County Boroughs ' and ' Non-County Boroughs.' The line between them was at first drawn at 50,000 inhabitants, but the County Councils pointed out that they would not be able to carry out the duties assigned to them if so many towns with concentrated rateable value were withdrawn from them. So the limit was raised to 75,000. But there are a number of ' special cases '—there generally are in British governmental schemes. For instance, Canterbury, with 25,000 people is a County Borough, while Willesden with 200,000 is not.

Though there are only fifty-two geographical counties in England and Wales, there are sixty-two ' administrative counties ' Yorkshire and Lincolnshire being each divided into three parts, Suffolk, Sussex, Hampshire, Cambridge and Northampton into two, while London has a County Council to itself.

The Government now had democratic local authorities able to take over the administration of social services of every kind. It at once gave them all such duties hitherto carried out by Justices of the Peace, except the licensing of inns and a share in control of the County Police.

Parliament having thus revived the Anglo-Saxon ' Shire Court ' as an administrative organ, did the same a few years later for the old ' Hundred ' and ' Township.' [1] These now took the form of District and Parish Councils, to which the County Councils could delegate such duties as required an intimate knowledge of each locality. There are some functions —*e.g.* the organisation of the police and the provision of mental hospitals—which can only be done efficiently on a fairly large scale. There are others—*e.g.* the checking of insanitary nuisances and the provision of allotments—which are better done for each neighbourhood by people on the spot. So by the *District and Parish Councils Act* (1894), Counties were divided into Urban and Rural Districts, each with an elected Council and paid officials, and each drawing revenue from the County Rate.

As a matter of fact the Districts collect the rates for the Counties, for this is obviously a job that can be best done by officials not too

---

[1] The Anglo-Saxon period has been called the Golden Age of local government.

remote from the ratepayer. The amount demanded from each householder is so much (depending on the cost of running the local services) for every pound of the assessed annual value (generally somewhat lower than the actual rental) of the buildings or land he occupies.

Under the *Local Government Act* of 1929 agricultural land is exempted from rates altogether, while factories and transport undertakings pay on only three-fourths of their annual value. But rates are not the sole source of income for Local Authorities. The Central Government gives them grants-in-aid for Education and Police, together with a block grant towards their general expenses. This varies according to population, but the figures are 'weighted' to meet local conditions. Thus, in 1937, the 120,000 people of Bournemouth (where there is very little unemployment) only counted as 272, whereas the 185,000 of Sunderland (where half the population were out of work) counted as 1,034,805.

The essential difference between Urban and Rural Districts is that the former undertake more duties. Many Rural Districts have little more than sanitary powers. But much depends on the policy of the County Council, which has a good deal of option as to what it will delegate to Urban Districts and non-County Boroughs, and what it will keep in its own hands.

There is no strict size-limit dividing Urban from Rural Districts, and there are many anomalies. The Rural District of Wrexham, for instance, has a population of 60,000, an area of 70,000 acres and a rateable value of £180,000, while Wem (Salop) with only 2,000 people, 900 acres and £11,000 is an Urban District.

County Boroughs, as we have seen, are self-contained and independent, and do not delegate any of their powers. They may try to extend their rateable area by taking in suburbs which would otherwise come under the County ; and many non-County Boroughs want to include adjacent parishes so as to qualify to become County Boroughs. But the County Councils generally oppose such ambitions, which would deprive them of rateable value. All such applications have to come before the Minister of Health, who institutes inquiries, and if the result is favourable puts through Parliament a ' Provisional Order ' authorising the change of status. But before the issue is finally settled there will probably have been a good deal of bickering and wire-pulling.

Areas under Rural District Councils are subdivided into 'Civil Parishes,' the boundaries of which are not always identical with those of ecclesiastical parishes, and are alterable by the County Council (with appeal to the Ministry of Health). The Local Government electors in each such parish hold an annual meeting in March when (if the population exceeds 300) they elect a Parish Council by a show of hands, or make arrangements for a poll.

Parishes in Boroughs and Urban Districts are not Local Government units. The Parish Council is essentially a device for giving a real measure of self-government to scattered sparsely populated areas, where the Rural District Council may be almost as remote as Parliament itself.

Parish Councillors hold office for three years, but choose a chairman annually. They have a clerk (part-time, paid or voluntary) and an honorary treasurer. They meet at least four times a year. Parish property is vested in them; they have charge of village-greens and recreation-grounds; they remove petty nuisances and see to the utilisation of existing water-supplies; they *may* provide public lighting and a library. But their chief function is to bring the needs of the parish as to housing, water, sanitation and road repairs to the notice of the Rural or County Councils. Not infrequently this takes the form of complaints to the County Council that the Rural District Council is not doing its duty by them.

There are at present over 12,000 Local Authorities in England and Wales, made up as follows : County Councils, 62 ; Metropolitan Borough Councils 28 ; Non-County Boroughs 300 ; Urban District Councils 602 ; Rural District Councils 478 ; Parish Councils 7,000 ; Parish Meetings 4,100. But nobody can be under more than three, and citizens of County Boroughs are under only one for all purposes.

Let us now note how many of the larger categories are contained in some typical geographical counties :

	County Boroughs	Non-County Boroughs	Urban Districts	Rural Districts
Lancashire . .	17	18	82	19
Devonshire . .	2	10	23	18
Berkshire . .	1	6	1	11
Merionethshire .	0	0	6	5

THE SCOPE OF LOCAL GOVERNMENT.—Upon the foundations laid in 1888 and 1894 there has been built up a structure of democratic local government, imposing in bulk if irregular in outline. Act after Act has added to the duties and powers of these Councils until to understand them in all their bearings has become a special branch of jurisprudence.

We may classify them under five main heads.

(1) *The Making and Maintenance of Roads.*—The Act of 1888 gave the County Councils charge of all ' main roads,' leaving them to decide which were ' main ' and which secondary roads. Some counties (*e.g.* Hertfordshire) at once ' mained ' practically all their roads, others (*e.g.* Surrey) practically none. Where important roads were left to the District Authorities they generally deteriorate ; and this became more noticeable with the growth of motor traffic. Moreover, there was constant warfare between Local Authorities as to whether the cost ought to fall on those who live along the roads or on those who use them. So in 1920 control over highways was given to a Ministry of Transport. The new Minister, having classified roads as Class I, Class II and Other, divided the country into six parts each with a Divisional Road Engineer with assistants and inspectors ; and with the help of these officials took over the duty of mediating between the Authorities.

This is an example of a general tendency in the last twenty or thirty years to create administrative areas consisting of several counties. Other services which can be more effectively dealt with thus are the supply of electricity and of water (where the natural watershed should be taken into account). But Authorities still sometimes show dog-in-the-manger feeling, which may have to be over-ridden by special Acts of Parliament.

(2) *The Maintenance and Control of the Police.*—By the Act of 1888 County Councils were to share with the Magistrates in the control over County Police. The County Boroughs were allowed to keep their independent Forces, but non-County Boroughs were encouraged to merge theirs in the County's ; for this is a service which cannot be efficiently run on a small scale. The Home Office keeps the various Forces efficient by sending round ' Inspectors of Constabulary ' (usually retired Army officers) on the strength of whose reports it meets half the cost of pay and uniforms.

(3) *The Management of Education.*—Towards the end of the last century education was improving rapidly in other countries ; Germany, in particular, was gaining great advantages in industrial and commercial competition by more enlightened expenditure of public money in this direction. So in 1899 the old haphazard Department under the Lord President was replaced by the ' Board of Education ' ; and two years later Balfour, the Prime Minister, introduced the Education Bill of 1902, which swept away the old School Boards and gave control to County and County Borough Councils. But the District Councils raised cries of indignation that their ratepayers should lose that personal touch with their schools that they had hitherto exercised through the School Boards. A County Council, they argued, sitting in a distant county-town, could not possibly have the interest in local conditions required to make the schools a vital force in the community. So amendments were passed giving the County Councils power to delegate control of elementary schools to non-County Boroughs of 10,000 and to Urban Districts of 20,000 inhabitants. Every school was to have a Board of Managers ; for the ' Provided ' Schools (*i.e.* the former Board Schools) the Local Authority nominated all the members ; for ' Unprovided ' (*i.e.* Denominational) Schools it nominated some of them.

By an Act of 1944 control of all education (' Primary ' from ages five to eleven, ' Secondary ' from eleven to sixteen, and ' Further '—Technical and Secondary) [1] is vested in County and County Borough Councils ; but Counties may, with the approval of the Minister, hand on these functions to ' Divisional Executives ' who will maintain the local interests of particular areas or municipalities. And non-County Boroughs and Urban Districts of more than 60,000 inhabitants may, if they so desire, be exempted from County control and prepare their own scheme for approval by the Minister. The old ' Provided ' schools are now called ' County Schools,' while ' Unprovided ' Schools have become ' Auxiliary Schools.'

(4) *The Administration of the Public Health Acts.*—As we have seen, it was for health services that Urban and Rural Districts were first created. Legislation piled up, year by year, dealing with such varied matters as the inspection of meat,

---

[1] Including compulsory part-time attendance at ' Young People's Colleges.'

the disposal of sewage, the supply of water, the upkeep of hospitals and clinics, the notification of infectious diseases, and provision for maternity and child welfare. A broadening outlook on such matters was shown when in 1919 the Local Government Board became The Ministry of Health and when in 1925 ' Inspectors of Nuisances ' became ' Sanitary Inspectors.' Eventually most of these Acts were codified in the great *Public Health Act* of 1936.

But there are still plenty of nooks and crannies in the regulations. For instance, in factories without mechanical power the local Sanitary Inspector has to see to cleanliness, overcrowding, temperature, ventilation and drainage ; whereas in factories with mechanical power his purview is limited to w.c.'s and fire appliances, all the rest being under the supervision of the Factory Inspector from the Home Office.

(5) *The Relief of the Poor.*—By the *Local Government Act* of 1929 the old Boards of Guardians were abolished, along with the Poor Law which they had administered, to make way for ' Public Assistance ' from Local Authorities. All this we shall investigate in a later chapter on the Social Services.

THE CONSTITUTION OF THE AUTHORITIES.—There is a general uniformity in the form of these bodies, from great County Councils like that of Lancashire with a population of millions and a Council of 150, to District Rural Councils like that of Colwyn (Radnorshire) with a population of a few hundred and a Council of five. Councillors are elected by the ratepayers to serve for three years, one-third retiring annually to give continuity. They choose Aldermen (not more than a third of their number and sometimes including people who are not members of the Council [1]) who serve for six years—another element of continuity. County and District Councils elect a Chairman, Borough Councils a Mayor to serve for one year (in Counties and Boroughs he, or she, is nearly always an Alderman).

Twelve towns have ' Lord ' Mayors—London, Birmingham, Liverpool, Manchester, Leeds, Portsmouth, Cardiff, Sheffield, Norwich, Nottingham, Bradford and Stoke-on-Trent.

[1] This enables the Council to call on the services of men and women who have been rejected by some mischance at the polls, or who would not care to face the heat and dust of an electoral conflict.

The position of Mayor has of course more dignity and ancient tradition than that of Chairman of newly-created bodies like County and District Councils. He wears a robe and chain of office, and personifies the town for civic ceremonial and hospitality, and the expenses of his office usually far outrun the allowance made to him for the purpose by the Council. In fact it is sometimes difficult to find anyone willing to give the time and money required.

The Councillors are mostly busy men, and full meetings are held only once a month (some County Councils meet only once a quarter). Most of the work is done in committees, which meet at any time to suit the convenience of members. The number of these committees depends, of course, on what duties the Council undertakes. A County Council will have a dozen, dealing with Police (' The Watch Committee '), Education, Housing, Public Assistance, Public Health and so on ; a Borough Council may also have a Public Transport Committee, a Parks and Playing Fields Committee, a Baths and Wash-houses Committee A Rural District Council, on the other hand, may have only one or two. Each committee appoints its own chairman, and works with its own professional expert—e.g. the Public Health Committee with the Medical Officer and the Sanitary Inspector, the Watch Committee with the Chief Constable.

The same chairman may preside over a committee for years (provided, of course, that he is re-elected triennially to the Council), and may become a specialist in the matters it deals with. But some authorities forbid this, on the ground that it weakens the democratic principle.

Under the larger Authorities the most important committee is the Finance Committee. It usually consists of the chairmen of all the others, and none of them can spend more than £50 without its approval.

Committees can co-opt a limited number of people not members of the Council ; and this, like the election of Aldermen to the Council, enables them to call on the services of people with special interest and knowledge which might otherwise be lost to the public service.

At Council meetings most of the business consists in the chairmen of the various committees presenting reports and putting forward proposals. The officials are generally present, but do not as a rule address the Council unless information is needed on some point arising out of the business. (They talk freely on their committees, of course ; in fact, they sometimes dominate them.) Ninety per cent. of the reports and proposals are passed by the Council without question, but the other 10 per cent. may arouse opposition, sometimes even ' scenes ' that give the local newspapers wherewithal to fill their columns.

Council meetings are nominally held in public, but most of the real work is done by Committees meeting in private ; and whenever the Council itself is going to discuss anything it does not want the public to know about it goes into ' Committee of the Whole Council,' from which the public are excluded.

Party politics do not as a rule count for much in these Councils, which are seldom concerned with broad issues of national policy. Nevertheless one would expect a Council with a Socialist majority to spend public money more freely than one with a Conservative majority.

The professional staff is under the general direction of the Clerk to the Council—in Boroughs he is called ' Town Clerk.' The Clerks to the larger Authorities are nearly always lawyers, for much of their work requires legal knowledge ; but as they are co-ordinators-in-chief of the work of the Authority they often acquire first-hand experience of one or other of the departments ; and the Clerk to a small Authority has often worked his way up from office-boy in its service. Every Authority has to have a Medical Officer of Health and a Sanitary Inspector, who are required by law to have certain qualifications, and whose salaries are in part paid by the Ministry of Health. The appointment of other officials depends, of course, on the size and status of the Authority.

There may be an Engineer, a Surveyor, a Director of Education, a Public Assistance Officer, an Electrical Engineer, a Treasurer or Accountant, a Librarian, an Analyst, and so on ; and on the staff of a large and important authority all these will have a number of assistants. The County Borough of Birmingham, for instance, employs nearly a hundred ' Chief Officers,' with nine qualified medical men in its Public Health Department, and six admitted solicitors in the Town Clerk's office. Salaries vary from three or four hundred pounds a year up to five or six thousand.

Many Authorities own their own tramways and sources of electricity, gas and water ; others leave the supply of these to private companies which though run for profit work more or less under control. Nearly all boroughs of any size have public parks, playing fields, libraries, baths and wash-houses ; many run markets and abbatoirs ; some have picture galleries, a few have orchestras.

How far municipal trading ought to go is a debateable question ; but most large boroughs have taken over at least their water-supply. Birmingham and Liverpool bring their water from the Welsh mountains, Manchester from Cumberland. For the outlay of many millions involved in such an enterprise a city has to raise a public loan. Of course, this needs parliamentary sanction. Liverpool led the way in 1880 with a special Act ; Birmingham followed in 1882 with a Provisional Order.[1] For loans of more modest dimensions—to buy up a tramway-system or build a civic centre—the sanction of the Minister of Health (only given after careful enquiry) may be sufficient.

How THE CENTRAL GOVERNMENT KEEPS CONTROL.—Since one of the chief ends of Local Government is to carry out the behests (either statutory—based directly on some Act of Parliament, or administrative—based on the discretionary power which some Act has given to a Department) of the Central Government, the latter must have some means of seeing that its will is done. Broadly speaking there are two such ' sanctions.'

In the first place, it is only by grants-in-aid out of the national exchequer that Local Authorities can give such costly services as Education and Public Assistance ; and the Government Departments usually make these grants dependent on favourable reports from their inspectors. Nowadays Government Inspectors do much by suggestion and advice. They seldom say ' You have failed to do so-and-so properly and the Department will therefore stop your grant.' More often they say, ' Don't you think it might be better if you . . . ? ' or ' When I was at so-and-so last week they seemed to get good results from . . .'

Secondly, the Departments' auditors have power to ' surcharge ' Councillors if they have spent public money in an

---

[1] A Provisional Order, issued by a Ministry, has the force of a statute, provided that Parliament has not objected to it within a certain time—usually a month (see p. 80).

unauthorised or extravagant way. (The Ministry of Health has a staff of fifty qualified auditors for the sole purpose of seeing that Local Authorities are using their revenues properly.) Then the Councillors (in theory, at any rate), will have to reimburse the funds out of their own pockets ; and although this penalty is rarely enforced, the possibility of it is enough to keep them in check.

There was a famous case of this sort in 1921, when a Socialist Borough Council of Poplar paid a minimum wage of £4 a week to its employees, on the ground that a ' Public Authority ought to be a model employer.' The auditor surcharged it (after warning) to the extent of about £60,000. The Council appealed to the Law Courts, to find out if this action was legal. (We have no *droit administratif* here, as they have in some countries : all cases come before the ordinary courts and are tried by the ordinary rules of law, whether the Government is concerned or not.) The question for the judge to decide was whether, in the absence of any limit fixed by statute, it was reasonable to pay wages much above Trade Union rates. Were there *no* limits to what a Council could pay its dustmen ? The High Court found for the auditor. The Court of Appeal reversed this decision ; but the House of Lords decided for the auditor again. That settled the legal issue ; but of course the Government did not even try to extract the money from the councillors.

Councils make ' Standing Orders ' for their procedure and ' Bye-laws ' covering the various departments which they administer. These are subject to the approval of the Ministry of Health and they are generally based on model sets which it provides.

THE LONDON COUNTY COUNCIL.—The Government of London has several distinctive features. Administrative forms suitable even for such great cities as Glasgow or Birmingham would be quite inadequate for such a vast agglomeration, with more inhabitants than most counties. So when the County Councils were set up London became an administrative County all to itself. It was certainly high time for an overhaul of its government, for the division of authority between the Metropolitan Board of Works and the old Vestries led to inefficiency, waste, and often corruption. Later twenty-eight ' Metropolitan Boroughs ' were founded, each with its own Mayor and Corporation and municipal officials. The

Boroughs of Wandsworth and Islington have greater populations than Norwich or Cardiff with their Lord Mayors.

Another peculiarity is the existence of 'The City,' right in the heart of the Metropolis, with a very small population, but with vast rateable value, ruled by a Lord Mayor and Common Council, and having its own police and officials, quite distinct from the government of all the rest of London.

APPENDIX TO CHAPTER III

SUMMARY OF THE RELATIONS BETWEEN CENTRAL AND LOCAL GOVERNMENT

COUNTY BOROUGHS are subject to the *Ministry of Health* for arbitration of disputes with other local authorities ; for approval of loans ; for audit of accounts ; for confirmation of bye-laws ; for approval of private bills ; for administration of Public Assistance ; for Public Health, both environmental (drains, etc.) and personal (treatment of disease, etc.) ; for Housing. They are subject to the *Ministry of Education* for primary and higher education, to the *Home Office* for control of police, to the *Ministry of Transport* for the maintenance of roads.

COUNTY COUNCILS are subject to the *Ministry of Health* as above ; to the *Ministry of Education* as above, though they may delegate their powers to 'Divisional Executives' primary education to the municipal boroughs and urban districts within their area. They share with the Home Office control of the police (except in some municipal boroughs). They are subject to the *Ministry of Transport* for the maintenance of classified roads, but can delegate this to urban districts and municipal boroughs.

NON-COUNTY BOROUGHS are subject to the *Ministry of Health* for arbitration with other Local Authorities ; for gaining promotion to be County Boroughs ; for the audit of accounts ; for the approval of Private Bills ; for the confirmation of bye-laws ; for Public Assistance (through Area Committees of the County Council on which the Municipal Borough Council is represented) ; for Public Health provisions ; for Housing. They are subject to the *Ministry of Education* for education, provided they have more than 60,000 inhabitants. Otherwise they come under the County Council. Some of them retain their own Police, with the financial assistance and superintendence of the *Home Office* ; but most are policed by the County. Some, acting as agents of the County Council, keep up the classified roads within their area, subject to the approval of the *Ministry of Transport*. All have control of their non-classified roads.

URBAN DISTRICTS are in the same position as Non-County Boroughs, except that there are no exceptions to the rule that they are policed by the County.

RURAL DISTRICTS are in the same position as Urban Districts, except that they are always under the County for education.

CHAPTER IV

THE GOVERNMENT

HOW IT IS MADE AND HOW IT ACTS

WHEN a Prime Minister has to inform the King that he can no longer carry on the Government for lack of support in Parliament, the King sends for the Leader of the Opposition and commissions him to form one.

CABINET-MAKING.—The new Prime Minister has already pretty well made up his mind about the distribution of the chief offices. He and the other leading lights of his Party (most of whom have held office before) have been sitting side by side on the Front Opposition Bench ; they have long anticipated this happy hour, and have discussed it round dinner tables and library fires. So after a day or two of hurried consultations the Prime Minister is ready to call on the King again with a list of his proposed Cabinet, and within a week or so he has filled up the list of ministers whose posts are not of ' Cabinet rank,' and of the Parliamentary Secretaries who act as adjutants to the principal ministers.

Many aspirants to office are disappointed, of course. Making a Cabinet is like putting together a jig-saw puzzle for which there are too many pieces, including some that do not fit. The Prime Minister and his inner circle of advisers have to weigh many conflicting considerations. All influential sections of the Party must be represented. Some important men want particular posts, while others refuse to join if they have them. (Hostile elements in the Cabinet kept Churchill out of office for a decade.) Others have to be included to prevent their ' turning sour ' in the House ; and promising young men must be given experience of office.

Thus the ' Government ' consists of three concentric circles. The Prime Minister (with perhaps two or three intimate counsellors) is in the middle ; the inner ring consists of the Cabinet, the outer of the subordinate ministers ; and there is a perimeter of ' Back Benchers ' whose main function is to support it by voice and vote.

It is for the Prime Minister to decide how many of the ministers are to be in the Cabinet, which is, in effect, the executive committee of the Government. Some always are—the Chancellor of the Exchequer, and the Secretaries of State ; but some men who are excellent administrators are useless in a committee through lack of capacity for give and take and the pooling of ideas. The tendency during the past century has been for the size of the Cabinet to increase, from about a dozen to about a score. This has been largely due to the growing complexity of life, and the more varied duties which the Government has to undertake. Sir Robert Peel had no need of a Minister of Transport or of Education or of Air or of Mines or of the Dominions. One drawback to the increase is that the meetings have grown more formal; there is now a secretariat which prepares the agenda (under the direction of the Prime Minister of course) and takes minutes. But what passes at the meetings is still kept a close secret. Members would not be able to talk freely if their remarks were going to be discussed in clubs and bar-parlours up and down the country.

All ministers have to be Members of Parliament. This fusion of Legislature and Executive is a characteristic feature of the British constitution—one in which it differs from the American, for instance. Our ministers have to be in a position to explain and defend their actions and policy, and to answer questions thereon. If the Prime Minister wants to bring into the Cabinet a man who has had the misfortune to be defeated at the last election, he may persuade a rank-and-file member with a safe seat (*i.e.* one where there is a substantial Government majority) to retire (not without hopes of a *quid pro quo*— a knighthood or baronetcy), and the proposed minister can stand at the resultant bye-election. Or, alternatively, it may be possible to make him a Peer : that depends largely on his social and financial standing.

Incidentally, Members of Parliament cannot actually retire— a rule which reminds us of the days when membership was an irksome duty. If for any reason a member wants to give up his seat he applies for the ' Stewardship of the Chiltern Hundreds,' a post which disqualifies the holder from sitting in Parliament. He then resigns from it—possibly the same day.

The Cabinet is nominally a Committee of the Privy Council. Ministers on attaining ' Cabinet rank ' become life-

members of that Council, and are styled ' Right Honourable.'
Normally the Cabinet meets once or twice a week—oftener
if there is anything in the nature of a ' crisis.' All members
may not always be present—some may be too busy in their
Departments ; and some discussions are carried on by ' Cabinet
Committees,' consisting of groups of ministers concerned in
some particular subject. But in the Cabinet itself, although
each member reports on the work of his own Department, he
may take an active part in discussions quite outside it. Otherwise there could obviously be no general discussion at all.

JOINT RESPONSIBILITY.—This brings us to the most distinctive of all British contributions to democratic rule. The
Government's policy on all matters is a *joint* policy. All
ministers must be ready to support it in the House and in the
country. Decisions are constantly taken with which all are not
in full accord. Members must often ask themselves (and, in
private, each other) whether they are justified in sharing
responsibility for a line of action in which they do not believe.
But though conscience is the warp, compromise is the woof, of
politics. If everyone insists upon every jot and tittle of his
political faith, democratic government becomes impossible.

Still, there may come a time when an upright minister will
say : ' This is going too far ; I cannot any longer support this
policy—indeed, I cannot refrain from opposing it.' If he is a
valued and important member the Prime Minister will strive
to dissuade him from going to extremes, for many supporters
of the Government may be swayed by his example ; and most
Prime Ministers have to expend a good deal of time and energy
in this way. If the malcontent stands firm and resigns his
office, he will explain to the House his reasons, but usually
more in sorrow than in anger, bearing in mind that he may—
probably will—be working with his late colleagues again some
day.

If a minister in the course of his duties arouses strong
opposition in the House and in the country, the Prime Minister
may repudiate his actions, in which case he will resign. Or he
may decide to back him up, and if necessary, call on the House
for the special Vote of Confidence.

There have been examples of both courses in recent times. In
1935, when Sir Samuel Hoare as Foreign Secretary made the
' Hoare-Laval Pact ' for the partition of Abyssinia, just after the

Government had won an election by promising to stand by that country, there was a great outcry. It is unlikely that Hoare would have acted without the sanction of the Prime Minister, but Baldwin let him resign—to reappear a few months later as First Lord of the Admiralty. On the other hand when in 1943 Herbert Morrison aroused a hornet's nest (especially in his own Party) by releasing Sir Oswald Mosley from detention, Churchill upheld the minister, and the uproar died away without any need for a Vote of Confidence.

The qualities that make a successful Prime Minister are not always those that make a successful Departmental chief. He must be a good judge of men, a good team-builder and team-captain. He must have the indefinable quality of personality, to attract the confidence of the public and the respect of his colleagues ; and that still less definable quality, judgment—the ability to grasp the essential points of a proposition and decide on its merits and consequences without hesitation or delay. And greater yet than all these is the need for courage and steadfastness.

Yet by a characteristic trait of our elusive constitution, there was until quite recently ' no sich a person.' Every schoolboy (and schoolgirl) knows how Walpole repudiated the ' slander ' that he was Prime Minister ; and the fiction was maintained all through the great days of the Pitts, Peel, Gladstone and Disraeli. These statesmen held sinecure posts (usually that of First Lord of the Treasury), and it was for these no-duties that they were paid. The nearest approach to recognition was their customary occupation of an official residence—Number 10 Downing Street. It was not until the Coronation of Edward VII (1902) that ' The Prime Minister ' appeared in the order of Court Precedence—and even then he was placed well down the list, after the Archbishops and the Lord Chancellor and the Speaker. The first mention of the position in a statute was in the Act (1917) authorising the use of ' Chequers ' as a country residence for ' the Prime Minister of the day.' Full recognition only came with the *Ministers of the Crown Act* (1937), which fixed the emoluments of the office at £10,000 per annum.

THE CIVIL SERVICE.—Ministers seldom remain long in the same post. There were four War Ministers between 1939 and 1943, during the greatest conflict of history. Winston Churchill in the first 25 years of his career was President of the Board of Trade, Home Secretary, First Lord of the Admiralty, War Minister, Air Minister, Colonial Secretary, and Chancellor of the Exchequer (and contrived to do something spectacular in each office). And more recently Sir Samuel Hoare within two years (May 1935–May 1937) had charge of the India Office, the Foreign Office, the Admiralty, and the Home Office. Obviously the work of a Department takes more knowing than the cleverest and most versatile of politicians could acquire at such short notice. This expert knowledge and continuity of service is provided by officials who remain in the same Office during their whole careers. As we have seen, they win their position in open competitive examination. This is framed to catch able university graduates just after they ' come down.' Is a knowledge of the Classics or Natural Science a good preparation for a career at the Board of Trade or the Ministry of Health ? The view taken in this country is that it is—that a man (or woman) who has disciplined his (or her) mind to take high honours in any line of study has made it an apparatus capable of tackling problems of other kinds. The career attracts able people of a certain type : it is not much in the public eye, but involves the working of administrative machinery by the use of intelligence and integrity. And it is safe. It begins with a living wage (about £300 a year at the age of 23) and may end with a Permanent Under-Secretaryship, a knighthood and £2,000 a year.

Although their work is nearly all done behind the scenes, some civil servants become well-known public figures, e.g. Sir Warren Fisher, Permanent Secretary to the Treasury, Sir Alexander Cadogan at the Foreign Office, Sir Findlater Stewart at the India Office. Some are taken from Departmental jobs to act as special advisers to the Government, e.g. Sir Maurice (now Lord) Hankey as Secretary to the Cabinet, Sir Horace Wilson as Industrial Adviser, and Sir Robert (now Lord) Vansittart as Diplomatic Adviser.

The work of a Government Department is a prime example of our combination of professional and amateur. The minister, being a non-specialist, brings the activities of the office into line with the general sense of the community. He is spokesman of the Department in the Cabinet and the House, and spokesman of the House and Cabinet in the Department. The Permanent Staff, headed by the Permanent Under-Secretary, give him the benefit of their accumulated experience (and card-indexed information on every conceivable topic connected with it) and the traditions of the Department. Its general policy depends for the time being on the Minister, and through him on the Cabinet ; but this affects only big issues. Thousands of decisions are taken daily by permanent officials, applying accepted principles to particular cases.

A full-size Department is represented to the outside world by a Cabinet Minister and a Parliamentary Under-Secretary, each with one or more Private Secretaries. There is a Permanent Under-Secretary who controls the work of the Department as a whole ; and a Deputy, who may take charge of some special branch of its activities—*e.g.* legislation. And there are a number of Principal Assistant Secretaries, each directing one of the activities of the Office—*e.g.* in the Home Office, one will be in charge of Police Matters, one of Factory Inspection, one of Approved Schools, and so on. Each has one or more 'Assistant Secretaries' attached to him, and perhaps two or three 'Principals' to draw up memoranda, collate facts and tabulate statistics. The Ministry of Health (to take a single example) may be concerned with matters of all dimensions from preparing a great new Housing Act, to deciding if John Robinson of Little Muddicombe must put a horizontal damp-course in his converted barn. Some-body (often the Deputy Secretary of the Department) has the daily task of deciding what questions are important enough to go to the Permanent Secretary, perhaps to be laid by him before the Minister (whence they may be conceivably taken to the Cabinet) ; or unimportant enough to be sent down to the appropriate Principal Assistant, and by him perhaps passed on to a mere Principal. Most of this passing on is done in writing, often in duplicate or triplicate, so that by the time a decision is reached quite a bulky docket may have grown up. And all this provides work for the Second Division clerks, whose scholastic qualifications are of Higher School Certificate type.

Taken all round a high standard of public service prevails at Whitehall. A Permanent Secretary and his staff will do their utmost to serve their Minister even though they may privately disagree with his politics and policy. Some of them exert great influence on public affairs, but it is all (or nearly all) anonymous : it is the Minister who gets all the credit or discredit and who has to defend the conduct of the Department in Parliament.

Sir James Grigg resigned his post of Permanent Under-Secretary to the War Office to become Secretary of State for War in the Churchill Coalition. Such an evolution may seem obvious, but it is unprecedented. Of course, a seat in Parliament had to be found for him.

THE CHIEF DEPARTMENTS.—Let us now take a glance at some of the very varied organisations housed in and near Whitehall.

First, the Fighting Services.

The Board of Admiralty is one of the very few Government 'Boards' that *are* Boards. There used to be a Lord High Admiral, but Charles II put the office 'into commission'— *i.e.* divided its duties and responsibilities among a number of persons who act collectively. The First Lord (who is seldom a Lord and never a sailor) is a member of Parliament and of the Cabinet. Other civilian members are the Financial Secretary and the Parliamentary Under-Secretary. The professional element is provided by five 'Sea Lords,' senior officers who may go back to sea when they have finished their turn of service at the Admiralty. The First Sea Lord is in charge of strategy and the disposition of fleets ; the Second sees to recruitment and training ; the Third to ship-building and dockyards ; the Fourth to the provision of fuel, medical services and victualling ; and a Fifth has recently been added to take charge of the Fleet Air Arm.

The War Office, now housed in a massive building across the road, has had a chequered history. For two centuries after Cromwell ruled England with his Major-Generals the nation was most anxious to keep the Army ' in its place.' Tradition grew up that it was a mere temporary expedient and that its officers required little training beyond the qualities inherent in gentlemanhood. Down to 1870 control was divided between a Secretary of State at the War Office and a Commander-in-Chief at the Horse Guards. Even the horrors of inefficiency in the Crimea (where operations, supply, and armaments were under entirely independent authorities) did not lead to amendment. It was not till the Boer War (1899–1902) had made Britain the laughing-stock of the world that a system which had worked so well for the Navy was adapted to the Army. An Army Council was now set up, consisting of the Secretary of State for War, a Parliamentary Under-Secretary ; the Chief of the General Staff, the Adjutant-General, the Quartermaster-General and the Master-General of Ordnance.

The Air Ministry, whose heart beats at Adastral House with limbs sprawling into several other buildings in the neighbourhood, has had—like the design of its 'planes—the advantage of late development. Its organisation is based on those which its elder sister-services had to work out by trial-and-error.

The co-ordination of the armed forces was undertaken by The Committee of Imperial Defence in 1904, reconstituted after 1918. In addition to questions of general policy it discussed problems of supply and the manufacture of munitions. It consisted of the Prime Minister, the ministers for the Services, the Chancellor of the Exchequer and the Secretary of State for the Dominions ; and experts were co-opted for particular purposes. A staff of permanent officials was attached. Its main sub-committees were concerned with (a) Strategy, (b) Man-power, (c) Supplies, (d) Organisation for war, (e) Research and Experiment.

Now let us turn to the Secretaries of State. There are altogether eight of them. We have mentioned two—those for War and for the Air ; the Departments of three—those for India, the Dominions and the Colonies—belong to later chapters of this book. The other three are for Foreign Affairs, for Home Affairs and for Scotland.

In Tudor times there was only one—the official who conducted the correspondence, on the Sovereign's instructions and often in his dictated words, with foreign rulers. In the next century it was found necessary to divide the work between one for the northern Powers of Europe and one for the southern. In 1782, when the Fox-North coalition forced itself into office, Fox took over all foreign relations, while the other Secretary, Shelburne, confined his attention to Home Affairs. The strain of the Napoleonic Wars and the capture of new overseas possessions led to another Secretary being appointed for ' War and the Colonies ' ; and at the time of the Crimean War the Colonies became a separate department. Then, in the re-organisation of the Government of India after the Mutiny, another Secretary of State was established to speak and act for it in London. Lastly, when the Dominions became virtually independent they could no longer be dealt with as ' colonies ' and a separate Secretaryship was set up.

Of the eight (each of which is constitutionally able to perform the duties of all the others) the Foreign Minister is preeminently THE Secretary of State. (His opposite number in the United States is still so styled.) Much of the work of the Foreign Office is routine—the issue of passports, the maintenance of the rights of Britons abroad and so on. Its Permanent Staff is divided into geographical sections, and the care and posting up of archives is a very special job. But a great load of work rests on the Minister himself. He has to read all the important papers—scores a day—that come in from ambassadors and other observers abroad ; to bring important points contained in them before the Prime Minister and the King, to discuss them in the Cabinet (where Foreign Affairs generally come first on the agenda) and to compose despatches in reply. The fate of nations may depend on the purport, and even the wording of these papers.

Two Prime Ministers (Lord Salisbury and Ramsay MacDonald) have been their own Foreign Secretaries, but either job is enough for any man. After 1918 Lloyd George short-circuited Lord Curzon with a foreign policy of his own, conducted in an annexe of No. 10 Downing Street nicknamed ' the Garden Suburb,' but this led to his downfall. Nor can it be claimed that Neville Chamberlain's intervention in European affairs had happy results —though in his case he took care to have a Foreign Secretary (Lord Halifax) of his own persuasion.

The Home Secretary is an odd-job man, but several of his functions are of the highest importance. He is the channel through which people address the King : he receives all petitions and presents such as he considers presentable. It is by his advice (given, often, after prolonged inquiry and painful doubt) that the King exercises the royal prerogative of mercy towards condemned criminals. He controls the police system, appoints Chief Constables, Stipendiary Magistrates, Recorders and Coroners. He is responsible for the Fire Service ; also for prisons, reformatories (euphemistically called ' Approved Schools,' nowadays), Inebriates Homes and Mental Hospitals. He has control over aliens, and grants them naturalisation if he thinks fit. He enforces the Factory Acts, the laws regulating Workmen's Compensation, the conditions of employment in shops, the prevention of cruelty to animals and children, and the preservation of wild life.

One of his former jobs, the supervision of roads and road-safety, was in 1920 handed over to the new Ministry of Transport ; and the control of Mines and Quarries he now shares with the Board of Trade.

For all these manifold duties his staff has to be divided and sub-divided into numerous departments, and he has armies of inspectors of various grades penetrating into all parts of the country.

The last of the Secretaries of State—only in 1926 promoted to that status from that of a mere Secretary—is for Scotland. The Scottish Office does for Scotland most of what the Home Office and the Ministry of Health do for England and Wales ; and the Members of Parliament for Scottish constituencies form a non-Party ' Grand Committee ' over which he presides.

There are several fictitious ' Boards,' supposed to be committees of the Privy Council. They nominally include a number of ministers, such as the Prime Minister and the Chancellor of the Exchequer, but they never meet, and their ' Presidents ' are really independent ministers. Some of them have now been transmuted. The old ' Local Government Board ' became in 1919 the Ministry of Health, which we have seen working through the Local Authorities. The ' Board of Agriculture ' has recently become the Ministry of Agriculture and Fisheries. But the ' Board of Education ' was actually designed as a phantom in 1899.

When asked about it in the House of Lords, the Duke of Devonshire said, ' As far as I remember the point was mooted when the bill was first prepared, but I quite admit I am unable to recollect the reasons which weighed in favour of a Board rather than a Secretaryship. . . . It has the advantage, at any rate, of numerous precedents, and it is perfectly well known that there will be no Board at all.'

The only surviving Board, apart from the Admiralty, is the oldest of them, the Board of Trade. Its original title in Stuart times was ' The Lords of the Committee of the Privy Council appointed for the Consideration of all Matters relating to Trade and Foreign Plantations.' It has lost control of the plantations (*i.e.* the colonies), but its functions are still almost as miscellaneous as those of the Home Office. It concerns itself with the development of industries, with weights and measures, with the Merchant Navy, with the bankruptcy laws, with gas undertakings, with trade-marks and patents, with statistics concerning world-commerce, industry and shipping. It has a special Parliamentary Under-Secretary for the Department of Overseas Trade, whom it shares with the Foreign Office. It used also to share with the Ministry of Labour control of a Department of Mines and Quarries ; but the exigencies of the second World War has turned this into a separate Ministry of Fuel and Power which looks like becoming permanent.

War led to the creation of special ministries in 1914–18 also, and some of these also became permanent. Among them were a Ministry of Pensions, a Ministry of Transport and a Ministry of Labour. This Ministry of Transport has charge of roads and road-traffic (including buses and trams), of railways, of canals and waterways. The Ministry of Labour was given charge of administering the Employment Exchanges and Unemployment Insurance ; it has an Industrial Relations branch to help in settling disputes between employers and employed, while its Statistics Branch collects facts and figures about strikes and lockouts, wages and hours, Trade Unions and the cost of living (which appear week by week in the *Ministry of Labour Gazette*).

A very special office is that of Postmaster-General, for the General Post Office is a huge business concern—the only office of State that brings in revenue instead of spending it. Its activities are many and varied. It collects and delivers letters and parcels ; it carries on the telegraph and telephone services ; it adminsters a Savings Bank ; it acts as an insurance office for life insurance and annuities ; it distributes Old Age and Widows' Pensions, and (in war-time) Separation Allowances ; it sells stamps to be affixed to National Insurance cards, and licences to keep dogs and wireless-receivers.

The best-paid ministers are the Law Officers. Their head is the Lord Chancellor, who presides over the Lords and is a member of the Cabinet. He appoints nearly all judges and magistrates, and has many formal functions handed down from medieval times. The Government has also an Attorney-

General and a Solicitor-General to give it advice and take action on its behalf in legal affairs. Of all these we shall have more to say when, in a later chapter, we come to deal with Law.

The Cabinet also includes holders of certain historical sinecures—the Lord Privy Seal, the Lord President of the Council, and the Chancellor of the Duchy of Lancaster. These posts are given to men whose counsel is desired in the Cabinet, but who for some reason cannot be given departmental office, or who are needed for some special duties that have cropped up.

In the Labour Government of 1929–31 J. H. Thomas was made Lord Privy Seal and Sir Oswald Mosley Chancellor of the Duchy, to deal with the problem of unemployment.

THE TREASURY.—And still we have not mentioned the most important Department—the ancient and bountiful mother who nourishes all the others. She is sometimes a stern and forbidding parent and keeps them in tight leading-strings, but they are proud of her strict probity.

There was a ' Lord Treasurer ' until George I put the office into commission and made it a Board. That Board is now a phantom. The First Lord, as we have seen, is the Prime Minister, who merely keeps a fatherly eye on the Department, while the other ' Lords of the Treasury ' are Government Whips, who have even less to do with it. It is the fifth member of the Board, the Chancellor of the Exchequer—once quite a subordinate official—who is really the national account-keeper. His importance is shown in the fact that he has an official residence alongside the Prime Minister's in Downing Street, with a garden door into the Treasury.

Even before the beginning of the session the Chancellor of the Exchequer consults his colleagues of the ' spending Departments ' as to how much money they will want in the coming year. The officials of the Departments will have already have had consultations with the Treasury officials before embarking on costly schemes ; the Estimates will now be discussed in the Cabinet.

Lord Randolph Churchill, father of Winston Churchill, would not agree to the amount demanded for the Army and Navy in 1886, and when the rest of the Cabinet supported the expenditure, he resigned. He thought this would compel Lord Salisbury, the Prime Minister, to give way, in default of anybody else capable of taking over the Exchequer. But he 'forgot Goschen'; and as matters turned out this was the close of his ministerial career.

When the Cabinet has accepted the Estimates it hears and discusses the Chancellor's proposals for taxation to meet this expenditure. It is remarkable how accurate his forecasts of income and outgoings usually are; and this is largely the work of the permanent officials at the Treasury.

Early in the session the First Lord of the Admiralty, the Secretaries of State for War and Air, and the Financial Secretary to the Treasury (for the rest of the Supply Services, commonly called the 'Civil Vote') present their Estimates for the approval of the House, giving an account of their stewardship and an opportunity for criticism.

These Estimates have to be detailed, stating the precise amount to be spent for various purposes. Money voted for soldiers' pay, for instance, cannot be spent on their equipment. And any surplus goes back to the Treasury; otherwise a Department might lay up a reserve which would make it independent of Parliament. Some items of expenditure are authorised by permanent statutes, and so do not appear in the Estimates. These are said to be 'charged on the Consolidated Fund.' They include interest on the National Debt, the grant to Northern Ireland, the King's Civil List, and other grants to the Royal Family, and the salaries of the judges, of the Leader of the Opposition, of the Comptroller and Auditor-General, and of the Unemployment Board. The object is to make these payments independent of party politics.

By this time the end of the financial year will be at hand. Early in April the Chancellor 'opens his Budget'[1]—that is to say, he lays the national balance-sheet before the House (sitting as 'the Committee of Ways and Means'), carefully keeping to the end of his speech the pronouncement which all have been so anxiously awaiting, on the taxation for the coming year. The Appropriation Bill by which the expenditure is authorised is debated at length in the course of the next three or four months, like any other Bill.

To deal with money matters the House becomes a 'Committee of the Whole' so that discussion may be less formal (see p. 75).

[1] In the eighteenth century the Chancellor brought his papers to the House tied up in a bundle and carried in a linen bag.

When discussing expenditure it is called the ' Committee of Supply ' ; when giving Ministers leave to collect taxes it is the ' Committee of Ways and Means.'

Here is the summary of the Budget of 1939.

ESTIMATED REVENUE (in millions sterling)		ESTIMATED EXPENDITURE. (in millions sterling)	
Customs	228	National Debt Services	230
Excise	116	Other Debt Payments	12
Death Duties	88	Army	86
Stamp Duties	24	Navy	94
Income and Property Tax	341	Air Force	74
Sur-Tax	62	Civil Votes :	
National Defence Contribution	20	Social Services	294
Post Office Profits	11	Education	121
Motor Vehicle Licences	36	Miscellaneous Outgoings	33
Miscellaneous	18		
	944		944

The Treasury receives all the taxes and pays them into the Bank of England. Down to the end of the eighteenth century the proceeds of each tax were ear-marked for specific purposes. It was Pitt who first established a Consolidated Fund, into which all receipts were paid and from which all expenditure was drawn. The ' cheques ' which the spending Departments draw on the Bank consist of Royal orders, and there is a ' Comptroller and Auditor-General,' independent of the Government, whose business it is to scrutinise each demand and see that it exactly accords with the ' appropriation ' passed by the Committee of Ways and Means.

This elaborate system of account-keeping (greatly admired by other Governments) owes much to Gladstone, who had a passion for national economy and first made his name as Chancellor of the Exchequer.

Of course, in the long run it is the House of Commons that decides upon expenditure, and the House reflects public feeling in the country. It was because Baldwin feared that House and Country would not face the cost of re-armament in 1935–36 that we plunged into a World War almost unprepared.

Only the Government may bring forward any proposal that involves the spending of public money. Other countries envy us this restriction, for it prevents private members from trying to curry favour with their constituents by getting the Treasury to pay for local or sectional enterprises.

SEMI-OFFICIAL AUTHORITIES.—With the advance of civilisation man requires a greater variety of things for his well-being, and many of these requirements are on such a scale and of such a nature as to be beyond the scope of private enterprise. The Government has taken more and more upon itself, sometimes directly and sometimes through Local Authorities ; but as a nation we dislike interference by ' bureaucrats,' provided that Parliament keeps a remote control to prevent the service going radically wrong. Hence the rise of what may be called semi-governmental institutions.

The most remarkable of these is the Bank of England ; but that institution, with its connections on the one hand with the Treasury and on the other with the City has such an important influence on our national life that we must give some account of it in an Appendix to this chapter.

Again one would have expected the Government of the the greatest seafaring nation in the world to look after the buoys and lighthouses round its coasts and pilotage in its estuaries ; but we prefer to leave much of this to a co-optative body of master mariners, dating back to Tudor days—the ' Elder Brethren of Trinity House.' No doubt if the Brethren neglected their duties the Board of Trade would step in and do something about it ; but there is never likely to be any call for this.

Again, there are few governmental functions more important than seeing that doctors are properly qualified ; but we allow this to be undertaken by a private body, the General Medical Council, to which an Act of 1853 gave control over medical schools and examinations, and authority to maintain a high level of professional conduct. The Law Society is in much the same position with regard to solicitors. So is the Dental Board, except that unqualified dentists are not absolutely prohibited from practising, provided that they do not call themselves ' Dental Surgeons.'

Some institutions are half-way towards nationalisation— e.g. the London Passenger Transport Board, which unified a number of private bus companies and tube railways under a Board responsible to, but not managed by, the Ministry of Transport ; and the Port of London Authority which has taken over the management of the London Docks from the old Dock Companies.

Others are practically Government departments made independent of changes of Ministry. Typical of these is the

Electricity Commission established by the *Electricity (Supply) Act* of 1919, for promoting and regulating the supply of electricity, with power to make Provisional Orders giving Local Authorities or private companies the right to distribute current to consumers in a particular area. It is most important offspring is the Central Electricity Board (of eight members nominated as vacancies occur by the Ministry of Transport), which concentrates generation at the most efficient stations, and supplies authorised undertakings with current ' in bulk ' along the main transmission lines known as the ' Grid.'

But the semi-official body most in the public eye (or ear) is the British Broadcasting Corporation. This started as an association of manufacturers and vendors of receiving-sets, to give their customers something to receive. But although the Government had done nothing to establish the service it soon saw that such a powerful influence over the nation's mind and spirit could not be left at the absolute discretion of a group of private individuals, primarily concerned with their own interests. So it chartered a Corporation, maintained by the sale of licences to work receiving-sets. As the Postmaster-General had to undertake the sale of the licences, to him fell ' responsibility ' to Parliament for the conduct of the Corporation. It is he who has to answer questions about it, to keep a distant eye on its proceedings and policy, and to speak for it when the time comes, every five years, to renew its charter. But nobody wants it to be under the direct control of a Minister or a Department, or to feel that its voice is the voice of the Government ; and in its day-to-day conduct, its Directors and staff act in what they consider to be the greatest good of the greatest number of listeners.

APPENDIX TO CHAPTER IV

THE GOVERNMENT AND THE BANK OF ENGLAND

THE Bank of England, as everyone knows, was founded by a group of City men who raised a war-loan for William III in return for a charter giving them certain banking privileges. Among these privileges was the right to issue notes up to the value of the sum lent to the Government. It steadily consolidated its position during the eighteenth century, until the Government's financial extremities during the Napoleonic Wars linked it up permanently with the machinery of state. Every time its charter was renewed by Parliament it gained greater privileges, and Peel's *Bank Charter Act* (1844) allowed it to issue notes up to an amount which increased in proportion to the value of the gold in its vaults.

For 250 years, throughout the nation's rise to industrial greatness, it remained a private corporation, paying dividends to shareholders who appointed its Governor and Directors, free from Government control. But it was never a profit-making concern; for its shareholders were mostly financial firms whose main concern was to safeguard it as a rock of safety round which the varied interests of 'The City' could cluster. And for all practical purposes its position remains much the same, even now that the Government has assumed the right to exercise supreme control over its policy.

It is the Bankers' Bank. It keeps the accounts of the commercial banks through which ordinary people and firms do their business, and also those of the bill-broking houses through which foreign trade is financed. Thus its finger is always on the pulse of the financial system not only of this country but of the whole world. For 'The Old Lady of Threadneedle Street' stands topographically as well as metaphorically in the centre of 'The City'—that agglomeration of Banks (British, Colonial and Foreign), Bill-brokers, Stock and Commodity Exchanges, Insurance and Underwriting firms, which growing up undesigned (like so many other British institutions), has made that square mile the hub of the financial universe.

The life-blood of industry and commerce is credit, and the flow of it is regulated by the Bank. It does this in two ways. (1) Every Thursday morning its Governors meet and decide the 'Bank Rate' for the ensuing week, *i.e.* they announce the interest they will, if called upon, charge for advancing money on 'bills' (= promises to pay at a fixed future date) backed by two sound London firms. (2) The Bank conducts Open Market operations— *i.e.* it buys or sells shares. If it buys, it pays out cheques which people pay in to their bank-accounts, thus enabling the banks to extend their credits: and vice versa.

Although the Bank is nominally independent of the Treasury the two institutions are so interlocked that it is difficult to say which has the more influence over the other. It is not only the Bankers' Bank—it is also the Government's Bank. Treasury officials are in constant touch with Bank officers. (It was largely due to the Bank of England that the Government decided to restore the Gold Standard in 1925 and to abandon it again in 1931.) Moreover the various Ministries keep their accounts with the Bank; all taxes are paid into it, and all expenditure drawn from it. When the Government wants to borrow it entrusts the placing of the loan to the Bank; and it often borrows for short terms from the Bank itself. The issue of £1 and 10s. notes with which the Treasury replaced gold coin in August 1914 was in 1928 handed over to it. The Bank, being unofficial, can do things for the Treasury which if done by a Government Department would make people afraid that the national finances were being 'Bolshevised.' The Chancellor of the Exchequer consults the Governor of the Bank over his Budget —in fact, our whole financial system depends on the connection. And behind and beneath the Bank is 'The City'—that spontaneous emanation of our national penchant for flexibility of organisation combined with imperturbable common-sense. Still, it is remarkable, to say the least of it, that a private concern should wield such immense power over the national prosperity.

CHAPTER V

PARLIAMENT
*

WHAT IT IS AND HOW IT INTERACTS WITH
THE GOVERNMENT

WE do well to feel affection and respect for our Parliament :
it is a natural emanation of our national spirit, and the oldest
assembly of the kind in existence—in some respects the parent
of all others. And whereas others are bound by written
Constitution, ours is a supreme sovereign body, with no
restrictions or limitations to its powers.

It has three parts : the Crown, the House of Lords and the
House of Commons. These parts it will be convenient to
consider in reverse order.

THE HOUSE OF COMMONS consists of 640 Members elected
by universal suffrage. All British subjects are eligible for
membership except persons under twenty-one, bankrupts,
peers, lunatics, and the clergy of the Churches of England
and of Rome.

The King opens each session of Parliament with a Speech
from the Throne in the House of Lords, the Commons, headed
by their Speaker, standing below the Bar as in the Middle Ages.
This Speech is really a statement by the Government on the
internal and external situation of the country, and the programme for the ensuing session. The Commons then assemble
in their own chamber for a debate on the Address to the King
thanking him for his speech. This affords the Opposition
their first chance to criticise the Government's announcements.

The Speaker is elected by the House, and normally is re-
elected for successive Parliaments until he resigns or dies. He
is a member of the Party in power at the time of his original
election, and is in effect chosen by the Prime Minister of the
day in consultation with the Leader of the Opposition. It is
not always easy to find a man with the necessary qualifications. He must be a man of character and of *savoir faire*, tactful
and quick-witted, and of a judicial temperament. He has to

renounce all ambition as a statesman, for his career as a party man will be over. To him will fall the interpretation of the rules of debate and the Standing Orders by which the House regulates its procedure, and he will have to give everybody a fair deal. Very seldom indeed has any suggestion of partisanship been made against a Speaker ; foreign observers are always struck by the unquestioning respect that is paid to him and his rulings. He has the power to suspend an obstreperous Member (with the consent of the House), but very rarely has occasion to use it ; for British people have an instinctive feeling that to turn an elected assembly into a bear-garden is to weaken the foundations of democratic rule.[1]

The Speaker wears the eighteenth century costume which we find helps to give dignity and authority to presiding officials (judges, for instance) : knee breeches, silver-buckled shoes, lace cravat and cuffs, and a full-bottomed wig. The Mace, ceremoniously borne before him by the Sergeant-at-Arms when he enters and leaves the Chamber, and lying on the table during debates, symbolises his authority, just as he himself personifies that of the House. The post carries with it the position of First Commoner of the Realm, £5,000 a year with a residence under the Clock Tower, and on retirement a pension and a peerage.

When he is first elected his proposer and seconder take him by the hand and lead him to the Chair with a show of force. This is a survival from the times when the duties might incur the wrath of the Court.

An important factor in the evolution of the British Constitution has been the fact that the benches in the Commons' debating chamber have always been ranged facing each other, and there is not enough room on them to seat all Members comfortably. Even when the Houses of Parliament were rebuilt after the fire of 1835 the new chamber was modelled on the old, with only 350 seats for over 600 persons. But this is not so stupid as it seems. It is only on very special occasions that all the Members want to be present at once, and on these occasions the side-galleries, though not suitable for speech-making, provide accommodation for listening to the

---

[1] David Kirkwood, a ' wild Clydeside Socialist ' tells in his memoirs how, after he made a ' scene ' in the House, old T. P. O'Connor came up to him and said : ' Don't do that sort of thing ! I've been through it. It does no good. You might as well stick pins in a crocodile. These people have a code. They will listen to argument, but abuse does not interest them.'

protagonists on the front benches. And if the House had full accommodation for all it would be too big to speak in comfortably. Speakers would have to shout, and it is difficult to shout counsels of moderation and good sense—as the Convention of the French Revolution found when it met in a riding-school. And the fact that members speak from their places, instead of going up into a rostrum as in other Chambers, discourages oratory. A sober appeal to good sense is far more effective in the House of Commons than flaming appeals to passion.

If a member uses notes, he has to hold them in his hand. The actual reading of speeches is forbidden by Standing Orders.

The oblong shape of the chamber (unlike the semicircles or horse-shoes of foreign parliaments) tends to a two-party system instead of the rainbow-shading of party-hue found, for instance, in the French Chambers and the Reichstag of the Weimar Republic. The leaders of the two teams sit face to face on either side of a table ; they lean across it and talk ' at ' the Honourable Gentlemen opposite. On the front bench to the Speaker's right (' the Treasury Bench ') sit the members of the Cabinet ; on that to his left sits the ' Shadow Cabinet ' of the Opposition. Members who are not out-and-out supporters of the chief parties sit below the gangway which divides the rows of benches on either side.

Highly characteristic of our Parliamentary system is the position of the Leader of the Opposition. He is always a Privy Councillor—if he has not already attained that position as member of a previous Cabinet it may fall to the Prime Minister to sponsor his membership. He draws a salary of £2,000 a year from the Consolidated Fund,[1] and has an office on the same corridor as the Secretaries of State. He stands beside the Prime Minister at the opening of Parliament, and is constantly consulted by the Government in arranging the business of the House. It is arguable that he personifies a main function of Parliament—to keep a watch on the Government of the country. When we read of members of the Opposition making nuisances of themselves in the House we shall do well to remember that this sort of thing is our constitutional

---

[1] It is therefore paid automatically, and does not depend on an annual vote. The salaries of the Speaker and of the Comptroller-General are in the same position.

safeguard against Parliament becoming a mere machine for registering the edicts of the Cabinet.

Other countries, struck by the merits of the system, have tried to imitate it—mostly with indifferent success. Kemal Atatürk organised an official Opposition in the parliament which he set up at Ankara in 1922, but the experiment came to an untimely end after a few months. To make such institutions work requires instincts inherited from centuries of parliamentary experience.

Speakers in formal debate do not address each other, but the Speaker, who is supposed to be going to convey the sense of the House to higher quarters. Nor do they mention each other by name, but as ' the honourable Member for So-and-so.'

A speaker may refer to a member of his own Party as ' My honourable friend.' If he is a soldier, sailor or airman, he is ' the honourable and gallant Member ' ; of a lawyer ' the honourable and learned Member.'

A ' session ' is a year's work, from February to December, with a short ' recess ' at Easter and a long one in late summer, when Members nurse their constituencies, make holidays, read, and perhaps think.

Each day's work is a ' Sitting.' It starts (in normal circumstances) with prayers, read by the Chaplain, at 2.45. (Mornings are devoted to meetings of the Cabinet, Commissions and Committees, Departmental business, deputations, private discussions of all kinds, interviews and correspondence). Then from 3 to 3.45 is ' Question Time,' one of the most notable features of our parliamentary system, and the House's chief check on the day-to-day conduct of the Government. Any member, however humble, can ask any Minister, however important, any question, however trivial, related to the Minister's Department. It is usually handed in a day or two in advance, to give the officials of the Department time to prepare the answer, which may be given orally or in writing. Each Ministry has its own day for answering questions : *e.g.* the War Office does so on Tuesdays and the Foreign Office on Wednesdays. Usually the Minister himself replies ; but if he is busy he may get his Parliamentary Secretary to speak for him.

Research into statistics may be involved (' What proportion of naval officers commissioned in 1941 came from the Lower Deck ? ')

or enquiry into obscure events and circumstances ('Is it true that Jane Jones while detained in a Remand Home at Little Muggleton was compelled to scrub floors?'). The question is not supposed to contain statements or arguments, but there are ways of evading these rules. A statement may take the form of 'Is the minister aware that . . . ?' And something very like a debate can be started by supplementary questions asked (and generally answered) on the spot. But Ministers are nearly always good-humoured and forbearing. They very seldom try to snub questioners, but assume that they are acting in good faith. To be too 'clever' and 'snappy' would injure their own standing and that of the Government in the esteem of the House.

If the question involves complicated figures the Minister may reply that he will publish them in the Official Report. (This refers to 'Hansard,' the verbatim report of each day's proceedings, on sale to the public at 6d. a number.)

Sometimes questions are asked in collusion with the Minister, when he wants an opportunity to make an explanation or a statement. Such matters are generally arranged by the Whips.

If a questioner is dissatisfied with a reply he often threatens to 'raise the matter on the adjournment.' Government business usually ends half an hour before closing-time, and it is then sometimes possible for a private member to move the adjournment and in doing so to initiate a more general debate than would be in order at Question Time. But speeches have to be short to give the Minister concerned time to reply to the points raised.

(And then the cry is 'Who goes home?'—a survival from days when the roads round Westminster were not safe enough for members to go singly.)

Yet another opportunity for calling a Minister to account is when he introduces the Estimates (of expenditure) for his Department. A motion can then be brought forward that his salary be reduced by £100. This is rarely pushed to a vote, but it gives an opportunity of criticising his conduct of his Department.

On one famous occasion, in 1895, when the Minister for War was accused of neglecting to lay in an adequate supply of cordite, the vote was actually carried, and the Liberal Government resigned.

The method of voting is a quaint survival. The Speaker calls on members to cry 'Aye' or 'No,' and according to his judgment as to the preponderance of sounds, says ' I think the Ayes (or Noes, as the case may be) have it.' The other side may challenge this by crying ' The Noes (or Ayes) have it ! ' The Speaker then orders the division-bell to be rung in the ante-rooms [1] and turns a two-minute sand-glass. Members come flocking in. When the sand has run out the main doors are locked and members file into the side-lobbies, the Ayes to the right, the Noes to the left, being counted by four ' tellers,' one on each side at each door, appointed *ad hoc* by the Speaker.

The most important power which the Government holds over the House is its control of the time-table, which enables it to decide what Bills shall be brought in and what subjects shall be debated. Every Thursday the Leader of the Opposition asks the Leader of the House (normally the Prime Minister) about the business for the following week. The statement may give rise to criticism ; but here again a reasonable spirit usually prevails. If the Prime Minister feels that any considerable section of the House wants a debate on any topic (*e.g.* Road Deaths, or Army Pay, or the Fall in the Birth-rate) he will endeavour to provide a day for it.

Sometimes, when the discussion of some great and controversial measure is so prolonged as to upset the Government's programme for the session, a member may propose ' that the question be now put.' Should the Speaker hold that this course is justified, the motion is put to the vote ; and if it is carried (provided that at least a hundred members have voted for it) the Bill, or some portion of it, is taken as having been passed. This is called the ' Closure.'

This curtailment of free discussion was never heard of until the Irish Party in the 1880's took to ' obstruction,' deliberately holding up public business by making interminable speeches in relays. The Irish and their grievances have long disappeared from Westminster, but the Government is often so pressed for time, with long and difficult Bills to get through, besides financial and other routine business, that some such method is sometimes unavoidable. But nobody likes it, and in this as in most matters connected with our constitutional methods, common-sense and fair-play generally prevail.

[1] The amenities of the House include a smoke-room, a bar, a restaurant, a library, and a writing-room. In fact it has been called ' the best club in London.'

Motions of censure, the closure, question-time, control of the time-table—these are the regular give-and-take of warfare between Government and Opposition. But each side holds in reserve a far more devastating weapon. If the Government has lost its hold over a considerable proportion of its back-benchers the Opposition may carry a Vote of No Confidence, when the Government will probably have to resign ; or the Government may dissolve the House so that a General Election may decide the issue between them and their opponents. Except on some matter of the highest importance, nobody wants to push matters to such extremes ; and usually the Government's mere announcement that it will regard a forth-coming vote as ' a matter of confidence ' (*i.e.* that it will resign if the House decides against its policy) is quite enough to bring its rebels to heel and restore its majority.

As an example of the loyalty of the rank-and-file of a Party to its Leader we may cite the parliamentary crisis of May 1940. Even after the set-back in Norway, when many Conservative members felt that the Prime Minister must be compelled in the national interests to resign, if Neville Chamberlain had called for a Vote of Confidence he would have got a substantial majority. But he saw that the time had come for a real National Government, and as the Labour Party would not join it as long as he was Prime Minister he resigned.

At least forty members must always be present in the House, or the sitting may be suspended and the time-table thrown out of gear ; and if a division is expected the Government must be sure of maintaining its majority. Otherwise it might be defeated on a ' snap ' division ; and although it would not necessarily, or even probably, resign in such a case, the incident would be damaging to its prestige. It must therefore have somebody to see that enough supporters to meet every likely contingency are always at hand. The Opposition party or parties are almost equally anxious to keep their members up to the mark, so as to be able to make as brave a show as possible in the division-lobbies.

The members who act in this capacity are called (by a sporting metaphor typical of the British people) ' Whips.' Those for the Government have salaries, being public servants without whom Parliament might come to a standstill. But by a characteristic fiction they draw these salaries not as Whips but as ' Junior Lords of the Treasury '—a Department with which they have no other connection. The Chief Whip is officially ' Parliamentary Secretary to the Treasury,' and draws £2,000 a year. He was formerly known as ' Patronage Secretary '—a title which suggests the means once employed to keep the Government majority together.

Even to-day he has a considerable voice in the disposal of honours and in the use of Party funds to contribute to members' election expenses. These powers help him to maintain discipline, for many members are under obligation to him—or hope to be.

The Government Whips have an office in the precincts. They have to be ' good mixers ' who know everybody and get on well with people, for they depend largely on personal influence and good-humoured banter. They form the liaison between the Prime Minister and the Party ; they tell him what back-benchers are saying in the lobbies, whether they are growing restive at what the Government is doing or not doing, and whether any particular group is likely to go so far as to vote with the Opposition. They have to be in constant attendance around and about the debating chamber, without much chance to shine inside it. But power is its own reward, and they have their feet on young ambition's ladder. They may well be in the next Cabinet.

Opposition Whips have no official positions and no salaries —merely hopes of these, and meanwhile great influence in Party counsels. They generally have a good understanding with the Government Whips, and arrange many matters in consultation with them ; and there is a ' gentleman's agreement ' between them not to play shabby tricks on each other. (See Appendix to this Chapter.)

It was once thought that the ' cordite vote,' which turned out the Liberals in 1895, was contrived by a plot of the Conservative Whips. A dozen of their members entered the House from the Terrace—just enough to defeat the Government in the ensuing division. If they had entered by the coat-room, where the Whips lurk to mark who goes in and out, the Government Whips would have rushed round to collect enough Liberals to balance them. As it was, the Government, being already rent with internal strife, seized its chance to resign. But it seems that the stratagem was carried out by the members themselves—their Whips knew nothing about it.

The word ' whip ' is also used for the lithographed slips sent round to members of the various parties almost daily, stating forthcoming business, and underlining expected divisions, once, twice or thrice. To disregard a ' three-line whip ' may lead to being black-listed as a deserter. If a member falls out with his Party, seriously and permanently, he ' no longer receives the Party whip.' When a non-party matter comes up (such as the suggested revision of the Prayer Book in 1927–28) the leaders of the Parties may ' take off the whips '—*i.e.* allow their supporters to vote as they please.

Discipline is stricter in the Labour Party than in the older Parties. Whereas the latter allow their members some latitude of private judgment, all Labour candidates have to sign a pledge that if elected they will vote according to the decision of the majority at the weekly meetings of the Parliamentary Party.

An important step towards genuine democracy was made when in 1911 members began to be paid £400 a year for their services. Of course, we do not want to encourage people to go into politics for what they can make out of it ; but nobody is likely to be attracted by a rate of pay which (even after it was raised to £600) does little more than cover the expenses attached to the position (such as living accommodation in London, and secretarial services to cope with correspondence from constituents and others) ; and it was obviously wrong that membership of the House should be limited to people with private means or with backing from a corporation, such as a Trade Union.

THE HOUSE OF LORDS is even older than the Commons, being directly descended from the Saxon Witenagemot : and it bears many marks of its antiquity. To-day, as a thousand years ago, it consists of the magnates of the realm, lay and clerical. During the Middle Ages the heads of noble families gained a customary right to receive a personal summons to Parliament ; and it is this right which to-day constitutes a peerage. There were once more prelates than lay peers, but the dissolution of the monasteries tipped the balance the other way ; and modern Prime Ministers (especially Pitt, Gladstone and Lloyd George) have found the creation of peerages such a convenient way of rewarding services that to-day there are about 750 laymen to 26 clerics. Very few peerages are more

than 200 years old. They are sometimes given for eminence
in the arts (though artists rarely have enough money to keep
up the position—no musician has ever attained it) ; oftener
to scientists, lawyers and warriors ; quite frequently to the
' tycoons ' of business and to politicians (a Cabinet Minister
can reckon on a viscounty, if he wants one, and an ex-Prime
Minister on an earldom. There are also a number of ex-
Governors of Dominions, Colonies and Provinces. And this
constant influx helps to keep the House up to date as a representative assembly of persons of established position.

In this country only the head of a family is a peer ; its other
members are commoners. They may have ' courtesy-titles ' :
the eldest son of the Marquis of Salisbury, for instance, uses his
father's secondary title, Viscount Cranborne ; his younger brother
is called Lord William Cecil ; both are eligible for election to the
Commons. Scottish ' lords ' may also be in the Commons ; for
when the Act of Union was passed in 1707 it was feared that a
crowd of impoverished Scottish peers would over-run the House,
and it was agreed that they should elect 16 of their number as
' Representative Peers,' the rest being eligible to the Commons.
A similar restriction formerly applied to Ireland also : Viscount
Palmerston was an Irish peer who always sat in the House of
Commons for English constituencies.

With the growth of population in the nineteenth century a
number of new bishoprics were created, but nonconformist
feeling opposed any increase in the parliamentary representation of the Church of England ; so the number in the House of
Lords was restricted to twenty-six. The two Archbishops,
and the Bishops of London, Winchester, and Durham are
always members, but of the others only the twenty-one most
senior in date of consecration.

Bishops are only life-peers, and though they are addressed as
' my Lord ' their wives continue to be plain ' Mrs.'

The House is presided over by the Lord Chancellor, seated
on the ' woolsack ' in front of the railed-off throne. Unlike
the Speaker he remains an active Party man, and often takes
part in the debates. He is always a member of the Cabinet,
and when the Government goes out of office, he goes too—to
enjoy a substantial pension along with the peerage which has
been conferred on him on appointment.

F

He also presides over the House when it sits as Supreme Court of Appeal—a function which it has inherited from the medieval Great Council. The other members of the Court are Lords of Appeal, who hold life-peerages, and seldom take any part in the ordinary work of the House.

The House of Lords never meets on Wednesdays or Saturdays, it always rises before dinner-time, and nine-tenths of its members only appear on special occasions. The quorum is three, and there are rarely more than a score of members present. At one time most of the Cabinet were peers ; but those days are gone for ever. In order that some vestiges of the House's old importance may be left to it there is a rule that at least three peers shall be in the Cabinet ; but the plain fact is that the life of the Government does not depend on what goes on in the Upper House, and that no man with political ambitions is willing to be relegated to it. Yet the general level of its debates is often higher than that of the Commons. Peers do not make speeches merely to ' get their name up,' or to impress constituents with their importance : they only speak when they have something to say which they feel needs to be said.

In modern times the main purpose of the House is to be a ' Second Chamber '—to act as a brake on headstrong legislation in the Commons. Bills pass through much the same stages in the Lords as in the Commons, but the process is abridged in some respects ; and the House is entirely free from the business which takes up a large part of the time and attention of the Lower House—Finance. For the Peers to touch a Money Bill would shatter that sacred palladium of our constitution—the principle No Taxation without Representation. Only once in modern times have they tried to break that rule and the result was most unfortunate for them—as we shall very shortly see.

THE CROWN.—In no aspect of the British constitution are appearances so unlike realities as in the Monarchy. In theory, the King reigns by Divine Right, as anyone can see by looking at a penny ; in fact, his position depends on an Act of Parliament. In theory, he is supreme lawgiver, administrator, judge ; in fact, he cannot act independently in any of these capacities. In theory, he has a veto on legislation, but it has atrophied from disuse, not having been exercised since the reign of Queen Anne.   In theory, he could disband the army, liberate all prisoners, make us all peers of the realm ; in actual fact, he could no more do these things than the reader or the writer of this book.   And though on appointment Ministers kiss his hand in token of subservience to his will, it is to Parliament that they are actually responsible for all that they do.

That is what is meant by the constitutional principle, ' The King can do no Wrong.' Technically a Prime Minister is responsible for his own appointment. Of course ' responsibility ' no longer implies impeachment and the scaffold—merely resignation enforced by the impossibility of carrying on the Government without parliamentary support. A natural corollary of ' responsibility ' is that our Kings have to be careful not to commit their ministers to any line of policy without their consent. (King Edward VIII in touring distressed areas aroused hopes, with warm-hearted impulse, of measures of relief which caused the Government no little concern.)

As the King has to act as an integral part of the Constitution, with ministries that may change every few years, he has to stand aloof from party conflict. It would be considered most improper for either Government or Opposition to mention his personal views on any controversial subject. Otherwise, if Parliament or the electorate decided against the line which he favoured, he and the monarchy itself would suffer a grievous loss of prestige.

Almost the only occasion when he has any real choice of action is when a Government has to be formed before the majority-party has elected a leader. When Bonar Law resigned in 1923 his natural successor was Lord Curzon, by far the most senior member of the Conservative Party then in power ; but George V—after taking expert advice, we may be sure—sent for the comparatively unknown Stanley Baldwin, on the grounds, presumably, that a Government can no longer be directed from the House of Lords.

Thus our Kings go through the motions of kingship without often affecting the course of events to any marked degree. They are kept informed of all that goes on in Parliament and in the Cabinet, especially in foreign affairs. Accumulated experience and freedom from the need to seek popularity sometimes enable them to contribute to the taking of wise decisions. But we do not expect or desire our Kings to be active statesmen, or supermen of any description. It is their function to personify the nation as a whole—especially its common sense. And symbols exert tremendous power over the human mind and spirit. The abolition of the Monarchy would destroy the last constitutional bond between the Dominions and the Mother Country, for the Dominions owe no allegiance—not even a 'courtesy' allegiance—to the Parliament at Westminster ; but Governors-General still represent the King, and exercise his functions on his behalf, in Ottawa, Canberra, Pretoria, and Wellington.

The authority of the Crown is often exercised through the medium of the Privy Council. This ancient relic consists of the whole body of the King's advisers. Historically the Cabinet is a committee chosen from it by the King. All Cabinet Ministers, past and present, are life members of it.

When the King holds a meeting of it, he summons only such members—perhaps half-a-dozen, including some Ministers and members of the Royal Household—as the Government thinks desirable. Its business is usually to make an ' Order in Council ' carrying into effect permissive powers granted by some statute to ' The King in Council,' and now considered necessary by the Government.

THE PARLIAMENT ACT.—The story of the Parliament Act of 1911 illustrates so well the constitutional position of the Houses, the Prime Minister and the Crown that we shall do well to recall it.

For a century the House of Lords had been a permanent asset of the Conservative Party : for peers are men of property, and property seemed to be endangered by many reforms advocated by Liberals. But the latter found the existence of a chamber able and eager to throw out their measures a grievous handicap in political warfare ; for working-men were encouraged to vote Conservative by the argument that the Liberals would never be able to get their high-flown projects through the Lords, whereas the Conservatives could carry their more moderate programme into effect. And after the election of 1906, which returned 500 Liberals (with their Irish and Labour allies) to 150 Conservatives, Balfour consoled his followers with the reflection that the House of Lords would still enable them to control the destinies of the country. One Liberal Bill after another, after passing the Commons by enormous majorities, was summarily rejected by the Lords.

For twenty years they had been declaring that the House of Lords must be ' ended or mended,' and this was felt even more strongly by the Labour and Irish Parties, who found the House an insuperable obstacle to reforms on which their hearts were set.

So in 1910 Lloyd George, Chancellor of the Exchequer and leader of the Radical wing of the Government, threw down a challenge to the Opposition and their aristocratic supporters. Several social reforms, such as Old Age Pensions (which the Lords had not ventured to reject), had recently been passed ; and he had others in view, including National Insurance. To pay for these he had to increase revenue by some 10 per cent. ; and he determined to do something to adjust the balance between rich and poor by taxes which would fall mainly on the former to pay for benefits which would accrue mainly to the latter. He had a stiff fight in the Cabinet about them, and his Budget was a month late. He called it a war-budget, for a conflict with poverty and squalor. Death Duties were raised to 10 per cent. on large estates ; Income Tax to the dizzy height of 9d. (rising to 1s. 2d. on incomes over £5,000 with a super-tax of 6d. on really wealthy people) ; and a new Land Tax of 20 per cent. was imposed on increase in land-values due to the growth of towns. The House of Lords was so shocked at this ' predatory taxation ' that it decided, for the first time in history, to throw out the Finance Bill.

That decision may have been heroic ; it certainly was not wise. The nation had not been much upset by the defeat of the Government's Education and Licensing Bills, but this was an attack on the basic principles of our democracy. Asquith dissolved Parliament to give the electorate a chance to speak its mind. The result was a Liberal-Labour-Irish majority of 124, and the Irish refused to support the Government unless it undertook to cut down the powers of the Lords. The only means by which the Conservative Peers could be coerced into accepting a curtailment of their powers would be by threatening to create enough new Liberal Peers to outvote them.

Queen Anne had actually created twelve Tory Peers to force acceptance of the Treaty of Utrecht, and the mere threat of such action had overcome opposition to the Reform Bill of 1832 ; but what was now threatened—the appearance of five or six hundred new Liberal Peers—would end for ever the prestige of the House and of the British aristocracy.

The Lords accepted the verdict of the Election and passed the Budget of 1910 (a year late) without more ado. But their rejection of it had raised the whole question of their powers. The Liberal Government was now debating whether it would be better to strengthen the Lords by making membership depend less on birth and more on capacity, or to weaken it by letting Bills become law over their veto. The former plan would have set up a rival to the Commons, and further dead-locks would have followed ; so it was the latter that was adopted.

The question now was whether the King would agree to put the necessary pressure on the Upper House. George V, who had only just become King, was faced with a difficult con-stitutional issue. Naturally he did not want the opening of his reign to be signalised by the virtual destruction of the House of Lords ; but if he refused to promise to make the new peers, Asquith would resign, and he would have to take a Conserva-tive Ministry with a Liberal House of Commons. This would be an utterly impossible position. Moreover, it would look as if he had thrown in his lot with the Conservative Party, and if another Election confirmed the Liberal majority the Crown itself might be endangered. So he gave the required undertaking, on condition that the issue was put directly to the electorate at another General Election.

The result of this was practically the same as the first, and the Government now went ahead with their Parliament Bill. It expressly forbade the Lords to touch any Bill certified by the Speaker as a ' Money Bill ' ; it enacted that a Bill rejected by the Lords was to become law over their heads if passed by the Commons in two more consecutive sessions ; and it shortened the life of a Parliament from seven to five years.   (See Appendix to Chapter VI.)

Even now it was for a time doubtful if the Lords would not commit *hara-kiri* by rejecting the measure. But in the end discretion prevailed ; most of the ' die-hards ' stayed away from the critical division, and the Bill became law.

Since then several projects have been brought forward for reforming the Upper Chamber, by reducing the merely hereditary element and including more life-members (like the

Bishops and the Law-lords) who would make it more representative of the best British character and intelligence. But right-wing politicians do not want to lose such staunch supporters as the ' backwoods ' Peers, while left-wingers do not favour a strengthening of what they regard as an obstruction to ' the people's will.'

APPENDIX TO CHAPTER V

HOW PARTY WHIPS COLLABORATE

The following imaginary conversation illustrates Parliamentary methods of conducting public business. The Opposition having given the Government notice that it wants to move a vote of censure on some topic of public interest, the Opposition Whip looks in at the Chief Whip's office.

Chief Whip : Of course, we'll do our best for you. But look here, old man, we've an awful lot of business to get through. Can't you raise this on the supplementary estimate for the Foreign Office, or wait until we bring in the Consolidated Fund Bill next week ?

Opposition Whip : I'm afraid not. Our men will get ruled out of order if they start raising on the supplementary estimate half the things they want to talk about ; and they won't wait for the Consolidated Fund Bill.

Chief Whip : Well, I'll make you an offer. If you'll close down the debate on the Shrimp Industry Reorganisation Bill at half past seven on Monday, and let us take the supplementary estimate for the Dominions, Colonies and Office of Works the same evening, we'll let you move your vote of censure on Tuesday.

Opposition Whip : Will that mean suspending the eleven o'clock rule on Monday ?

Chief Whip : I'm afraid so, but I'll try to stop our men from talking if you'll do the same.

Opposition Whip : All right. Thanks very much.

(Adapted from Ivor Jennings : *Parliament* (C.U. Press).

Chapter VI

THE BIRTH OF A STATUTE

ITS PREPARATION AND PASSAGE THROUGH PARLIAMENT

The last chapter illustrated only one of Parliament's activities —its watch on the Government. Down to about a hundred years ago that was its chief function ; but nowadays most of its time is taken up with legislation. Besides the routine of Estimates, Budget and Appropriations, the work of a session often includes the passing of three or four large-scale measures, besides scores of lesser statutes of which the general public scarcely hears.

We will now sketch the life-history of an important piece of legislation from its first inception to its becoming part of the law of the land.

DRAFTING THE BILL.—Let us suppose that at the time of the election which put the Government in power the question of housing was much in the public mind, with newspapers full of the plight of the homeless, exhibitions of model dwellings, articles in reviews and talks on the radio discussing the way to tackle the problems. The Prime Minister, feeling that a strong housing programme will appeal to the electors has made grandiloquent allusion to it in a great meeting in the Albert Hall, and his followers have pledged themselves to it in their election addresses. But for the first two years of its life the Government has been busy with other matters, and now the public impatience has risen to dangerous heights. Protests are made in the House that there was no mention of it in the King's Speech at the opening of the second session ; a ' ginger group ' among the Government's supporters urges immediate action. So towards the end of that session the Cabinet decides that an effort must really be made. Before they break up for the summer recess they decide upon the general lines of the measure—how far it shall consist of slum-clearance, and what attempt shall be made to attract industry and population to new areas. The main task of preparing it will fall to the

Ministry of Health, but other departments will be vitally affected—in particular the Ministries of Transport and of Labour ; and, of course, the Treasury, which will have to finance the scheme.

The Minister of Health and his Parliamentary Secretary and the permanent heads of various branches at the Ministry have been discussing the matter in a desultory way ever since the Government came into power, and some preliminary enquiries have been made. But a Departmental Committee must now be set up, with a secretariat of its own, to work out the various aspects of the proposed Bill—how land, building materials, labour and transport are to be provided ; what size of house, at what rent, will be most in demand and most economic. They will call into consultation architects, surveyors, contractors, road-engineers, representatives of Local Authorities, and so on.

By the time the new session opens all this is in full swing. An allusion is made in the King's Speech to the Government's intentions ; whereat the Opposition will, of course, express regret that the measure outlined does not go far enough—or that it goes too far. Weeks slip by ; sarcastic enquiries are made at Question Time. But unexpected obstacles have cropped up in the Cabinet. Several Ministers have strong (and divergent) views on the subject ; the Minister of Health has a hard fight to keep his Bill in the shape which he and his men at the Ministry have decided on. A good deal of the discussion at Cabinet meetings will turn, not on the merits of the Bill, but on the effect it will have on the electorate.

By this time the Department's legal staff will have enquired into the bearing of the proposed Bill on existing statutes, and have sketched out its general design, dividing it into clauses and sections. Then, the Prime Minister having won general approval of the measure in the Cabinet, it is sent to the Government draftsmen to be put into formal legal phraseology.

These draftsmen are officially called ' Parliamentary Counsel to the Treasury.' We laymen are sometimes disposed to scoff at ' legal jargon ' ; but the aim in drafting a Bill is to make its intention clear, not to ' the man in the street ' but to the professional lawyers who will have to interpret it ; and they have a technical language which has necessarily to be more precise than the easy-going speech of every-day life.

THROUGH THE LOWER CHAMBER.—At last the great day comes, foreshadowed for some weeks past, and definitely announced by the Leader of the House on the previous Thursday. But it is not really very exciting—in fact, it is a mere formality. The Minister asks leave to introduce a Bill for the Better Housing of the Working Classes ; and this is granted without discussion. This is the ' First Reading.'

Formerly the Bill was read aloud by the Clerk of the House. But with modern Bills, some of them long enough to fill a good-sized book, this infliction is mercifully pretermitted. A roll of parchment, often a mere dummy, is brought in and laid on the table. The actual Bill has already been printed and circulated among Members.

Moreover, as this is a measure of first-class importance, the Government will probably have issued a ' White Paper ' explaining its intentions. These are on sale to the public, and form an interesting development in British Democracy ; for they enable the public to study the Government's proposals, and to bring the pressure of public opinion to bear, by writing to Members of Parliament or to the newspapers, or by holding public meetings of protest.

A week or two later comes the ' Second Reading.' This time there is a debate on the general principles of the Bill. The Minister of Health will probably open the debate ; if the Government want to make an impressive display the Prime Minister himself may close it. There will have been some criticism from the Opposition—that is what an Opposition is for ; but if the measure seems to have general approval of the Government's party in the House, no serious attempt will be made at this stage to throw it out.

A less important measure than the one we are considering would now be sent before a Standing Committee. No great legislative assembly could do in full session a tithe of the work that has to be done. The members have neither the time nor the special knowledge to discuss all the details of all the Bills that come before it. So at the beginning of a new Parliament the Party leaders put their heads together and nominate a ' Committee of Selection,' consisting of eleven Members representing all shades of opinion, under the chairmanship of a member of the Government Party. This Committee of Selection remains in existence throughout the life of a Parliament, and chooses ' Standing Committees ' and ' Select Committees.'

The three Standing Committees consist each of from thirty to fifty permanent members (permanent, that is, for the session), with another twenty or thirty members added for each particular Bill from Members of Parliament specially interested in the subject concerned.   The Committee of Selection is enjoined by Standing Order No. 48 to ' have regard to the composition of the House '—that is, to see that the parties are represented on the Committee as nearly as possible in proportion to their strength in the House. They sit during mornings in committee rooms in the Parliament building ; Bills before them are said to have been sent ' upstairs.'

Thus Standing Committees are miniature Parliaments, and their chairmen (chosen by the Government) are in much the same position as the Speaker ' downstairs '—*e.g.* they can proceed by closure if members are obstructing progress by making too many speeches ; and questions are decided by vote.   Thus when the Committee ' reports ' to the House it makes definite recommendations—there are no ' Minority Reports ' as with a Royal Commission.

Note the distinction between a Committee of Selection and a Select Committee. A Select Committee consists of four or five Members chosen by the Committee of Selection to inquire into some matter on which the House wants information.   Unlike a Royal Commission, it can compel the attendance of witnesses and put them on oath, and can require the production of documents. When it has fulfilled its purpose and made its report it is dissolved.

Note also that whereas Standing Committees and Select Committees report to the House, a Royal Commission reports to ' The King's Most Excellent Majesty '—*i.e.* to the Government.

But there will be no need for our Housing Bill to be analysed by a Standing Committee—there is already a wide knowledge of it and interest in it.   It will go to the ' Committee of the Whole '—the entire House sitting not as a House but as a Committee.   The Speaker is not present ; his place is taken by the ' Chairman of Committee ' (generally the Deputy Speaker, with some prospect of the succession), who sits not in the Speaker's Chair but at the Clerk's table.   The Mace, the symbol of the authority of the House, is not in its place ; the atmosphere is more informal, and Members can speak more than once to the same motion.   The Bill is now examined and debated clause by clause, section by section.   Amendments to any part of it may be moved by members of the Opposition, or by the Government's own supporters. Some—brought forward merely to draw attention to a possible weakness in the Bill—are withdrawn if the Government spokesman firmly opposes them ; some may be pressed to a division though the mover may know quite well that they will be heavily defeated ; some the Government will accept, and work into the Bill. But suppose a Member moves that all workmen employed on the Housing scheme shall be paid a penny an hour more than the standard Trade Union rate, in order that the Government may set an example to other employers of labour. There will be strenuous support for the motion from some quarters of the House, strenuous opposition from others. The Minister and his Under-Secretary will hastily consult the Prime Minister behind the scenes. The Prime Minister decides that to accept this amendment would involve a matter outside the scope of the Bill, on which the Government is not prepared to commit itself. The Minister will return to the Chamber and in winding up the debate on the amendment will intimate that the Government will resist it tooth and nail. The Whips will already have been at work, and members will hurry in for the division. In all probability the Government will have no difficulty in defeating the amendment ; but if it is carried, it must either withdraw the clause, or drop the Bill altogether, or resign, or dissolve the House.

In 1944 the Government, by a threat of resignation, forced the House to cancel an amendment it had carried ; but the circumstances were exceptional, for the break-up of the Churchill Coalition at that moment would have been a disaster for the whole world.

It is this ' Committee Stage ' of a Bill that takes the time. It may last for weeks. The Government may have to bring the closure into play to get it through in time for other essential business of the session ; or it may have to employ the ' guillotine,' by which a Bill is divided into sections and the date announced in advance on which the debate on each will be cut short.

' Seeing the Bill through the House ' is a very harassing time for the Minister and his Parliamentary Secretary. They have to be always ready to explain the meaning of clauses and the reasons for them, to correct false impressions, to make

minor concessions, to discuss the strategic position with the
Prime Minister and the Whips, and to drive the thing along
in the House and in the Lobbies with persistence but with
good humour.

The Minister may have to send his Parliamentary Private Secretary to get information from a Ministry expert on the topic in
hand, who will be sitting in the ' Box,' a little enclosure under the
gallery behind the Treasury Bench.   We have an amusing account
of the varied errands for which a henchman is used by a Minister.
Mr. Walter Long, President of the Board of Trade, is seeing a
Metropolitan Water Board Bill through the House.   Sir William
Bull, his Parliamentary Private Secretary, ' sat behind the Minister
all through. . . . Long never turns his head, but gives directions
this-wise :
    ' Bull, ask the Whips on the other side if we will give them two
more representatives on the L.C.C. will they let the clause through
to-night ? '
    ' See Sir A. Provis and see if he approves of Amendment 51.'
    ' Stanhope is outside—say I can't come out, and find out what
he wants.'
    ' See what Gladstone said in 1886 about unconstitutional
amendments.'
    ' Bull, take a note of what Tim Healy is saying.   I shall be
back directly.'
                    (Sir Charles Petrie :   *Walter Long and his Times.*)

When the Committee Stage is at last ended, any amendments passed in the course of it have to be ' reported ' to the
House as a House, with Mr. Speaker back in the chair.   The
main purpose of this ' Report Stage ' is to allow the House to
review and debate the Bill as affected by the amendments.

When Disraeli brought in the second Reform Bill of 1867 its
scope was quite moderate ; but he had no reliable majority in the
House, and Gladstone and the Liberals were able to force through
one Radical amendment after another.   Disraeli accepted them
rather than withdraw the Bill or resign, for he was determined
that his Party should get the credit for enfranchising the working-
man.   The result was that by the time the Bill became law nobody
would have recognised it as the same measure that had shyly come
before Parliament six months earlier.

After the Report Stage follows the Third Reading—a mere
formality like the First.

THROUGH THE UPPER CHAMBER.—Now our Bill is sent to 'another place.' (The House of Lords is never mentioned by name in the Commons.) There it goes through much the same stages as in the Commons, piloted by one of the three Cabinet Ministers which every Government must have there. If amendments are passed the Bill goes back to the Commons for these to be considered. The Commons may accept them, or may send the Bill up again in its original form. Before the *Parliament Act* of 1911, if the Lords insisted on amendments unacceptable to the Commons there was a deadlock, as a result of which the unfortunate Bill usually died a natural death. But nowadays, if the majority in the Commons is really in earnest they have only to pass the measure in two more consecutive sessions to by-pass the Lords altogether.

This may not be easy, however, in a case like that which we have been examining, where the Bill has been brought in late in the five-years' life of a parliament. Good fortune as well as good management will be needed to get it through ; for the dissolution will probably come before the fifth year has expired, and this automatically destroys all Bills still pending.

For really vital matters of national importance the stages of legislation can be telescoped. For instance, an Act authorising the use of Treasury Notes in place of gold was passed through both Houses and received the Royal assent within twenty-four hours in August 1914.

THE ROYAL ASSENT.—Last scene of all comes in the House of Lords. ' Black Rod ' (so called from his ebony wand of office with a golden lion on top), the official messenger of the Lords, is seen approaching. The Serjeant-of-Arms, who has been on the watch for him, shuts the door in his face. This is a reminder, dating from days when kings were often at loggerheads with their parliaments, that the debates of the Commons are sacred from outside interference—even that of a king. Black Rod knocks three times ; whereupon the Serjeant-at-Arms, having received a nod from the Speaker, and looked through the grating to make sure that the King has not sent an armed guard to coerce the House, opens the door. Black Rod walks half way up the House, bows three times to the Speaker (who rises), and once to each side of the House (where Members remain seated but remove their hats), and says : ' Mr. Speaker, the Lords Commissioners desire this honourable House to attend immediately in the House of Peers ' ; then he retires backward as far as the Bar.

The same historic ritual is observed on other formal occasions, such as the opening, prorogation and dissolution of Parliament. The marks made by the rod could be seen on the door of the old House of Commons, destroyed in 1941.

The Speaker and the Clerk of the House then file out, followed by such of the Members as care to attend the ceremony. In the House of Lords they find the Clerk of the House and certain Commissioners representing the King. After customary greetings and bowings, the Clerk of the Lords reads out the title of a Bill—there may be a dozen or so in the batch, or there may be just one. After the reading of each title the Royal Commissioner says ' le Roy le veult '—the Old French being a relic of the Plantagenet days when this was the usual speech of the English upper classes.

If the King were to veto a Bill this would be couched in the euphemistic formula : ' Le Roy s'avisera '—the King will think it over. But this has not happened since 1708.

The Speaker, on his return to the Commons says : ' I have to acquaint the House that the House has been to the House of Peers, where it has been announced that His Majesty has been graciously pleased to give by Commission his assent to the following Bills . . .'

PRIVATE BILLS AND PRIVATE MEMBERS' BILLS.—What we have been tracing is the passing of a Government Bill. There is no technical reason why the initiative should not be taken by any ordinary Member. But the Government controls the parliamentary time-table, which is so overcrowded that many of its own Bills have to be dropped or postponed. It is therefore very chary of giving up any of this precious time to discussing the fancy projects of private Members. But that the latter have *some* rights is recognised by the provision in Standing Orders for dealing with Private Bills and Private Members' Bills.

These are not at all the same thing. A Private Bill is a measure giving a Company or a Local Authority permission to carry out some project which will affect public interests. Most of our railways and canals were authorised by such Acts.

As we saw in Chapter III, Local Authorities usually proceed nowadays by Provisional Order from the Ministry of Health. This is a much cheaper and quicker alternative, for the Ministry merely sends down an Inspector or a small Commission to make inquiries on the spot, and if it approves the scheme, makes a Provisional Order, which is put through Parliament (probably in a batch with several others) before Question Time. But Private Acts are still sometimes necessary. The applicant has to give notice to every Authority or firm or individual likely to be affected by the project. If there is opposition to it the Government sets up a Select Committee before which counsel argue the case and cross-examine hostile witnesses. The ' Parliamentary Bar ' is a very highly-paid branch of the legal profession, and the costs of the Bill may run into many thousands of pounds. If the report of the Select Committee is favourable Parliament will probably pass it without much ado ; but an unfavourable report kills it stone-dead.

The tendency is to reduce the need for private legislation as much as possible. Until 1857 it was the only means of obtaining a divorce, and until 1870 the only means of becoming naturalised.

A Private Members' Bill, on the other hand, is a Bill which some Member or group of Members conceives to be in the public interest, but which the Government has failed to include in its programme—either from lack of time or lack of interest. The short sitting on Friday afternoons, and in the early part of the session (before financial business fills up parliamentary time) a few evening hours on Tuesdays and Wednesdays, are given up to these Bills. Members have to ballot, a month ahead, for an opportunity to bring in their Bills. Only about one in ten is successful, and even then the time available is so short that if there is any strong opposition it generally fails to get a Second Reading. If, however, it gets past that stage and is sent before a Select Committee, its chances are quite bright, for the House will probably accept the Committee's verdict without demur.

A notable example of a successful Private Member's Bill in recent times is the *Matrimonial Causes Bill* of 1937. A. P. Herbert entered Parliament in 1936 for the express purpose of trying to make divorce easier and fairer, and by a remarkable combination of good fortune and good management got his measure through within fifteen months of taking his seat. Students should read his entertaining account of the process in *The Ayes Have It*.

The difficulties in the way of private legislation have one good effect which we realise when we note what happens in legislatures where it is easy. See later, p. 199.

DELEGATED LEGISLATION.—Complaints are often heard that Parliament is apt to give the Departments powers which it ought to keep in its own hands. Many modern statutes leave to Ministers (which in effect often means the officials of their Departments) an extremely wide discretion in applying Acts. Sometimes Acts merely express the intention of Parliament in general terms, giving a Department *carte blanche* to make rules for carrying it into effect. Thus the *Rating and Valuation Act* (1925), declares that

> If any difficulty arises in connection with the application of this Act . . . the Minister (of Health) may by Order remove the difficulty . . . or do any other thing which appears to him necessary or expedient.

The Bye-laws of Local Authorities (which cover every conceivable subject from building houses to leaving litter in the streets, but have to have the approval of the Ministry of Health) come into the same category.

As we have no *droit administratif* in this country, any minister or official or Local Government officer who exceeds the powers granted to him by an Act can be proceeded against in the Divisional Court under Writ of *Certiorari*. But recent legislation sometimes circumvents this possibility by a clause like the following (in the *Roads Act* of 1920) :

> An Order made by the Ministry (of Transport) under this Act shall be final and not subject to appeal to any Court of Law, and shall on the application of the Minister be enforceable by Writ of *Mandamus*

(which compels a Local Authority to fulfil its statutory obligations).

What make matters worse is that many of these powers are conferred on Ministries and Local Authorities by Provisional Orders which, as we have seen, often slip through Parliament almost unnoticed.

Of course, there is much to be said for the practice. Parliament has not the time or patience or special knowledge to foresee every possible contingency in which an Act might be applied ; and if they tried to provide for them all, Acts would swell to unmanageable bulk and take months instead of days to pass through the Committee Stage. Nevertheless this form of legislation needs watching. It is contrary to the spirit of the Constitution, and might develop into a mild form of fascism.

Fortunately our officials as a class have a full share of British reasonableness, and rarely show a disposition to develop into petty despots.

APPENDIX TO CHAPTER VI

A sample Act of Parliament will show the form into which statutes are cast, especially the Preamble, the Enacting Words, and the Title-clause. The *Parliament Act* of 1911 has been chosen as an illustration because of its historical importance and its brevity. (The *Public Health Act* of 1936, cited earlier in this book, covers 680 pages.)

PARLIAMENT ACT, 1911
(1 & 2 Geo. 5. Ch. 13) [1]

An Act to make provision with respect to the powers of the House of Lords in relation to those of the House of Commons, and to limit the duration of Parliament.   (18th August, 1911.)

WHEREAS it is expedient that provision should be made for regulating the relations between the two Houses of Parliament.

And whereas it is intended to substitute for the House of Lords as it at present exists a Second Chamber constituted on a popular instead of hereditary basis,[2] but such substitution cannot be immediately brought into operation :

BE IT THEREFORE ENACTED by the King's most Excellent Majesty, by and with the advice and consent of the Lords Spiritual and Temporal, and Commons, in this present Parliament assembled, and by the authority of the same, as follows :

I. [*Powers of the House of Lords as to Money Bills.*]   (1) If a Money Bill, having been passed by the House of Commons, and sent up

---

[1] I.e., the thirteenth Act passed in the session which was partly in the first and partly in the second year of the reign of George V.

[2] An anticipation not fulfilled up to date.

to the House of Lords, at least one month before the end of the session, is not passed by the House of Lords without amendment within one month after it is so sent up to that House, the Bill shall be presented to His Majesty and become an Act of Parliament on the Royal Assent being signified, notwithstanding that the House of Lords has not consented to the Bill.

(2) A Money Bill means a Public Bill which in the opinion of the Speaker of the House of Commons contains only provisions dealing with all or any of the following subjects, namely, the imposition, repeal, remission, alteration or regulation of taxation ; the appropriation, receipt, custody, issue or audit of accounts of public money ; the raising or guarantee of any loan or the repayments thereof ; or subordinate matters incidental to those subjects or any of them. In this subsection the expressions ' taxation,' ' public money ' and ' loan ' do not include any taxation, money, or loan raised by local authorities or bodies for local purposes.

(3) There shall be endorsed on every Money Bill when it is sent up to the House of Lords and when it is presented to His Majesty for assent the certificate of the Speaker of the House of Commons signed by him that it is a Money Bill.

II. [*Restriction of the Powers of the House of Lords as to Bills other than Money Bills.*] (1) If any Public Bill (other than a Money Bill or a Bill to extend the maximum duration of Parliament) is passed by the House of Commons in three successive sessions (whether of the same Parliament or not), and having been sent up to the House of Lords at least one month before the end of the session, is rejected by the House of Lords in each of those sessions, that Bill shall, on its rejection for the third time by the House of Lords, be presented to His Majesty and become an Act of Parliament on the Royal Assent being signified thereto, notwithstanding that the House of Lords have not consented to the Bill : Provided that this provision shall not take effect unless two years have elapsed between the date of the second reading in the first of those sessions of the Bill in the House of Commons and the date on which it passes the House of Commons in the third of those sessions.

(2) When a Bill is presented to His Majesty for assent in pursuance of the provisions of this section, there shall be endorsed on the Bill the certificate of the Speaker of the House of Commons signed by him that the provisions of this section have been duly complied with.

(3) A Bill shall be deemed to be rejected by the House of Lords if it is not passed by the House of Lords either without amendment or with such amendments only as may be agreed to by both Houses.

(4) A Bill shall be deemed to be the same Bill as a former Bill sent up to the House of Lords if it is identical with the former Bill

or contains only such alterations as are certified by the Speaker of the House of Commons to be necessary owing to the time which has elapsed since the date of the former Bill in the preceding session. . . .

Provided that the House of Commons may, if they think fit, on the passage of such a Bill through the House in the second or third session, suggest any further amendments in the Bill, and if agreed to by that House, shall be treated as amendments made by the House of Lords and agreed to by the House of Commons.

III. [*Certificate of Speaker.*] Any certificate of the Speaker of the House of Commons given under this Act shall be conclusive for all purposes, and shall not be questioned in any court of law.

IV. [*Enacting Words.*] In every Bill presented to His Majesty under the preceding provisions of this Act, the words of enactment shall be as follows, that is to say :

> ' Be it enacted by the King's most Excellent Majesty, by and with the advice and consent of the Commons in this present Parliament assembled, in accordance with the provisions of the Parliament Act, 1911, and by the authority of the same, as follows.'

V. [*Provisional Order Bills excluded.*] In this Act the expression ' Public Bill ' does not include any Bill for confirming a Provisional Order.

VI. [*Saving for existing rights and privileges of the House of Commons.*] Nothing in this Act shall diminish or qualify the existing rights and privileges of the House of Commons.

VII. [*Duration of Parliament.*] Five years shall be substituted for seven years as the time fixed for the maximum duration of Parliament under the Septennial Act, 1715.

VIII. [*Short title.*] This Act may be cited as the Parliament Act, 1911.

Chapter VII

PARTIES AND ELECTIONS

HOW THEY ARE ORGANISED AND CONDUCTED

SOME people deplore Parties. 'Why,' they ask 'should the nation have the use of only half its best brains, with the other half hindering instead of helping? Why should not the tasks of government always be tackled without party bias, as in war-time?' But it is essential to democracy that opinions should differ, and should be allowed to differ. Those who want a permanent 'National Government' assume that it would always govern according to their ideas. Totalitarianism, with one creed imposed on all, and one party monopolising power, does not produce the kind of government that suits our national temperament.

A TWO-PARTY SYSTEM WITH THREE PARTIES.—Our national polity has grown up on the basis of an in-side governing and an out-side criticising, the criticism being tempered by the fact that the critics will sooner or later become the in-side themselves.

One reason for the success of this system in our country is that party differences do not go very deep, and none of them affects great political principles. It is largely a question of emphasis. Conservatives may be pre-eminently Imperialist, but nobody wants to weaken or destroy the Empire. The Liberal tradition is based on Liberty, Equality and Brotherhood but nobody would repudiate those ideals. Labour works for the extension of State control, but nobody proposes to abolish it. Moreover everybody in British politics (apart from negligible Communist and Fascist minorities) wants to make our parliamentary democracy work, and shares our national instinct that this cannot be done without moderation, good sense and fair play.

Little as the one-party system would suit us, the multi-party system of the French and German Republics and of pre-Fascist Italy would scarcely suit us better. For where there are a number of groups in Parliament, none of them strong enough to form a ministry alone, the result is a constantly-shifting series of coalitions, with group-leaders chaffering for places behind the scenes.

Yet now, after laying down the principle that ours is a two-party system, we have to admit that it is more than seventy years since there were only two Parties in Parliament. From 1870 to 1914 the Irish Nationalists formed a *tertium quid*, while the Labour Party appeared in 1905. Thus for the overlapping period of nine years there were actually four parties and four whips circulating in the House. But the enormous preponderance of the Liberal Party during most of that period minimised the ill-effects ; it could outvote all the rest of the House put together. And even after the elections of 1910, when the reduction of the Liberal majority put the life of the Government in the hands of the Irish and Labour parties they dared not use their power lest they should bring in the Unionists, and their last state be worse than their first.

And then at the end of the first World War a surprising concatenation of political circumstances led to a marked advance of the Labour Party at the expense of the Liberals. We shall find it instructive to note how this came to pass.

How Labour Ousted Liberalism.—The story of the rise of British socialism in the 1880's and how it leavened Trade Unionism in the 1890's to form the Parliamentary Labour Party belongs to a later chapter. Here we will start with the appearance of that Party, some forty strong, as part of the great Liberal revival of 1905–6. These Labour members, mostly Trade Union officials, professed to be Socialists, but there was nothing ' red ' about them. One of them, John Burns, became President of the Local Government Board under Campbell-Bannerman, and they seemed so anxious to be loyal allies of the ' Great Liberal Party ' that impatient left-wing elements sprang up in the Trade Unions, urging ' direct action '—the taking over of mines and factories, by violence if necessary—in place of the slow attrition of parliamentary methods. The Party joined the Coalition Government of Lloyd George in 1916 (just as it joined that of Winston Churchill twenty-four years later), and was represented in his War Cabinet.

At the Armistice (1918), it at once broke with Lloyd George and came out of the Coalition to form an Opposition party,

But the Liberals were divided.   Half of them resented the way Lloyd George had ousted Asquith from office in 1916, and criticised his conduct of the war ; the other half remained in the Coalition. At the election of December 1918 Lloyd George and Bonar Law gave a ' coupon ' of approval only to those Liberals who had stood by the Government, and opposed the Asquithian Liberals by Conservative candidates. This was an astute move on the part of the Conservative party-managers ; for the electors rushed to vote for the Coalition which had ' won the war,' and was now promising to ' Hang the Kaiser,' to ' Make Germany pay ' the whole cost of the war, and to create a ' Britain fit for heroes.' The result was a Parliament consisting of 33 Asquithian Liberals, 63 Labour members, and 526 Coalitionists—of whom all but about 70 were Conservatives.

But big majorities generally split into factions. Many Conservatives disliked Lloyd George's foreign policy, and at heart they felt that it was beneath the dignity of their great historic Party to continue under the leadership of a Radical whom they had formerly reviled as a pettifogging little Welsh attorney. So at a meeting at the Carlton Club in November 1922 the majority of them re-asserted the independence of the Party under Bonar Law. A few leading members refused at first to go with the crowd, but the split soon healed.

The breach that divided Liberals, on the other hand, proved unbridgeable ; and just as nothing succeeds like success, so nothing fails like failure. Electors will not go on wasting their votes on a Party too weak and divided to have any prospect of ever forming a government. Thus Labour was now the only Party able to resist Toryism with any prospect of success, and many former Liberals went over to it. Its status had completely changed. Whereas before the War it had represented only the particular stratum of society implied by its name, it could now look forward to undertaking some day the government of the country. With this in view it had, even before the end of the War, broadened its constitution, by setting up local labour parties which included not only affiliated branches of Trade Unions and Socialist organisations but individual ' workers by brain as well as by hand ' , and in the General Election of 1923 it deprived Liberalism of all claim to be standard-bearer of ' Progress.' Its leader,

Ramsay MacDonald, instructed members of the Party in constituencies where there was no Labour candidate to vote Conservative rather than Liberal. The result was the return of fairly equal numbers of Conservatives and Labourites, with the Liberals holding the balance. Asquith (rather magnanimously, in the circumstances) decided that he would be acting in accordance with the spirit of the constitution and the general will of the nation by voting with Labour to defeat the Conservative Government on a Vote of Confidence at the first meeting of the new Parliament.

The resultant Labour Government did better than had been expected, but it existed only on sufferance. It could bring in no Socialist measures for fear that the Liberals would vote with the Conservatives and turn it out ; and the mere suspicion that it was in touch with Bolshevik Russia was enough to overthrow it within a year.

The Party had another innings in 1929, but this time it was overtaken by the world slump. Unemployment rose to dizzy heights. Foreign creditors were drawing out their deposits at the Bank of England, and it seemed as if the Bank might have to stop paying out gold. To prevent what seemed like a disaster to British credit MacDonald called for drastic cuts in Service pay and in Social Services. Most of his Cabinet resigned rather than countenance this ; but the Conservatives and Liberals came to the rescue, and the public was scared into giving the Coalition a handsome majority at the ensuing election.

No intelligent economist now believes that ' cuts ' are the right course of action in such circumstances. To check unemployment purchasing-power must be increased, not diminished. Loans are, economically, quite justified so long as they bring in good returns : nine-tenths of the expansion of production by private enterprise is done on borrowed money. And, incidentally, the Government had to stop payments in gold, after all, a few weeks later, without any of the disastrous results it had prophesied.

As there were few Liberals, and still fewer Labour members who supported the ' National Government,' this meant that the Government was Conservative with a slight tincture of the other Parties. And we saw a phenomenon unique in our constitutional history—a Prime Minister without a Party !

For the next ten years the Labour Party gradually recuperated from the shattering blow of 1931. The election of 1935 increased its strength in the House from 49 to 151 ; but this was not enough to challenge the Government. The rise of Nazism, involving the sudden and complete disappearance of German Trade Unionism and Social Democracy, hitherto regarded as the strongest labour organisation in the world, taught the British Labour Party a lesson—but the opposite of what might have been expected. It did not make a vigorous and united stand against Conservatism. On the contrary, it argued that the rise of Nazism from its three elements (militarism plus big business plus the gangsterism of unemployed youth) was the reaction of the middle classes to Communism ; and that Labour must therefore demonstrate its moderation and constitutionalism. That was why it repeatedly refused to affiliate the Communist Party, and drove the left-wing Independent Labour Party outside its fold, and expelled Stafford Cripps for proposing a united front.

Thus for ten years there was no effective criticism of the Government from any party or group of parties capable of replacing it. First under Ramsay MacDonald, then under Stanley Baldwin, and then under Neville Chamberlain, the National Government continued in office until the disasters of 1940 necessitated a reconstruction under Winston Churchill —a real coalition replacing a sham one.

PARTY ORGANISATIONS.—All political parties need organisations to marshal their forces. Before 1832 the chief cohesive power in politics was adherence to some great personage who joined forces with other great personages to form a political group. But the Reform Bill so increased the electorate that Parties had to create some more widespread and impersonal form of organisation. Peel was the first to realise this, with his call to his followers in the Tamworth Manifesto (1834) : ' Register ! Register ! Register ! ' For in those days people had to prove their right to be placed on the list of voters. Soon local organisations for both parties sprang up in big towns. But the election of 1868 showed Disraeli that, with the electorate doubled by his recent Reform Act, these local organisations must be supported and controlled by a central office in London ; and the result of this prescience was seen in the Conservative triumph of 1874. The Liberals now learned the lesson, and the driving energy of Joseph Chamberlain produced a parallel organisation which won them the election of 1880.

Henceforward each Party had a Central Office at Westminster, more or less under the control of the Whips (though the Conservatives have also a paid Manager) with a central fund to be spent on winning elections. Alongside this, each Party has a federation of local 'parties.' The central fund comes mainly from wealthy supporters.

It used to be rumoured that some of these subscribed in the expectation that the leader would remember their names when it fell to him to propose New Year and Birthday Honours to the King— that £15,000 for the Party Chest would buy a knighthood, £25,000 a baronetcy and £50,000 a barony. But the Liberals have now so little chance of again being in power that for them, at any rate, this selling of honours is no longer a source of income ; while the Labour Party has always depended for its revenue mainly on the Trade Unions.

The local organisations consist of the leading spirits of the Party in the constituency, with a paid agent who is usually employed by the candidate. Until registration was undertaken by the Government (in the *Representation of the People Act* of 1918) the agent had to see that the members of the Party were on the register ; and even now the rival agents periodically appear before the local Registration officer [1] to urge the claims of their own supporters and deprecate those of others.

Of course the great business of the local organisation is to select a candidate. Unless they have somebody living in the constituency with the necessary qualifications, the committee may ask the Central Office to send down likely candidates to address them and answer their questions about himself and his views. They may demand one well enough off to ' nurse ' the constituency with subscriptions and hospitality, and to pay most of his own election expenses. On the other hand, the Central Office may urge them to adopt somebody for whom it wants to find a constituency but whom the Committee do not find attractive ; and this sometimes leads to friction which may lose the seat.

It is noteworthy that whereas in the United States all candidates must be resident in the constituency, the great majority of our

---

[1] Usually a Local Government official, such as the Town Clerk.

candidates are ' carpet-baggers ' who come in from outside. Another contrast between the two democracies is that whereas in America a different candidate is often chosen for each election, in this country there is a feeling that a former candidate has claims to re-nomination.

The older Parties are based on traditions going back to the Civil War, and their organisation has been growing up for a century ; but the birth of the Labour Party is more recent, its parentage more peculiar and its organisation so complicated that it requires special mention. It has an Annual Conference, attended by delegates from all local Labour Parties, Trade Unions and affiliated Socialist Societies. These have voting power in proportion to their membership, which gives great preponderance to the Trade Union element. The Party elects a different President every year. It also has a National Executive Committee which can meet and act on its behalf all the year round, having a secretariat and offices in Transport House, Westminster. The members of the Party in Parliament also elect their own leader annually, but usually re-elect the same man. Policy is decided by yet another body, the National Council of Labour, which consists of the Executive Committees of the Labour Party itself, of the Parliamentary Labour Party and of the Trade Union Congress.

ELECTIONEERING.—When Parliament is dissolved, arrangements at once begin for the General Election which will follow in a month or so. (Unofficial preparations will generally have begun some time before, for a dissolution seldom comes unexpectedly.) The King, acting through the Lord Chancellor, sends out a writ to each constituency, authorising it to elect a Member of Parliament.

The boundaries of constituencies are changed from time to time—nowadays by Commissions acting under Registration Acts. The aim is, of course, to make them all about equal in voting-strength, but it is impossible to keep pace with changes in local conditions and movements of population, and gross inequalities exist. The Redistribution Act of 1945 removed some of these anomalies by dividing a number of constituencies, thus increasing the total from 615 to 640.

But at least the Party in power is never guilty of ' gerrymandering ' in this country. Gerrymandering is arranging constituencies for party advantage. For instance, a town returning four members,

with a working-class centre and middle class suburbs, will if divided
into four quarters through the centre return four middle-class
members ; but if the centre forms one constituency and the outer
ring is divided into three parts, it will return one Labour candidate
and three of the others.

The writs are addressed to the sheriffs of counties and
county boroughs who leave the routine work to their paid
under-sheriffs and a specially engaged staff. Returning-
officers are appointed for each constituency, and these arrange
for polling-stations (usually at elementary schools) in every
district, hire carpenters to rig up partitions to preserve the
secrecy of the ballot, and prepare the metal ballot-boxes which
have been stored away since the last election.

Then comes nomination day. The regular party candidates
have probably been fixed long ago, but independents sometimes crop up a few days or even hours before the closing of
nominations. To stop freak candidates putting up ' for fun '
without any real backing (thereby causing extra trouble and
confusion to all concerned), candidates have to deposit £150
with the Returning Officer, which is forfeited by any who does
not poll at least one-eighth of the total number of votes cast.
In some constituencies, where one party has a large permanent
and unshakeable majority, no other candidates come forward
(e.g. the City of London, which has long returned two Conservatives). In that case the Returning-officer declares the
nominated candidate ' returned unopposed.'

But if the seat is contested, the campaign now opens. It
is a time of furious activity for the Party agents. Committee
Rooms (i.e. branch headquarters) are opened, handbills are
distributed, and posters (some sent down from the Central
Office, others printed locally) are put up on hoardings. Every
candidate can send an address, usually garnished with a por-
trait, to each constituent post free. Halls have to be engaged
for public meetings, and celebrities (if possible) brought in
to speak at them. Above all, arrangements must be made for
canvassers to call from door to door, arguing, persuading
cajoling the voters. This is by far the most effective form of
electioneering ; women are said to be particularly good at it.
Public meetings bring in very few votes—they are attended
mostly by adherents or by hecklers : but they afford the best
opportunity for the candidate to show himself and let his

voice be heard—people will not vote for a name without an apprehensible personality attached to it. He must keep his temper with the hecklers—a clever flash of good-humoured repartee may do him more good than the most crushing display of learning and logic.

Electioneering costs money—from £200 or £300 if there is plenty of voluntary help and the constituency is compact, to £1,000 or so if everything buyable or hirable has to be paid for in a widely spaced country division. Payment for some services is illegal—canvassing, and the conveying of voters to the poll, and ' treating ' ; a candidate's whole expenses must not exceed 5d. per head of the electorate in boroughs and 6d. per head in counties. After the election the agents have to render account to the Returning-officer, and an elected Member may be unseated if the other side can prove that his agent has exceeded the legal limit. The object of the restriction is to give a fair chance to candidates without much money to spend ; but of course well-to-do candidates always have advantages— for one thing they are more likely to be able to borrow cars from their friends.

Candidates have to be cautious about giving public pledges to support this or that policy in Parliament, for such matters are settled by Party leaders, and it is their policy that he will be expected to follow in the House. If he fails to do this he may be refused the ' Party whip.' In that case the Party Committee of his constituency may call on him for an explanation, and if it is unacceptable they may ask him to resign his seat. But they cannot force him to do so.

Incidentally it must be borne in mind that our Members of Parliament are not expected to concern themselves with the local or personal interests of their constituents to anything like the same extent as those of France or the United States. True, a Member for Bolton would probably be active when the interests of the cotton industry were concerned, and a Member for Cardiff about anything affecting coal-exports ; but this sort of thing is far more intense in other democracies.

Also it must be remembered that a British Member of Parliament is not a delegate sent to speak and vote in the name of his constituency. He is a member of a sovereign body in which he is supposed to obey the dictates of his own mind and conscience. Burke expressed this once for all when his Bristol constituents called him to account for acting against their wishes. ' Authoritative instructions, mandates which the member is bound to obey, vote and argue for, against the conviction of his judgement and conscience—these are utterly unknown in the laws of this land. . . . Parliament is not a congress of ambassadors from different and hostile interests, but a deliberative assembly of one nation, with one interest—that of the whole.'

On polling-day (the same date everywhere, nowadays) the polling-stations (usually elementary school-rooms) are open for twelve hours, to give everybody a chance to vote. At the station the voter gives his registration-number, and receives a ballot-paper so numbered, torn out of a counterfoil-book. The presiding officer marks it with a rubber-stamp, the design of which is kept a close secret until polling-day.

All this is to prevent anybody voting twice, or personating some other voter. The elector can find out his registration number in advance, and a copy of the register can be consulted at the polling-station.

He then takes the paper, on which the names of the candidates are printed, to one of the booths, makes a cross opposite the name of the candidate he favours, folds the slip and ' posts ' it in the sealed ballot-box. If he makes any mark on it besides the cross, it is invalidated. (This is to prevent anyone finding out how particular electors voted.) When closing-time comes, the boxes are taken, still sealed, to the headquarters of the constituency—e.g. the Town Hall. There the votes are sorted into bundles of a hundred for each candidate. When this is complete, the bundles are counted, and the Returning-officer reports the result, first to the anxious candidates and their friends in the building, then from an upstairs window to the waiting crowd below. The candidates generally appear in public together and make speeches complimenting each other on a clean fight, and claiming the result as a victory (actual or moral, as the case may be) for their respective causes, and all is over.

ELECTORAL REFORM.—Many people complain that our electoral system is not fair, and not democratic. The best that can be said for it is that ' it works '—it gives us fairly stable government, fairly representative of the general trend of public opinion. But it is argued that a more precise reflection of that feeling is called for, especially when there are more than two candidates for a seat. For if there are three or more the great

majority of the electors may have voted against the candidate
who becomes the sole representative of the constituency in
Parliament.   In the 1929 Election this was the case in 309 out
of 608 contested constituencies.

Let us take a concrete example.   At the election of 1924
in the counties south of the Thames, returning an aggregate
of 85 Members, the Conservatives polled approximately 1½
million votes, the Liberal and Labour candidates about half
a million each.   A fair representation of the views of the
electorate would have been 51 Conservatives, 17 Liberals and
17 Labour Members ; whereas the actual result was 84 seats
for the Conservatives, 1 for the Liberals and none for Labour.

Several remedies have been suggested.   One is the Alternative Vote, by which in a three-cornered contest the voter would
indicate his second choice as well as his first.   If the candidate
at the top of the poll had not a clear majority over the other
two, the candidate at the bottom would be eliminated and
the second choices of his supporters distributed to the others.

But this would still leave an unrepresented minority, and
there is more support for ' Proportional Representation.'
This would lump together a group of small constituencies,
making them jointly return eight or ten Members.   If 180,000
votes were cast in an eight-member constituency, any candidate
who polled 20,001 would obviously be sure of election.   But
out of the (let us say) 20 candidates, each elector has put
figures 1 to 8 opposite the names of the candidates he favours.
When in the course of counting first choices a candidate reaches
20,001, the Returning-officer declares him elected, and any
further votes cast for him are counted to their second choice.
This process if repeated often enough (with certain complications into which we need not enter here) would give 8 candidates the qualifying number of votes, and no elector would
have cause to feel that his franchise had been wasted.   Opponents of the system complain that it is too complicated for
the ordinary elector to grasp ; to which its supporters reply
that it is not the voter who will have the headache, but the
Returning-officer and his staff.

Returning-officers would presumably be whole-time experts
(keeping the Register up to date between elections) under such a
system.   The Inland Revenue officials who work out our Income
Tax for us tackle infinitely more complicated problems.

Another common objection is that all sorts of cranky minorities would have a handful of Members, that no one Party would be able to get a working majority that would enable it to govern with a sense of responsibility, and that we should have rule by unstable huckstering groups. To this it is replied that it is the essence of parliamentary democracy for all shades of opinion to be adequately represented, and that the political genius of the nation would enable it to adapt itself to the changed conditions. Proportional Representation in Eire has put one party in office for ten years, and the other for an even longer period. And it is further pointed out that the present system, which admittedly gives majorities in the House out of all proportion to the feeling of the country, can have, and has had, disastrous results. For instance the ' coupon election ' of 1918 gave Lloyd George and his colleagues 526 seats and the Opposition 96 (leaving out the Irish members who did not take their seats), whereas a House proportionate to the votes cast would have given him only 337 seats to 295. Would not the presence of a strong minority in the House have enabled him to make a better Treaty and to give the nation a better start towards internal peace and social security ? And the equally fantastic results of the 1931 and 1935 elections give cause for similar doubts.

At least, that is the contention of the disciples of Proportional Representation.

CHAPTER VIII

INDUSTRIAL DEMOCRACY

THE ORIGIN, STRUCTURE AND METHODS OF BRITISH TRADE UNIONISM

ALONGSIDE the political democracy machinery has grown up by which the wage-earning classes (the great bulk of the nation) seek to improve and safeguard their standards of life by means of collective bargaining with employers. The Trade Unions which perform this function won the rights of existence by a long struggle. Like our political institutions, they lack uniformity and consistency, having developed piecemeal under pressure of very varied circumstances. Even to-day, when they are accepted as an essential part of the national life, their organisation is of many types ; and though their representatives meet in annual Congress, they jealously guard their independence. It is impossible within the limits of this chapter to examine in detail a structure so complex ; but nobody can understand British democracy without at least recognising the existence of this aspect of it.

SELF-HELP FOR THE WORKING-CLASSES.—The mass-production that began with the Industrial Revolution required the sinking of large sums in machinery, buildings, raw material and the maintenance of labour. It widened the gulf between masters and men, between capital and labour, between owner and worker. The owners were able to take the whole of the increased value which manufacture added to the raw material, and this gave them a strangle-hold on the livelihood of less fortunate (or less purposeful) people. The workers had just one weapon of defence—they could combine to withhold labour from employers who would not pay an adequate wage. But as yet they had no votes, and Parliament accepted the point of view that employers were creating wealth and affording a living to work-people who were ungrateful for benefits received. Pitt's *Combination Acts* (1799–1800) made it punishable with six months' imprisonment for a workman to combine with other workmen to get a rise in wages, or to attend a meeting for such a purpose.

Combinations were regarded as a foolish and dangerous attempt to interfere with the working of Divine Providence. Malthus taught that the vast majority of mankind must necessarily live just on starvation level (see p. 15). Economists had a theory that, there being only a certain amount of wealth available for wages, those who got more than the minimum were leaving their mates destitute. And Benthamites declared that ' The Greatest Good of the Greatest Number ' could only be attained through ' enlightened self-interest ' working with the least possible interference. All these arguments led to the comfortable conclusion that, however much one might deplore the evils suffered by the poor, there was nothing much that anyone could do about it.

But other ideas in the air had burst into the incandescence of the French Revolution, with its assertion of Liberty, Equality, the Rights and Brotherhood of Mankind. In 1825 Francis Place and his friends contrived to get the Combination Acts repealed. Henceforth Trade Unions were not illegal, provided they did not have recourse to ' obstruction ' or ' molestation.'

This opening victory kindled an over-confident spirit which courted disaster. Robert Owen spent the fortune which he had acquired as a mill-owner in pioneering towards a Promised Land for the working-classes. He was the first British ' Socialist '— it was one of his disciples who invented the word ; but most of his efforts were wasted in trying to create a Utopia as by a wizard's wand. Among his projects was one for a ' Grand National Consolidated Trades Union ' which was to call a General Strike and bring the whole edifice of capitalism down with a resounding crash, making way for a new industrial world in which Fair Price and Mutual Aid would replace cut-throat competition. But this was expecting Trade Unionism to run before it had learned to walk. The General Strike collapsed almost before it had begun, and the employers followed up their success by refusing to employ men unless they accepted ' The Document,' abjuring Trade Unions.

For the next generation self-help moved, very tentatively at first, along three lines.

(A) ' The People's Charter ' was an agitation for reforms to do what the Act of 1832 had so signally failed to do : make

Parliament hear the voice of Labour as well as that of Capital. This was to be achieved by Manhood Suffrage, Vote by Ballot, Abolition of Property Qualification for Members of Parliament, Payment of Members, Equal Electoral Districts, Annual Elections. The Chartist Movement achieved nothing at the time, and faded out after 1848 ; but it was the beginning of political education for the working-class, and accustomed the public mind to the idea that the Act of 1832 was not the last word on democracy. And most of the six demands have long since been met.

(B) The Co-operative Movement was the beginning of what we may call 'practical Socialism.' Several people (Robert Owen among them) had conceived the idea that trade should be carried on not for the profit of individuals with prices fixed by supply and demand, but by the community itself, with prices fixed by cost. These schemes had all failed until in 1844 some Rochdale workers clubbed their pennies to start a store to supply themselves and their neighbours with flour and oat-meal. The novel feature of their scheme was that the store was to be open to non-members, who were to share the profits in proportion to their purchases. Thus all customers had an interest in extending the business. The Toad Lane Store prospered ; it was imitated in other industrial towns of the North and Midlands and in Scotland. Later on these stores were federated to gain the advantage of large-scale buying, and manufacture was added to distribution. To-day the capital behind the movement is 225 millions sterling, and nearly half the households in Great Britain belong to it. But its great importance in early days was that it gave the working-man self-respect, opportunity and motive for thrift, ' a stake in the country,' and practice in combining for the general good.

(c) Trade Unionism, left for dead in 1834, revived in a different form. The new Unions were associations of skilled craftsmen who paid comparatively high contributions out of which sick pay and other benefits were provided. They had whole-time paid officials—usually respectable, law-abiding men who husbanded their finances too carefully to indulge in reckless strikes, and supported the Liberal Party now evolving from old-time ' Whiggery.' The leaders formed a ' Junta '— a sort of informal parliament of labour which later developed into the Trades Union Congress.

But they could not escape the hostility of employers towards organisations that pooled labour-power, and in 1866 a thunderbolt fell upon them. The Boilermakers having prosecuted a defaulting treasurer, the Judge pronounced that a Trade Union, as ' an institution in restraint of trade ' had no legal rights.

It had long been a maxim of Civil Law that no contract is binding which tends to hinder commerce.

The Unions helped the Liberals to win the election of 1868 in the hope that they would pass a law to rectify this, but the *Criminal Law Amendment Act* of 1871 was a disappointment to them.

It protected the funds of registered Unions, and provided that no Union could be refused registration because its rules were in restraint of trade, but it expressly warned them against violence and intimidation, and judges had given some forced interpretations of these words : ' black looks ' and ' threatening to strike ' had been punished as forms of intimidation.

So at the next election (1874) they voted for Disraeli and the Conservatives, and they reaped their reward in the *Employers and Workmen Act* of 1875, which safeguarded their right to strike.

This was the Magna Carta of the Trade Union Movement for a quarter of a century, and gave Britain a long lead in the organisation of labour.

SOCIALISM.—One of the most unfortunate effects of Industrialism is ' the Trade Cycle.' When new markets open, manufacturers borrow money from the banks or sell shares to the public in order to supply them. Activity and prosperity spread around. Everybody is busy, everybody has money to spend on houses, furniture, clothes, amusement—even on books. But sooner or later the market is glutted, the banks stop lending, private investors lose confidence, factories close, workpeople are dismissed and can no longer buy ' consumer goods.' This alternation of feverish activity and sluggish hebetude is wasteful and injurious to the whole community, but its worst effects fall upon the poor. Well-to-do folk can ' live on their hump ' in bad times, but the poor can never accumulate enough ' hump ' to carry them through prolonged unemployment.

The worst of all slumps, that of 1929–32, has led to an intensive study of the phenomenon, and in future we may at least be able to mitigate its evils. But during the nineteenth century mass-production was too novel for people to understand the forces at work, and the distress caused by the double slump of 1877–79 and 1881–84 left permanent marks on our national life. It re-awakened a sense of responsibility for the well-being of our fellow-men which had been soothed to slumber by such phrases as 'The Law of Supply and Demand' and 'The Survival of the Fittest in the Struggle for Existence.' Toynbee Hall, the first University Settlement for the study and relief of poverty in the East End, was founded in 1882. 'Slumming' became a fashionable pastime for young ladies from Mayfair. The Salvation Army, recently started to save men's souls, now found that it had first to save their bodies by relief works. Charles Booth, a wealthy shipowner, devoted himself to collecting statistics about poverty—showing, for instance, that one-third of the people of London lived permanently on the verge of stravation. Above all there was a revival of Socialism in a new and original form.

In 1847 two Germans, Karl Marx and Friedrich Engels, had published 'A Communist Manifesto' which expounded a 'scientific' Socialism very different from the haphazard Utopianism of Robert Owen. Their view was that Capitalism was a mere phase, that the conditions which had produced it were already passing, and that it behoved all men of good will to engage in a ' class war ' to hasten the cataclysm which would end it. Out of the debris they would be able to build a better world in which there would be no owning class, the proletariat would collectively own the machinery and raw material, and would produce by co-operative energy for the common good. Marx was expelled from Germany as a revolutionary, and spent the next twenty years in London, producing *Das Kapital*, a long, learned and abstruse exposition of the historical and economic basis of this creed. But his ideas made no impression in this country until they were taken up by H. M. Hyndman, a man of means who had been to Cambridge and played cricket for Sussex. In 1884 he founded the Social Democratic Federation to propagate the gospel of

' the Socialisation of the means of Production, Distribution and Exchange in the interests of the entire community, and the complete emancipation of Labour from the domination of Capitalism and Landlordism.'

By way of 'palliatives for immediate adoption' it suggested such bagatelles as the repudiation of the National Debt and the Nationalisation of the Land.

Side by side with the Social Democratic Federation was the Fabian Society, which attracted a remarkable number of clever young men and women, including Bernard Shaw, Sidney and Beatrice Webb, Graham Wallas and H. G. Wells. Its methods were indicated by the name of the Roman general who beat the Carthaginians by avoiding battle : it sought to change the basis of society by what revolutionary Socialists mockingly called 'the inevitability of gradualness,' by promoting collectivism through Acts of Parliament and Local Government activities like municipal trams, gasworks, washhouses and so on.

But all this seemed very remote from cold and hungry working-people, and the old Trade Unions haughtily held aloof from any kind of Socialism, until in 1889 a great strike in the London Docks opened a fresh era in the organisation of labour. It was controlled by a new type of Trade Union leader—powerful street-corner orators like John Burns and Tom Mann, who were members of the Social Democratic Federation. Public sympathy was on the side of the strikers, and they gained practically all their objectives—sixpence an hour for spells of not less than four hours. This resounding triumph gave great impetus to Trade Unionism, and deflected it into fresh paths. Unions sprang up for unskilled, low-waged workers, who paid a few pence into what was practically a war-chest to provide strike-pay with which to fight employers and eventually bring 'the Capitalist system' to an end. Henceforward Trade Unionism became more and more associated with Socialism.

THE TRADE UNIONS AND THE LABOUR PARTY.—The Trade Union Congress, reconstituted in 1895, appointed a Parliamentary Committee to promote its 'legislative programme'; but inasmuch as it had no representatives in Parliament this 'programme' was a castle in the air. Even when in 1899 the Congress joined the Socialist organisations to form a 'Labour Representation Committee' it only managed to win two seats at the 'Khaki Election' of 1900.

But soon after that election something happened which put the new Labour Party on its feet. In August 1900 a strike occurred on the Taff Vale Railway. The Amalgamated Society of Railway Servants had taken no part in the quarrel, but it sent down its General Secretary to negotiate. In order to pacify the angry strikers and hasten a settlement, he organised strike-pay and persuaded ' black-legs ' imported by the Company to go back home. But as soon as the men had returned to work the Company sued the Society for the losses incurred during the strike ; and to the surprise of almost everyone the action was successful. The judge laid it down that the Act of 1875 did not entitle Trade Unions to use their great wealth without legal responsibility for the harm they might do to others. This judgment was reversed by the Court of Appeal but confirmed by the House of Lords, with the result that the Amalgamated Society of Railway Servants had to pay £23,000 damages, and as much more for costs. The Unions were thus deprived of their only weapon against employers—the concerted withholding of labour. A new Act was needed to restore it, and the Unions at the next election used all their voting-power to extort pledges from the Liberal candidates, wherever no Labour candidate was standing. This was one of the main causes of the tremendous Liberal majority of 1906, and of the election of forty members of the new Labour Party. The outcome was the *Trade Disputes Act* (1906) which declared that Unions could not be held responsible for employers' losses during strikes.

The employers now took another line of attack—against the right of Unions to support Members of Parliament. The Labour Party consisted mainly of Union officials, dependent for subsistence on their Unions ; so in 1909 one W. V. Osborne, a branch secretary of the Amalgamated Society of Railway Servants was put up by an Employers' Association to refuse to pay the ' parliamentary levy ' of a shilling collected annually from all members of the Unions affiliated to the Labour Party, As a Conservative, he said, he objected to being taxed to support political opponents. The High Court dismissed his claim, but the Appeal Court upheld it, and so did the House of Lords. This was a test case, the result of which would be accepted by the Courts in all similar cases.

Here was another judicial decision to be countered by

legislation ; but the Liberal Government was in no hurry about it. Payment of Members (1911) somewhat eased the situation for the Labour Party and the admission of Trade Unions as ' Approved Societies ' for administering National Insurance gave a great fillip to the movement. Even nondescript Unions of unskilled labour formed special departments for the work, and the membership of one of them, the General Workers, rose from 5,000 to 200,000 in three years. But it was not until 1913 that the Labour Party managed to extort from their Liberal allies an Act allowing Unions to finance Members of Parliament, and even then they were not to do so unless a majority of their members agreed, while dissentients could withhold the levy without losing their rights of membership.

These four years during which the Labour Party had been kept waiting on the parliamentary mat had encouraged the growth in some Unions of a revolt against the staid respectable Party at Westminster—a revolt in favour of ' direct action.' The years 1910–14 were filled with a growing chaos of industrial unrest, the outstanding features being gigantic strikes of dockers, railwaymen and miners. A new leaven was at work. The purpose of some of these strikers was no longer merely more pay and less work : they felt themselves to be preparing for a mass-attack on Capitalism. The final cataclysm could only be brought about by concerted action among the chief Unions, and a start was made, just before the first World War, with a ' Triple Industrial Alliance ' between three of the most powerful of them, the Miners' Federation of Great Britain, the National Union of Railwaymen (the reconstituted Amalgamated Society of Railway Servants) and the Transport Workers.

THE GENERAL STRIKE.—The War suspended this revolutionary movement. The British Trade Unions, like their counterparts in Germany, ceased from activities which might hinder ' the national war effort ' : and when Lloyd George's coalition was formed a prominent Trade Union official was admitted to the War Cabinet as representative of the labour-force without which the war could not be won. There was no longer any reluctance to recognise the right of Unions to speak for the workers ; on the contrary, the Government was very glad to have workers subject to organisations controlled by responsible officials, and it increased the power of these officials by authorising them to issue tickets exempting craftsmen from conscription.

But discontent with the official quietism of the Unions soon arose again. There was indignation over the 'dilution of labour' by semi-skilled workers now employed, sometimes at fancy wages, to do work which had always been reserved for fully fledged craftsmen. Moreover, the ordinary machinery of negotiation with employers having broken down in the confusion of war-conditions, the employees of a particular workshop would elect a 'shop-steward' *ad hoc*; and it was generally 'leftward' young men who, being the most prominent in voicing grievances, were deputed to carry them to the management.

Thus when the War ended the big Unions were divided between the old-fashioned leaders and a younger generation inspired by the Russian Revolution, who were spoiling for a fight, and were determined to maintain in peace the gains they had made in war—especially a share in the control of industry. When the Miners refused to accept a cut in wages the other members of the Triple Alliance promised to support them by a 'sympathetic strike.' But at the critical moment the 'safety first' leaders of the Railwaymen and Transport Workers recovered control, and on 'Black Friday' (April 15, 1921) the Alliance perished.

But this was not the end. Conditions turned against the Unions. Mass unemployment depleted their funds and weakened their bargaining-power, and strikes only worsened matters by making overseas customers seek more stable sources of supply. The Government's return to the Gold Standard in 1925 and its agreement to pay war-debts to the United States in gold still further crippled trade. In 1926 the Miners appealed to the Trades Union Congress for support in resisting a further wage-cut. The Trades Union Congress entered upon negotiations with the Government, but Baldwin, the Prime Minister, announced that 'all the workers in this country will have to accept reductions,' and this seemed to threaten the standard of living of the whole working-class. The adventurous element in the Unions had been nursing the idea of a General Strike; and the Government, urged on by a group of Ministers who wanted to end the long-drawn crisis by a 'show-down,' suddenly closed the discussions and challenged the Trades Union Congress to carry out its threat. Trade Unionists responded with a solidarity which surprised even themselves. For a week there was no transport by road or rail, except that run by amateur strike-breakers organised by the Government; mines, factories and workshops closed; there was no postal service and no newspapers. But the worst sufferers were the workers themselves, and we British are not given to revolutions. A General Strike can only succeed by bringing constitutional government to its knees. It is a fight to a finish. The very reluctant dragons of the Trades Union Congress began at once to try to make terms. But the Government, inspired by Winston Churchill, insisted on unconditional surrender, and got it (May 9, 1926). It followed up its victory with a new *Trades Union Act* (1927). This attacked the funds of the Labour Party by decreeing that Union members had to ask to pay the parliamentary levy instead of dissentients having to ask to be excused. It also declared illegal any strike which had aims beyond a trade-dispute in which the strikers are actually engaged, and which was designed to coerce the Government either directly, or by inflicting hardship on the community.

Thus a strike of busmen in sympathy with a strike of railwaymen would be illegal. The illegality did not render an individual striker liable to punishment; but any action by a Union in support of such a strike would make its funds liable for damages.

Furthermore Unions of Civil Servants were not to be affiliated to the Trades Union Congress or any similar federation; and Local Authorities were forbidden to do what some Town Councils with Labour majorities had done—make membership of a Union a condition of employment, or require contractors to employ only Trade Union labour.

The collapse of the General Strike disillusioned the rank and file of the movement, and the effects were completed by the Great Slump and the split in the Labour Party. The era of organised strikes which had lasted (with an interval during the first years of the War) since 1910 was closed. The militant party was crushed; the direction of affairs was in the hands of sober-minded officials who sought to make the best possible terms with Capital rather than to destroy it, and devoted much of their time and attention to keeping a firm hand on local branches, preventing unofficial strikes, and curbing irresponsible fire-brands who might make the Unions liable under the Act of 1927. Most of the stoppages of work since 1926 have been spontaneous affairs in which the officials have intervened to pacify their followers rather than to lead them in battle.

STRUCTURE OF TRADE UNIONISM.—British Trade Unionism is very British in its planlessness. It grew up piecemeal, in response to needs felt by one body of workers after another, and the result is a congeries of conflicting, overlapping organisations. But there is a growing tendency towards order. Amalgamation has made Unions fewer and larger. Industry has become so highly organised, mass-production has gone so far, Capital has become so trustified, that the Unions have been pushed in the same direction. There are still little single-branch Unions here and there, and some of them are very reluctant to sink their identity in a huge impersonal organisation directed by officials in London ; but it is only by so doing that they can find the strength to stand up to modern industrial conditions.

The formation of one big union out of many small ones calls for rare organising power, energy, and skill in handling men. A masterpiece in this direction was achieved in the building up of the Transport and General Workers' Union (mainly by Ernest Bevin) out of a number of unions of dockers, lightermen, busmen, tramwaymen and lorry-drivers. It is now the biggest organisation of its kind in the world, and its headquarters, Transport House, also contains the offices of the Labour Party and of the Trade Union Congress.

Another remarkable organisation is that of the Building Trade, which federates Bricklayers, Masons, Painters, Glaziers, Plasterers and Woodworkers. It sends twenty delegates to a National Joint Council for the Building Trade, where they join twenty representatives of employers to regulate the grading of labour according to skill and district, the cost of living bonus, allowances for travelling and for bad weather and similar matters.

It should be noted that these represent two different processes by which small unions grow into big ones : amalgamation and federation.

The chief centripetal force in the world of organised labour is the Trades Union Congress. This grew up as an annual conference of delegates from local Trades Councils. (The latter consist of representatives of all the Unions in a town or district). Only in 1895, after the first great expansion of the Unions, was it re-organised in its present form ; and it was not until after the first World War that it instituted a General Council, as a permanent General Staff of paid officials, chosen from different sections of Congress according to their numerical strength. And even now neither Congress nor Council has any compulsive control of the Unions. They do not form a super-state but a League of Nations—and a League without even the moral force of a Covenant. Among the Council's chief functions are arbitrating in disputes between Unions, and representing the Trade Union movement in the councils of the Labour Party and of the International Labour Office.

Only about four-fifths of the Unions belong to Congress. The member-Unions send to its annual meetings (about 1,000 strong, held in a different town each year) a delegation of workers and officials whose voting-power depends on the paid-up membership of the Union. Important decisions are often taken as a result not of public debate in the Congress-hall, but of agreements behind the scenes by delegates who wield the vast card-vote of a few powerful Unions. Some people regret that the delegates are not sent, as before 1895, by local Trades Councils. But the high officials who control the central executives of the Unions deprecate the activities of ' irresponsible busybodies ' ; for Trades Councils tend to be more ' leftward ' than Congress.

The strength of the various Unions and groups of Unions at a recent Congress was (in thousands) as follows :

Transport Workers : 606. Mining : 545. Railways : 449. Engineering : 449. General Workers : 342. Distributive Trades : 275. Cotton : 185. Building : 327. Printing and Paper : 169. Iron and Steel : 119. Wool : 105. Non-manual : 134. Boots and Leather : 103. Ship-building : 78.

In all about 4 million members were represented, out of about 5 million members of all Unions.

The essence of Trade Unionism is collective bargaining. Most of the early struggles of the Unions aimed at wringing from employers the right to negotiate on behalf of their members. Employers long resisted this as interference with ' freedom of contract ' ; but of course master and man were not on a level footing. It makes little difference to the employer of a thousand hands if one of them ceases to work for him, but it makes a world of difference to the ' hand ' to be dismissed. But this is a matter in which ' Socialism ' in the broadest sense of the term, has triumphed. Productive enterprise has developed enormously in scale and in complication. Most ' employers' nowadays are great corporations, the Directors of which appreciate the advantage of bargaining with officials who know the ropes and can speak for the employees *en masse*—professional negotiators who by the nature of their job want industrial peace and a good bank-balance for their Union, and believe that the strike is a weapon most effective when kept in its scabbard.

Expert skill is especially required in negotiating about piece-rates, and the grading of labour in time-rates. (Piece-rates are the basis of wages in mining and textiles, time-rates in railways. Some industries fluctuate between the two. Building workers mostly want to preserve time-rates against employers who would like to introduce piece-rates, *e.g.* so much per thousand bricks laid.)

The Unions mostly maintain that, equitably, organised Labour ought to have as much voice as organised Capital in the control of industry. Nobody regrets more than they that, with Capital claiming the right ' to do what it likes with its own,' the only influence which the workers can exert has to take forms which limit output, and so raise costs ; and nowadays they point to the results achieved in the USSR, where the distinction between Capital and Labour has ceased to exist. But of course it would be quite wrong to regard Trade Unions as primarily strike-organising institutions. In 1935, a typical pre-war year, the global expenditure of the British Trade Unions was as follows (in thousands sterling) :

	£
On Unemployment Benefit (additional to the £1,801 provided by the State)	703
On Sick Pay	584
On Funeral Benefit	342
On Superannuation Benefit	1,070
On Strike Pay	234
On other benefits	336

The contributions payable to the Unions still varies almost as widely as when ' the New Unionism ' began in 1889, from the

6*d.* a week to the National Union of General and Municipal Workers (which provides little beyond ' dispute-pay ') to the 12*s.* a week of some Printers' Unions, which provide as much as £2 a week Superannuation Benefit.   (But the Printers have long been the aristocrats of the Trade Union world.)

As we have seen, most of the Unions subscribe to the funds of the Parliamentary Labour Party ; but the money devoted to this purpose has by law to be collected and kept separately from that spent on industrial and social purposes. As the designers of the Act of 1927 knew, it is not everybody who will take the trouble to contract into a payment of this kind when they can evade it by merely neglecting to do so.   The Miners contribute almost to a man, but only about half the Railwaymen do so, and an even smaller proportion in other Unions.

As we saw in Chapter VII, the Parliamentary Labour Party is an amalgam of Trade Unions, Socialist organisations and private individuals. Of the 160 Members elected in 1935, half were financed by the Trade Unions (35 by the Miners), 71 by Divisional Labour Parties and 9 by the Co-operative Party.

TYPES OF ORGANISATION.—Trade Unions are of two distinct types : Craft Unions which include those who follow a particular calling, wherever they may be employed—*e.g.* engineers ; and Industrial Unions which include all the workers who co-operate in producing some commodity—*e.g.* colliery employees. But there is much overlapping and often jealousy between Unions—*e.g.* as to whether men permanently employed in railway workshops ought to belong to Engineers', Woodworkers' or Upholsterers' Unions, or to regard themselves as railwaymen.

The infinite variety in organisation can best be illustrated by thumb-nail sketches of two of the largest and most typical Unions.

First, the Miners, so often in the news. The coal-mining industry is concentrated in particular areas, shut away from the outside world. Miners have long felt strongly that the mineral wealth of the country ought to belong to the nation, and that the industry ought to be organised on a nation-wide agreement as to wages and conditions. Until 1942 the owners resisted this and the National Union of Mine-workers (formed in 1944 out of the historic Mineworkers' Federation of Great Britain) is still made up of District Associations—South Wales, Scotland, Durham, Yorkshire and so on —each with its full-time officials and its own scales of contribution and benefit. The Union has offices in London, and its Executive (elected annually from the officials of the District Associations) deals with the Government Ministry of Mines over such matters as safety regulations. But the basis of the organisation consists of the Pit Lodges, each with its elected Chairman and Secretary, who represent the employees of the mine in relation with the management, and advise them over insurance and compensation (one miner in five is incapacitated by injury every year).

In old-fashioned pits one of the Lodge officials usually acts as ' checkweighman ' at the pithead, to see that each miner gets fair-play over his piece-work earnings.

Each group of Lodges appoints by ballot a Miners' Agent (who has generally graduated to the position as a Lodge Official) to represent them on the Coalfield Executive which negotiates with the District Coal-owners' Association.

Local solidarity is intensified by Miners' Institutes for recreation, and Miners' Co-operatives for supplies, and this concentration gives mine-workers great electoral power. They usually elect ex-Agents whom they know personally and who represent them more fully than most Members of Parliament represent their constituents.

Railwaymen, on the other hand, are scattered about over the whole country, and often take a leading part in local Trades Councils. They have three Unions entirely independent of each other. The footplate grades nearly all belong to the Associated Society of Locomotive Engineers and Firemen (about 60,000 strong) ; there is a Railway Clerks' Association for the clerical and supervisory staff (also about 60,000) ; the other half-million belong to the National Union of Railwaymen. Railway workers, like miners, aim at nationalisation, but they feel much less bitterness towards their employers. For as a matter of fact a large measure of nationalisation already exists. During the first Great War the Government had to group the 130 Railway Companies into four, which work under statutory machinery governing fares and wages.

THE EFFECTS OF THE WAR. The second Great War, like the first, brought financial prosperity to the Unions. Unemployment was reduced to a minimum, and such strikes as took place were unofficial—*i.e.* they were not authorised by the Unions and therefore unsupported by ' strike-pay.' The Unions again, as in 1914–18, agreed to the ' dilution ' of labour by untrained and semi-trained workers ; and their ranks were swelled by thousands of men and women not previously engaged in industry. By the end of the War the Amalgamated Engineering Union had over a million members, and a reserve of 5 millions sterling : and the reserve funds of the whole movement had risen from about £20,000,000 to about £50,000,000.

Once again, as in 1914–18, the demand for war supplies made the survival of Great Britain dependent on the industrial capacity of its labouring-classes, and renewed in those classes a desire to participate in ' the policies and purposes of industry ' (to quote the Report of the 1944 Trades Union Congress). But the Unions learned by their experience after the last war that their movement requires solidarity to withstand the shocks and strains of the post-war period. The combined membership of two-thirds of the Unions did not amount to 1 per cent. of the whole. There was far too much overlapping and competition for members—more than 50 Unions catered for the Lancashire Cotton Trade alone. They therefore intensified the trend towards unification. The Mineworkers consolidated their Federation into a simpler and more centralised type of organisation ; a Joint Working Committee was set up by the three Railway Unions ; and similar tendencies are to be observed in other trades.

CHAPTER IX

THE SOCIAL SERVICES

WE hear the phrase ' Social Service ' so often to-day that we forget how modern it is. Apart from elementary education, the only personal public services provided for Queen Victoria's subjects were some bleak Poor Law Institutions and few isolation and mental hospitals. It was not until the beginning of the present century that the spirit shown in the 1880's by the inquiries of Charles Booth and the propaganda of the Fabian Society began to take substance in Acts of Parliament.

THE FIRST PHASE.—The prelude to this development was a new *Workmen's Compensation Act* (1897). Up to then a workman could not claim compensation for injuries received at work unless he could prove that they were due to wilful negligence by the employer, and were not caused by a fellow-workman. Henceforth it was payable even if no fault lay with the employer or anybody acting under his orders. At first this applied only to certain dangerous trades (railways, mines and building) but a later Act (1906) extended it to practically all occupations.

Most employers insured against the risk—mine-owners were compelled to do so. In cases of prolonged incapacitation the weekly allowance was often commuted for a lump sum, but the bargain had to have the approval of a County Court judge.

This of course was not a ' social service ' rendered by the State —the State merely compelled employers to render it.

Then a new era opened with the appointment in 1905 (by a Conservative Government) of a Royal Commission on the Poor Laws. This was no mere routine affair : it was planned on a comprehensive scale. Everybody realised that ' the ideas of 1834 ' [1] were outworn—that poverty must no longer be treated as a disgrace to the individual—it was a responsibility to the community. As a matter of fact the Commissioners were so many and so varied that they had to work in two independent groups.

[1] See p. 17.

I

The minority, of which Sidney Webb was the moving spirit, adopted the Fabian Society's plan of sending social workers about the country to study the facts on the spot ; and some of these investigators produced valuable monographs, such as Cyril Jackson's on *Boy Labour*.

Yet, when after four years of intense activity the Commission issued its twofold Report, its most striking feature was the extent to which the groups, despite their difference of approach, were of the same mind. They agreed that the existing Poor Law was obsolete ; that its methods were actually promoting squalor ; and that there ought to be more differentiation between different classes of paupers, and more effort to check the *causes* of destitution ; and that the chief of these causes was sickness.

It was found that of every hundred paupers, 12 were insane, 25 were children (mostly orphans or with invalid parents), 38 were infirm or aged or both, and 12 were ' casuals.' Only 13 were able-bodied, and of these half had some temporary sickness.

But the Minority Report went further ; it called for a complete Public Health Service, untainted by pauperism, with provision for unemployment based on the Socialist dogma of the ' Right to Work.' Unfortunately, this conception of an all-in social service was thirty-five years ahead of the times.

However, a stream of piecemeal reforms had already begun to flow under the Liberal Government which came into office just after the Commission was set up. Among the rude shocks which the South African War (1899–1902) gave to our national complacency was the revelation that only a minority of the men medically examined reached the very moderate standards set by the War Office. An Inter-Departmental Committee on Physical Deterioration found that the main cause was under-nourishment and neglect in childhood. This spurred the Government to a bold innovation. Acts passed in 1906–7 permitted Education Authorities (not, be it noted, the Guardians, who were associated in people's minds with pauperism) to provide mid-day meals for necessitous children, and required them to provide medical inspection in all elementary schools. And two further medical services quickly followed. The Government gave financial help to Local Authorities to combat tuberculosis (' The White Plague ') by dispensaries, hospitals and sanitoria, and to treat ' mentally deficient ' people who were not certifiably insane.

For persons certified insane by two doctors, County and County Borough Councils already had to provide asylums, by the Lunacy Laws as revised in 1890–91.

And by the time the Report appeared Lloyd George had launched ' a frontal attack on Want ' with a scheme for Old Age Pensions (1908). At the age of seventy old folk were to draw 5s. a week, provided that this did not bring their weekly income above 15s. This was not munificent, but it was the first recognition of the debt owed by the community to people who had built up its wealth by lives of labour at low wages. In 1920 the amount was doubled to meet the increased cost of living resulting from the war of 1914–18.

The idea had been started in Germany by Bismarck in the 1880's, to reconcile the German working-class to long hours and low pay ; and the experience of New Zealand since 1898 had shown its value in removing the depressing fear of a pauper old age. It was not wholly a debit to the Treasury, for it encouraged people to give their aged parents a home and keep them out of the hated ' House.'

In 1909 John Burns at the Local Government Board opened a new line of attack with a *Housing and Town Planning Act*. Hitherto Local Authorities had been unable to prevent the growth of ugly suburbs which devoured open spaces and destroyed natural amenities. They could now buy up land to provide ' lungs ' for town-dwellers, and could control the activities of the jerry-builder.

This Act was only permissive, and John Burns' policy at the Local Government Board did not encourage Local Authorities to spend much money on Housing. Compulsion only began with the *Housing and Town Planning Act* of 1919, which required the Authorities to submit plans forthwith. But even this was success-fully evaded, and various amending Acts have stimulated Local Authorities with grants from the Exchequer.

Then young Winston Churchill, in his first Cabinet post as President of the Board of Trade, started ' Labour Ex-changes ' to bring together employers wanting work-people and work-people wanting jobs. These were very successful—

they were soon bringing about an average of 2½ million engagements a year. In 1916 they were transferred to the new Ministry of Labour, and re-named ' Employment Exchanges.'

NATIONAL INSURANCE FOR THE WORKING-CLASSES.—But this Government's most spectacular contribution to social service was the *National Insurance Act* (1911). This, together with Old Age Pensions, was what Lloyd George had in mind when bringing in his ' People's Budget.' Part I of the Act provided medical care, and Part II provided against unemployment. The two Parts had very different histories. The first, like Old Age Pensions, had prototypes in Germany and New Zealand, and after surviving furious opposition in Parliament entered upon a quiet and uneventful existence. The second was experimental, and after becoming law almost unnoticed led to developments which brought the country to the brink of ruin.

Health Insurance had to be compulsory ; otherwise people who were ' good risks ' would have stayed out of the scheme, leaving it overweighted with the ' bad risks.' As the State was to take control it subsidised the Fund, adding 2d. a week to the 4d. of the worker and the 3d. of the employer. (Lloyd George cheered wage-earners with the thought that they were getting ' ninepence for fourpence '). After a certain number of these weekly premiums had been paid (by stamps affixed to a card), insured persons were entitled to free medical and dental attendance, medicine, appliances, and hospital treatment.

At first the Act applied only to manual workers and to salary-earners getting less than £150 a year ; but this income-limit was raised to £250 in 1919 and to £420 in 1942.

There had long been voluntary organisations for these purposes. Friendly Societies, such as the Royal Ancient Order of Buffaloes and the Oddfellows, combined sick and funeral benefits with general brotherliness ; to which some of them add mumbo-jumbo of secret rites, and a certain amount of conviviality. The more prosperous Trade Unions, too, provided their members with medical services ; and some of the great Insurance Companies, such as the Prudential and the Pearl, had special branches for this kind of work, sending agents round to collect the weekly premiums. These organisations had accumulated a valuable fund of experience, and Lloyd George drew upon it by employing them to carry out the Government scheme. Provided that they fulfilled certain conditions to ensure financial stability, they could be registered as ' Approved Societies ' for the purposes of the Act.

The scheme was ridiculed by the Opposition as ' trying to make people thrifty by Act of Parliament,' while the doctors (led by their professional organisations, such as the British Medical Association) jibbed at the system by which they had to apply to be placed on the local panel, and were to receive only 4*s*. per annum for each insured person who registered with them. That 4*s*. was too low a figure was proved by the fact that it was raised by a Government Amendment to 9*s*. without upsetting the finances of the scheme. And doctors soon became reconciled to the panel, despite the time spent in filling up forms and giving certificates. For the average number of patients on a doctor's list is about 2,000 (the legal limit is 2,500), and £900 a year is a useful foundation for a private practice. And though inconsiderate people sometimes abuse their right to free treatment, the Chinese basis of doctoring, that it should pay the physician better to keep his patients well than to have them ill, has much to commend it.

Health Insurance Committees were formed in every Local Government area representing the insured, the Authority and the doctors. It was intended that these should supervise the whole working of the scheme, but eventually the terms were made on a nation-wide scale, and the Committees merely employed a clerical staff to keep registers and distribute payment to doctors and chemists.

The Unemployment part of the Act was limited to trades most liable to fluctuations (building, ship-building and engineering), and covered only two million workers. Employer, workman and State each paid 2½*d*. a week ; an unemployed person was to draw 7*s*. a week for one-fifth of the number of weeks for which he had paid premiums. Nobody knew how the scheme would work out, and it was understood that if it proved actuarially unsound the Government would come to the rescue.

The war which soon followed produced jobs for all, and in the course of it the fund accumulated £25 millions. So in 1920 a new Act was passed, bringing in eleven million more people and doubling both premiums and benefits.

The benefit even when raised to 15s. seems very small ; but it was never intended as a subsistence—merely as a nucleus round which the unemployed person could rally his own resources.

But the revised scheme was hardly launched when it ran into heavy weather. The war-boom was followed by the inevitable slump. Unemployment, below half a million when the Act was passed, rose to two millions in 1921. All calculations went by the board. The Fund's nest-egg was quickly consumed. Many of the unemployed had not paid enough contributions to entitle them to benefits. Something had to be done for them ; and rather than force them to ' go on the parish ' (which would have cost as much in the end, and might have fanned smouldering discontents into flame) the Government decided to let them draw a weekly ' dole ' outside their contract rights, and to pass a special Act authorising the Fund to raise a loan to meet the cost. This hand-to-mouth system was continued (by Coalition, Conservative and Labour Governments in turn), until by 1929 eighteen Acts of Parliament had extended the Fund's borrowing-powers to a total of £115,000,000 and it was falling £1,000,000 deeper into debt every week.

Then came the world slump, and unemployment became worse than ever. The anxious search for cause and cure drew attention to the state of the Insurance Fund. Two Commissions of experts agreed that to save the nation from bankruptcy cuts must be made in national expenditure, especially in the ' dole.' It was over this that the second Labour Government broke up, to be replaced by a National Government which immediately issued a number of ' economy orders.' One of these substituted ' transitional benefit,' paid directly from the Treasury, for payments through the exhausted Insurance Fund, and required applicants to prove to a local ' Public Assistance Committee ' that the total resources of their household did not exceed the minimum required to keep body and soul together. This ' Household Means Test ' caused more bitterness of spirit than any other public measure since Chadwick created his ' Bastilles.'

British people particularly resent inquisition into their family affairs. But the view taken by the Government was that many expenses are naturally shared by all the members of a household— rent, heating, and rates, for instance—and that it was only fair to the tax-payer that all these considerations should be weighed in assessing his burden.

DECLINE AND FALL OF THE POOR LAW.—During the years 1914–18 there was great difficulty in providing the hospital treatment promised in the National Insurance Act. Apart from Voluntary Hospitals (few and far between) there were only Poor Law Infirmaries available. The Guardians were quite ready to throw these open to insured persons, but hatred of the Poor Law was so bitter that patients were very reluctant to be sent to them. So after the war it was decided to turn the Local Government Board into a 'Ministry of Health' with the special task of using its loan-granting powers to stimulate Local Authorities to provide for Hospital treatment, Maternity and Child Welfare, and Care of the Blind.

In 1925 the new Ministry set up a third branch of National Insurance—Contributory Old Age Pensions of 10s. a week at the age of sixty-five for widows and other persons not touched by the Act of 1908. But the new Act, clashing with the old, produced fearful complications, and confusion was worse confounded by further Acts in 1929, 1937 and 1940.

Though the Ministry of Health still administered the Poor Law, the Boards of Guardians were kept more or less in the background to deal with the hard cases whose needs were not met by any of the extensions of Insurance and Pensions. It was hoped that this would be a very small residuum, but during the following years, with the unemployment figures hovering round the 2,000,000 mark, the demands upon the Guardians became so great that they could not cope with the situation. Public opinion, even on the Boards themselves, forbade the 'workhouse test.' Scales of outdoor relief were raised, but the Poor Law had got a bad name. No amount of sympathetic handling by the Guardians could eradicate the fear and hatred acquired by their predecessors.

Thus the Poor Law was both bankrupt and outmoded, and the Baldwin Govermnent of 1924–29 (with Neville Chamberlain as Minister of Health) decided that the time had come to abolish it, lock, stock and barrel. The *Local Government Act* (1929) transferred the main functions of the Guardians to 'Public Assistance Committees' of County and County Borough Councils, while their hospitals and institutions for the care of the blind and of infants were delegated to the existing Public Health and Education Committees of those Authorities.

Note the mild phrase ' Public Assistance ' replacing the harsher ' Poor Relief.' The Committees appointed ' Public Assistance Officers,' and other paid officials. County Committees had local branches consisting of members of District Councils, the local members of the County Council, and co-opted members, of whom some had to be women.

The Act also required Counties and County Boroughs to prepare schemes for General and Isolation Hospitals, but did not fix a strict time-limit within which this had to be done, and there continued to be an unfortunate lack of uniformity between one Authority and another. On the whole the County Boroughs, moved by civic pride and close contact with the needs of their citizens, were more enterprising than the Counties.

The severities of 1931 were never intended to be permanent. As soon as the dangerous corner was turned a new plan was devised for dealing with unemployed persons not entitled to insurance benefit. There was set up in Whitehall an ' Unemployment Assistance Board ' nominated by the Minister of Labour with a ' field staff ' dispersed about the country in local offices, to investigate claims. The great advantage of this scheme was that it could be worked upon definite principles and uniform scales.

But people whose needs (often in some sudden emergency) were not met by National Insurance Acts or the Unemployment Assistance Board still had to get ' Public Assistance,' and the co-existence of two independent systems of relief caused much confusion.

For instance, to draw relief from the Assistance Board (the word ' Unemployment ' was dropped from its title in 1938), a man had to be ' available for employment.' So if he fell sick he had to go to the Local Authority's Public Assistance Officer—to be returned to the Assistance Board as soon as he recovered.

The administration of Old Age Pensions was even more complicated. It was in the hands of the Commissioners of Customs and Excise, who investigated claims through their local Pensions Officers, with the assistance of Pensions Committees appointed by Local Authorities ; while the Ministry of Health had a special department for hearing appeals. Payments were made through

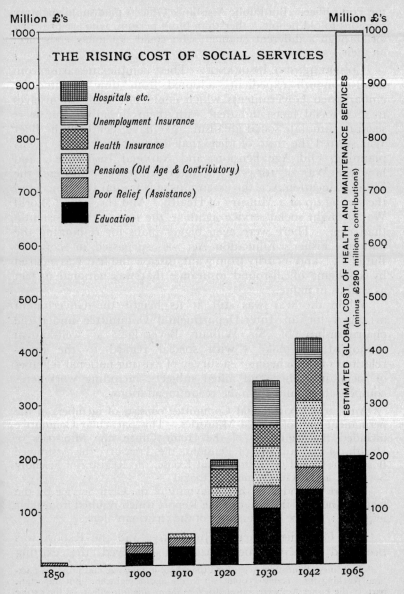

THE RISING COST OF SOCIAL SERVICES

Hospitals etc.

Unemployment Insurance

Health Insurance

Pensions (Old Age & Contributory)

Poor Relief (Assistance)

Education

ESTIMATED GLOBAL COST OF HEALTH AND MAINTENANCE SERVICES
(minus £290 millions contributions)

Million £'s 1000

Million £'s 1000

GROWTH OF SOCIAL SERVICES

the Post Office. But Public Assistance Officers paid supplementary pensions to old people (other than blind persons, who are provided for through a different channel) who could not make ends meet on their 10s. a week.

COMPREHENSIVE INSURANCE.—These complexities arose from hand-to-mouth expedients adopted from time to time by embarrassed Governments which could not bring themselves to face social facts and deal with them broadly. But wars seem to stimulate social idealism. We have seen how the Boer War started the train of ideas that led to school meals, town-planning, Old Age Pensions and National Insurance ; and how the War of 1914–18 produced Universal Suffrage, the Fisher Education Act, the extensions of National Insurance and the setting up of a Ministry of Health. And the second World War brought social service again to the fore, more insistently than ever. There were even bigger plans for re-housing the nation ; Fisher's Education Act was surpassed in scope by Butler's ; [1] and security from want, disease and fear was secured by a scheme of all-round insurance that was national in fact as well as in name.

While the war was still at its height the Government arranged for an Inter-Departmental Committee under the chairmanship of Sir William Beveridge, a well-known economist, to make ('with special regard to the inter-relations of the schemes ') a survey of existing national schemes of social insurance and allied subjects, including workmen's compensation, and to make recommendations.'

An Inter-Departmental Committee consists of members of the permanent staff of several Ministries. This particular Committee included representatives of the Home Office, the Ministries of Health, of Labour and of Pensions, the Treasury, the Assistance Board, the Board of Customs and Excise, the Registry of Friendly Societies, and a Government Actuary.

We are reminded of the anonymity of the Civil Service by the fact that none of these signed the Report which resulted from their inquiries : it bore the signature of the chairman alone.

The Committee met in June 1941 and the Report was presented in November 1942. It surveyed the existing

---

[1] Both these Education Acts raised the school-leaving age and provided part-time teaching for ' Young People ' up to the age of eighteen. But important parts of the Fisher Act were repealed before they came into effect, on the excuse that the country could not afford such luxuries with a million unemployed.

muddle, showing that 7s. 6d. out of every £1 paid to industrial Insurance Companies went in overhead expenses, including the collector's commission ; that the distinction between Health and Unemployment benefits frequently halved an unemployed man's income when he fell sick ; that workmen sometimes failed to get compensation for crippling injuries because they could not afford to go to law, or because their employer went bankrupt. Its proposals were revolutionary. It recommended that *all* social services should be rendered to *all* people in return for sticking a single stamp on a card each week.

It emphasised the people's preference for contributory schemes. As a nation we like to feel that we can claim services as a right, not have to beg for them as a charity ; and we are ready to pay considerable sums for the sake of this feeling. Of the eighteen million persons covered by National Health Insurance, five millions paid into hospital contributory schemes, though they could get the same treatment free. And the resentment against the Means Test came largely from the feeling that it was unfair to penalise ' what people had come to regard as the duty and pleasure of putting pennies away for a rainy day.'

The Government's response to the Report appeared in September 1944 in the form of a White Paper on Social Insurance. Its proposals may be summarised under the following ten heads.

I. A flat weekly subsistence payment for people unemployed or laid up by sickness : 24s. for a single man or woman, 40s. for man and wife.

II. Complete free medical service, including general practitioner, surgeon, specialist, dentist, hospital and sanatorium treatment, and all medicines and appliances.

III. ' Retirement Pensions ' (35s. joint, 20s. single) to men at 65, to women at 60. Orphans' allowance of 12s. a week to age 16.

IV. Maternity Grants of £4, Death Grants up to £20.

V. A National Assistance Fund in reserve to meet special necessities.

VI. A consolidated contribution of 3s. 10d. from men, 3s. from women ; together with 3s. from employer for men and 2s. 5d. for women. One weekly stamp on card.

VII. Family allowances of 5s. a week for each child after the first, and free meals and milk at school. (This is outside the financial scheme, being payable entirely by the State.)

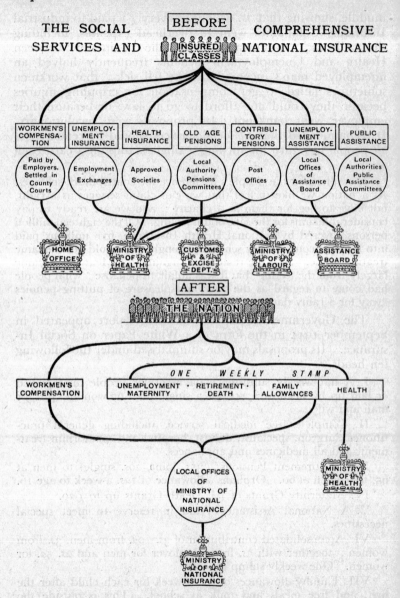

THE SOCIAL SERVICES BEFORE AND AFTER COMPREHENSIVE NATIONAL INSURANCE

VIII. These services are to be without Means Test. They cover the entire population—' rich man, poor man, beggar man, thief,' giving expression to the solidarity and unity of the nation.

IX. Workmen's Compensation is to be within the general scheme, instead of being a matter of contention between employer and employed (or between Trade Union and Insurance Company). But the funds for it are to be kept separate, and maintained by a weekly payment of 6d. for a man and 4d. for a woman, divided equally between employer and employed.

X. The whole scheme is to be managed by a new Ministry of National Service, with a network of local offices at which the public can lodge claims, seek information or guidance, and obtain payment of certain benefits. (But Pensions are to be paid through the Post Office, Unemployment pay through Employment Exchanges.)

The Government Actuary has worked out the following estimate of the cost :—

ESTIMATED EXPENDITURE (IN £ MILLIONS)

	1945	1955	1965	1975
Retirement Pensions . .	169	203	272	324
Other Social Insurance Benefits	205	225	228	218
National Assistance . .	69	73	70	67
Family Allowances . .	59	60	56	52
Health Services . . .	148	170	170	170
Totals. . .	650	731	796	831

ESTIMATED INCOME (IN £ MILLIONS)

	1945	1955	1965	1975
Insurance Contributions .	283	280	275	259
Interest on Funds . . .	15	15	15	15
Balance to be met from Exchequer or Rates . .	352	436	506	557
Totals. . .	650	731	796	831

The rising cost is largely due to the fall in both the birth-rate and the death-rate ; for this will increase the proportion of people drawing pensions as compared with the number working and paying contributions.

The Government Actuary estimated that whereas in 1945 the number of pensioners would be 3,400,000 and the number of contributors 21,000,000, in 1975 the figures will be 6,100,000 and 20,000,000.

The deficit is a lot of money, but it is not more than 5 per cent. of the estimated national income, which will grow with the increasing mechanisation of production. And it may be argued that such a redistribution of spending-power will help to diffuse among all classes the goods and services which were locked up for lack of it in the depression which followed the last war. And it is further arguable that if the country's productive capacity will not enable it to provide a minimum income of 24s. a week for adults and 5s. a week for children, then it is time that some more efficient economic system was introduced.

And so ends the story that was opened by the Lloyd George Act of 1911. It is now for the nation, freed from debilitating worries, to justify the scheme by a fresh outburst of that productive energy which has given it wealth and power in the past, and which is even more vitally necessary to-day.

Chapter X

THE LAW

HOW THE COURTS ADMINISTER IT, AND THEREBY HELP TO MAKE IT

OUR Law, like our Constitution and our Empire, is something all our own, which grew up from our national disposition to avoid laying down principles and get on with the job in hand. And, as with those other institutions, the process has gone on until the result is too massive to be amenable to planning.

COMMON LAW.—The basis of our legal system is the ' Common Law '—the record of earlier judgments. As far back as history goes judges have assumed the existence of a body of Law not made by King or Parliament. Statutes have been bringing it into touch with changing conditions ever since the thirteenth century, and their bulk grows by a stout volume every year ; but these are merely the addenda and errata of the Common Law which originated with tribal ideas of right and wrong current among our cave-dwelling forbears. No statute declares in set terms that we must pay our debts and refrain from cutting our neighbour's throat. And this applies to our political liberties—the right to free speech for instance ; our ancestors did not trouble to proclaim such rights—they merely provided legal remedies by which to enforce them.

Most other nations have digests of their Law, setting forth the principles on which their Courts are to act. France and Germany, after all the changes and chances of war and revolution, look back to the Code which the all-embracing genius of Napoleon Bonaparte imposed upon them, bringing order out of chaos, at the beginning of the last century ; and the *Code Napoléon* was itself based on the *Institutes* by which Roman law and custom were codified in the sixth century under the Emperor Justinian. In applying such systems to varied circumstances judges create an incrustation of case-law not unlike our own ; but the principles underlying their judgments are all set forth in a brief pamphlet.

When the Japanese adopted a legal system on the Western model they would have preferred to base it on British Common Law ; but, unable to find it set forth in any clear form, they had to fall back on the *Code Napoléon*.

British settlers overseas, on the other hand, took the Common Law with them as part of their racial inheritance. It is in force not only in the Dominions and Colonies, but in the United States. There are two exceptions : in South Africa Roman Dutch Law prevails, and the Province of Quebec still uses the French civil law.

Of course, a statute may reverse a doctrine of Common Law—that follows from the Sovereignty of Parliament. But its words have to be interpreted by judges whose professional minds have been formed by familiarity with the Common Law.

This was shown over the Trade Unions.[1] Judges argued, consciously or unconsciously, ' The Common Law is the basis of the Laws of England ; Parliament cannot have intended to undermine that basis ; therefore the Act of 1875 cannot mean that Unions can with impunity injure employers by depriving them of labour.' The most explicit Acts had to be passed to break down this Common Law outlook.

There is a fiction that judges do not *make* law by their decisions—that they are merely applying to the case before them rules enshrined in earlier judgments on similar cases. But the moment the new judgment has appeared in the *Law Reports* everyone begins to assume that it has made the law somewhat different from what it was before.

The *Law Reports* go back to the sixteenth century. Only those cases appear which the compiler considers of permanent legal importance. It is characteristically British that they are not edited or published by the Government, but by private firms, who print different selections of cases.

LAWYERS.—A striking peculiarity of the legal profession in this country is its division into two branches—solicitors and barristers. Numerically barristers seem to form a special branch and solicitors the main body, but historically barristers are the main body and solicitors an offshoot.

In the Middle Ages all lawyers, in England as on the Continent, were advocates, who both prepared their cases and

[1] See p. 103.

argued them before the courts. But there arose a class of
' attorneys ' who did much of the routine work about the
courts—applying for writs, marshalling witnesses, and so on.
The importance of this humbler class grew, and in 1739
' Solicitors ' (as they came to be called) formed an association,
which a century later became ' The Law Society,' to regulate
entry into the profession and standards of professional conduct.

Solicitors are legal men-of-all-work. They prepare con-
veyances, leases, mortgages, settlements, deeds of partnership
and the articles of Limited Companies, and carry out various
kinds of financial business. And if one unfortunately has to
go to law, or (more unfortunately) is proceeded against by
someone else, or (most unfortunately of all) is charged with
some offence or crime, it is to a solicitor that one goes for advice
and through whom one takes any legal steps that may be
necessary. If the case comes before a Magistrate's Court or a
County Court, the solicitor can appear on one's behalf, question
witnesses and address the Bench. But if the matter goes before
the High Court, either in London or at the Assizes, he has to
' instruct ' a barrister.

These ' instructions,' which give a statement of the facts, an
outline of the client's case, and a summary of the evidence for it,
are typed out on ' brief-paper.' The outside of the ' brief ' is
endorsed with the fee which ' counsel ' is to get for taking it.

A member of the public cannot make professional contact
with a barrister except through a solicitor. (This is not a
matter of law, but of professional etiquette as rigid as the
strongest law ever made.) Even if one merely wants ' Counsel's
Opinion ' about a point of law or one's prospects of success in
the courts, one's solicitor has to be present at the interview in
the barrister's chambers.

A future solicitor has to be articled for five years to a
solicitor in practice, gaining experience from work done in
his office ; and to pass two examinations conducted by the
Law Society.

The ' articled clerk ' may have to pay a fee up to £500, and the
stamp on the articles costs £80. Thus only people with some
money to spend can enter the profession. Those with a bent for
the law who cannot afford the expense become unarticled clerks.
The confidential clerk of a busy firm may by constant practice

K

become a better practical lawyer than his employers—and through his knowledge of clients' affairs be more indispensable than some of the partners.

Barristers belong to one of the ' Inns of Court '—the Inner Temple, the Middle Temple (which took over the premises of the Knights Templars, suppressed under Henry III), Lincoln's Inn and Gray's Inn.   They are of the same nature as Oxford and Cambridge Colleges, with Benchers in place of Fellows. When an aspirant has fulfilled certain conditions, including dining in Hall thrice a term for three years and passing examinations (a good deal easier than those for solicitors), these Benchers ' call him to the Bar.'   He then has to work in a barrister's chambers for a minimum of six months, paying about 100 guineas for tuition.   Thereafter he can set up in practice.

But briefs may come slowly, unless he has busy solicitors among his friends.

(' I soon got tired of third-class journeys and dinners of bread and water, So I fell in love with a rich attorney's elderly ugly daughter,' sings the Judge in *Trial by Jury*.)

If he makes a reputation for winning cases he can charge high fees (as much as 500 guineas with a 100-guinea ' refresher ' for every day the case lasts) ; but for years he may have to live on private income, or his wits, with an occasional brief marked Five and One (*i.e.* 5 guineas with 1 guinea for the preliminary consultation), or even One and Nothing.   Still, many lucrative posts are open to a barrister which do not involve pleading in court—as Town Clerks, and on the legal staff of Government Offices ; while for those who have gained some standing in the Courts there are posts as Stipendiary Magistrates, Recorders and County Court Judges ; and above all, judgeships of the High Court.

Successful barristers used to become ' Serjeants-at-Law ' ; nowadays they can apply to the Lord Chancellor to be made ' King's Counsel.'   A K.C. never takes a case alone—he always has at least one ' Junior Counsel' with him.   He wears a silk gown instead of a ' stuff ' one, and is said to have ' taken silk.'   Judges are nearly always selected from successful K.C.s.

In most countries judges are not former advocates ; they form a separate branch of the profession.

Judges are appointed by the Government, the Lord Chancellor having the chief voice in the selection. Formerly judgeships were often a reward for political services to the party in power, but this is less frequent now. Puisne (rank-and-file) judges are paid £5,000 a year, Lords of Appeal and Law Lords rather more, up to the Lord Chancellor's £10,000. These are higher salaries than are paid to judges in other countries ; but we want first-class men on the Bench, and most of the candidates are earning big incomes at the Bar. Many of them accept the position mainly because it is less strenuous for a man who is getting on in years than the waging of forensic battles on the floor of the Court. And, of course, it is highly dignified.

An English judge in his full-bottomed wig, his scarlet and ermine, is an impressive embodiment of the majesty of the law. Counsel also wear wigs, gowns and bands. Solicitors when pleading in County Courts wear gowns and bands but not wigs.

THE HIGH COURT OF JUSTICE.—The courts in which our Law is administered have grown up, like the Law itself, out of changing needs and circumstances. Not until 1875, after seven centuries of development, was there any attempt to rationalise them. Only one entirely new court has been created—and even then an old name was revived for it.

Nowadays we regard justice as a part of government, like the Post Office or the Army. But in feudal times it was a source of profit to territorial nobles as well as to the King. In this matter as in others the King eventually gained supremacy ; for, having good lawyers at hand engaged in administration, he was able to provide suitors with reliable judgments. Gradually a class of specialist judges arose. Henry II developed it as an asset to his power ; and under his son the barons tried vainly in Magna Carta to check the growing monopoly of the royal courts of justice.

By the time of Edward I three such courts were sitting regularly at Westminster : Common Pleas, for disputes between subjects ; King's Bench, for disputes in which the Government was involved ; and Exchequer, for revenue matters. The judges went on circuit from time to time, carrying the King's justice to all parts. When they returned to Westminster from these Assizes they naturally discussed their cases and their judgments, and thus created a truly 'common,' uniform system, superseding the local customs peculiar to different parts of the country.

Assize Courts are primarily criminal courts ; civil suits are still supposed to be heard in London.

The distinction is not always easy to draw. Of course, murder and burglary are clearly criminal, the payment of debts and the fulfilment of contracts are clearly civil. But slander or negligent driving may be either—it depends on whether retribution or compensation is sought.

Actually the civil business at Assizes is often heavier than the criminal. Civil actions are formally begun in London, to be heard there *nisi prius* ('unless beforehand') Assizes are held in the County ; and this generally happens, saving the cost of taking the parties and their witnesses up to London to complete the trial.

Assize Courts are commonly built in pairs, opening off a central lobby. Criminal cases are heard in the CROWN COURT (which has a dock), civil cases in one bearing the inscription NISI PRIUS (without a dock). The judge presiding in the former wears scarlet, while the judge in the Nisi Prius court wears black with a crimson girdle.

But English justice has always been completed—and complicated—by another set of principles, besides Common and Statute Law. By the time of Edward I the Common Law was already hardening into shapes which produced unfair results in particular cases. But the King still had a reserve power of getting justice done. Besides the judges (who, when the letter of the law works unjustly can only shrug their shoulders and say 'This may be hard luck, but the law is law !') there was the King's Chancellor, his general secretary, an ecclesiastic who 'kept the royal conscience'—*i.e.* who decided what was rightful in governmental affairs. People who felt aggrieved by the ordinary courts addressed themselves to him, and he kept a court of his own in which to hear their tales of woe. He could not reverse the judgment of the law, but he could summon the other party to the suit and say to him 'The King commands you not to avail yourself of the unfair advantage which the law has given you. If you do I shall put you into gaol.' This is to-day called 'granting an injunction.'

Such decisions became precedents for later decisions, as in the law courts, and grew into a system of 'Equity.' It filled such a deeply-felt want that it developed. Soon the Chancellor himself had to be a lawyer.

Bishop Williams under Charles I was the last Lord Chancellor to be a cleric ; Lord Shaftesbury under Charles II was the last one not to be a lawyer by vocation.

'Masters in Chancery' (especially the Master of the Rolls) had to be appointed to help with the growing volume of work, but still the court fell into arrears and became the by-word for the 'law's delays' depicted in *Bleak House*. The pressure of other duties made the Lord Chancellor give up attending in person. There was constant confusion and overlapping between the courts—a suitor might have to get damages in one court, an injunction in another and his costs in a third ; and might lose his case by applying for the wrong writ.

At last the whole system was overhauled as part of the spate of reforms set flowing by the Gladstone Government of 1869–73. The *Judicature Act* (1873), created a single High Court of Justice, consisting (as amended later) of three Divisions, all eventually housed in the Law Courts in the Strand (completed 1886). In the Chancery Division are heard cases in which the rules of Equity are specially appropriate—*e.g.* Settlements, Trusts, Mortgages, and Partnerships. Then there is a division for Probate, Divorce and Admiralty.

This may seem a queer assortment of matters ; but Death and Marriage are occasions with which the Church is specially concerned, and when the old Ecclesiastical Courts were abolished their jurisdiction was handed over to the same lay court. As to Admiralty, it was natural that a maritime nation should have disputes arising from collisions at sea, the chartering of ships and so on ; but there were not enough of them to justify keeping a separate court, and this work was given to the Probate and Divorce Division—seemingly for lack of any more appropriate home. Elder Brethren of Trinity House sometimes sit on the bench with the judge to assist when questions of seamanship arise.

All other civil suits come before the King's Bench Division. Besides sitting in London, most of its twenty-one judges go on circuit three times a year, one sits in the Central Criminal Court (commonly called 'The Old Bailey'), and two join the Lord Chief Justice in a 'Divisional Court' to hear appeals from Magistrates' Courts and Quarter Sessions, and cases under Writs of *Certiorari* and *Mandamus*.[1]

The Old Bailey is the busiest criminal court in the world. It is in almost continuous session, often with several courts sitting simultaneously under the Recorder of the City of London, the Common Serjeant, and a King's Bench judge. Its jurisdiction covers primarily crimes committed in Greater London, but cases are often sent up from the provinces, especially if strong local feeling makes it unlikely that a local jury would be really impartial.

COURTS OF APPEAL.—If a litigant thinks he has not had a fair deal from the High Court and is willing to risk the loss of more money for costs, he can carry his suit to the Court of Appeal. This consists of the Master of the Rolls and eight 'Lords Justices of Appeal.' Three of them sit together to form a Court, and thus three cases can be heard simultaneously. Witnesses do not (normally) appear—their evidence is taken from the report of the original hearing ; but counsel argue points of law, the appellant generally claiming that the High Court Judge overlooked part of the evidence, or misconstrued some previous judgment, or misdirected the jury.

If our suitor is still dissatisfied, and has money to burn, he can (by permission of the Court) appeal to the House of Lords. For this purpose that House consists of the Lord Chancellor, any ex-Lord Chancellors available, and seven 'Lords of Appeal'—former judges who are made life-peers. They sit in the House, and counsel remain outside the Bar. It is the most inconvenient law-court in the world—but the most lucrative for those who practise before it. The members of the Court give their judgments separately, and the issue is decided by 'Vote of the House.'

Thus a suitor might have the support of six out of nine judges (the High Court judge, the three Appeal Court judges, and two of the five Law Lords) for his case, and still lose his case.

Until 1907 there was no opportunity of revising the verdict or sentence of a Criminal Court ; but there is now a Court of Criminal Appeal, consisting usually of the Lord Chief Justice

[1] See p. 81.

BRITISH COURTS OF JUSTICE

Courts with Civil Jurisdiction .... ═══════
Courts with Criminal Jurisdiction ...... ▬▬▬▬▬▬▬

HOUSE OF LORDS	JUDICIAL COMMITTEE
[FINAL COURT OF APPEAL FOR GREAT BRITAIN]	OF THE PRIVY COUNCIL
	[FINAL COURT OF APPEAL FOR THE DOMINIONS]
Lord Chancellor & 7 Lords of Appeal in Ordinary	Personnel as for House of Lords plus certain overseas ex-Judges

COURT OF APPEAL

Master of the Rolls and
8 Lords Justices of Appeal

COURT OF CRIMINAL APPEAL

Lord Chief Justice and
2 Puisne Judges

HIGH COURT OF JUSTICE

CHANCERY DIVISION	PROBATE, ADMIRALTY & DIVORCE DIVISION	KING'S BENCH DIVISION	ASSIZES [NISI PRIUS]	CENTRAL CRIMINAL COURT
5 Puisne Judges	President and 5 Puisne Judges	Lord Chief Justice and 20 Puisne Judges	ASSIZES [CROWN]	A K.B. Judge Common Serjeant Recorder of London [OLD BAILEY]
		DIVISIONAL COURT		

QUARTER SESSIONS

County J.Ps or
(in County Boroughs)
Recorders

COUNTY COURTS

60 County Court Judges

COURTS OF SUMMARY JURISDICTION
Petty Sessions under J.Ps.
18 Stipendary Magistrates
27 Metropolitan Police Magistrates

MATRIMONIAL
COURTS

and two other Judges of the King's Bench Division. As with the civil Court of Appeal, it accepts the evidence of the lower Court (though fresh witnesses may be called, with its express permission), and hears counsel argue for and against the findings of that Court from a legal point of view. It can increase, affirm or reduce the sentence.

Of the 'Conciliar Courts' like Star Chamber and High Commission, only one survived the Civil War : the Judicial Committee of the Privy Council. It consists of the Law Lords and certain Indian and Dominion Judges, and sits (usually without robes or other paraphernalia) to hear appeals from the courts of the King's overseas Dominions.

THE LOWER COURTS.—Until 1846 civil suits could only be brought in the High Court, which meant that justice was mostly too expensive for humble folk. But in that year an Act instituted 'County Courts' within the reach of every locality and every purse. The areas they serve do not necessarily coincide with counties, but when a name had to be found for them it seemed a good plan to give them the prestige of the ancient shire-courts. There are at present sixty County Court judges. Some have only one court, serving a big town ; others go on a little monthly circuit. They are appointed by the Lord Chancellor from senior barristers, and are paid about £2,000 a year. Each Court has a clerical staff under a Registrar, who is a solicitor and takes smaller cases himself. The main business of these courts is compelling the payment of small debts. Over a million summonses of this description are issued annually, 95 per cent. of them for sums under £20 ; but only about 30,000 cases are actually heard—the mere serving of the summons makes most debtors pay up before incurring further costs. The Courts also settle claims under the Workmen's Compensation Acts, especially the sanctioning of lump-sum settlements ; they hear claims for compensation arising out of accidents ; and settle small equity matters concerned with mortgages, partnerships and bankruptcies ; also suits about titles to land, hire-purchase and tenancies.

The lowest grade of criminal court was re-organised at about the same time that the County Courts were set up for civil matters. It was a statute of 1848 that brought system into the haphazard proceedings of magistrates which we noticed in an earlier chapter. Justices of the Peace are still

local 'amateurs,' guided in matters of law by their clerk—
generally a local solicitor ; but they have lost nearly all their
administrative powers,[1] they have to hear cases in a proper
court-house ; and they are nominated by an inclusive committee—not merely by the Lord Lieutenant of the County.

Complaints are sometimes heard that nominations are too
often a reward for services to a political party ; that magistrates
are too old, and have too little understanding of working-class life.
But it is difficult for people earning their living to attend the court
one or more mornings every week.

Some County Boroughs engage a barrister as a whole-time
'Stipendiary Magistrate,' and London has 'Metropolitan
Police Magistrates.' A Stipendiary may have Justices of the
Peace sitting with him—technically he is only chairman of the
Bench ; but a Metropolitan Magistrate is monarch of all he
surveys.

These courts used to be known as 'Police Courts'—an
unfortunate name which induced a false impression—sometimes
in the magistrates themselves—that they were connected with
the police. They are now called 'Courts of Summary
Jurisdiction.'

There are statutory limits to the offences that can be dealt
with by them, and to the penalties which they can inflict.
A single Justice of the Peace can imprison for fourteen days and
fine up to £1 ; two or more can imprison for six months and
fine up to £50. But for serious crime they have to indict the
accused to stand his trial at Quarter Sessions or the Assizes.

There are cases of intermediate gravity, in which the accused
can choose whether he will be committed for trial by jury or be
dealt with summarily. He generally chooses the latter ; conviction may be more probable, but sentences tend to be lighter
and a term of imprisonment starts sooner. Magistrates prefer
this course too ; for committing a prisoner for trial involves taking
down depositions of witnesses in writing. Only about 15 per
cent. of 'indictable offences' are actually tried by jury.

Assizes we already know something of. Quarter Sessions
can be attended by any or all of the Justices of the Peace of a
county ; there are often as many as a dozen on the Bench.
They choose their own chairman, but it is of great advantage

[1] They still license public houses.

for the magistrate so chosen to be a trained lawyer. If not, great responsibility falls on the Clerk of the Peace, who is usually Clerk to the County Council.

The question whether a case goes to Assizes or to Quarter Sessions is settled by various considerations. Really serious charges, such as are punishable by death or penal servitude for life, and those that involve difficult legal points have to go to Assizes. In other cases the decision may rest on which comes next in date, or upon the qualifications of the Chairman of the Sessions.

County Boroughs have their Quarter Sessions taken by a ' Recorder,' appointed by the Lord Chancellor. This is an attractive post, for it provides a barrister with a regular income in return for a few days' work every three or four months, leaving him free at other times to practise as counsel ; and it often leads to a judgeship.

Magistrates have special courts for matrimonial disputes, which consist largely in wives wanting ' separation orders ' under which their husbands will be compelled to pay a weekly sum for their maintenance. These are held in private ; as are Children's Courts, in which care is taken to prevent young delinquents from being brought into contact with crime and criminals.

Excellent work is done in connection with these two courts by Probation Officers. These were at first provided by religious organisations, but they now form a regular public service. They visit people in their homes, give them advice, and keep magistrates in touch with their domestic circumstances.

Coroners' Courts are not criminal courts, but they some-times lead thereto. Coroners are lawyers or doctors, appointed by County and County Borough Councils. When a death occurs without a doctor being able to certify the cause, the circumstances have to be reported to the Coroner, who may decide that they justify an inquest—a public inquiry, with the compulsory sworn evidence of witnesses, and (if he thinks it necessary) a jury. A Coroner's Court simply pronounces upon the cause of death ; it cannot punish anybody for anything. But its verdict may cause the Coroner to commit somebody for trial.

JURIES.—We are justly proud of our legal system. Our judges are free from governmental influence—they can only be dismissed by a complicated process which includes a vote of both Houses of Parliament and the consent of the other judges. *Habeas Corpus* compels the Government to bring prisoners to speedy trial. Trials are held in public.[1] Officials are subject to the same law as private persons. Evidence as to a person's character must not be produced in court before he is found guilty. The procedure of the police in dealing with accused persons is carefully circumscribed to prevent anything in the nature of 'third degree.' But our most cherished tradition is the right of every Englishman to 'trial by his peers' (*i.e.* his equals in rank). This was once a safe-guard for accused persons who might otherwise be at the mercy of a despotic king and his judges. We are no longer in need of such protection ; and there is to-day a tendency (embodied in the *Administration of Justice Act*, of 1933) to restrict jury-trial to heavy criminal charges and important civil suits in which the common sense of a cross-section of the public may be a corrective to the narrower outlook of a judge. At least that is the theory. A jury supplies an 'amateur' element like that which we found in our Central and Local Government. Obviously, cases which involve intricate legal arguments or the prolonged examination of documents are unsuitable for jury-trial. Either party to a suit can ask for a jury ; but he knows that it will prolong the case, for counsel take longer to examine witnesses and drive home their arguments when they have to convince a dozen laymen than when they are addressing themselves solely to a professional lawyer on the Bench. And time is money in the courts. The decision, jury or no jury, lies with an official of the court, with right of appeal to the judge.

Magistrates' and County Courts never have juries, nor do the Chancery or Probate, Divorce and Admiralty Divisions of the High Court ; and since 1933 they are used in less than 10 per cent. of the cases before the King's Bench.

A panel of jurymen is summoned by the Under-Sheriff from the householders of the neighbourhood ; the jury for each case is chosen by ballot. Juries may be either ' common ' or ' special.' The latter are people who live in more ex-pensive houses and are therefore presumed to be better able to follow a difficult case. Verdicts have to be unanimous. If a jury disagrees the case has to be re-tried with a fresh one.

---

[1] Unless the Judge specially directs that it be held *in camera*, in the public interest.

PROCEDURE.—This history of our courts has made their methods differ from those of Romanesque courts. A French judge makes it his business to find out as much as possible about a case before it comes into court, whereas our judges (and, where they are employed, juries) are in the position of referees seeing fair-play in a contest conducted before them, and deciding which side has won on points. Civil suits are cited as *Somebody* v. *Somebody Else*, and criminal cases as *Rex* v. *Somebody*.

Our system of ' pleadings ' is designed to narrow the issue, like the ropes of a boxing-ring. In civil cases the Writ states exactly what is claimed ; in criminal cases the Indictment states exactly what the charge is. This and nothing else is what the plaintiff or the prosecution have to prove in order to be successful. (Hence the much-quoted claim that our courts assume a person to be innocent until he is proved guilty.)

In civil cases the plaintiff employs a solicitor to work up his case, and counsel to present it in court. In criminal cases it is usually the local police who set the prosecution going. Counties and County Boroughs often keep a whole-time solicitor to manage prosecutions—to hunt up witnesses (serving them, if necessary with writs of *subpoena* to compel their attendance), to prepare depositions, to engage counsel and so on. The accused person has to provide for his own defence, though by the *Poor Persons' Defence Act* (1930) certificates covering the cost may be granted by magistrates or Assize Court officials ' whenever the interests of justice would be served thereby.'

Difficult and ' heavy ' cases (*e.g.* murder, coining, fraudulent bankruptcy) are undertaken by a Government-appointed Director of Prosecutions, with a specialist staff of solicitors and clerks. He distributes briefs among a small group of counsel nominated by the Attorney-General, though the latter may appear in person against prisoners charged with political offences.

The details of court-procedure are governed by rules amended from time to time by a committee under the Lord Chancellor. The general course is the same in nearly all contested cases. Counsel for the plaintiff (or prosecution) opens it with a brief statement of the claim or charge and of how he proposes to make it good. Then he calls his witnesses and examines them. Counsel for the other side may try to break down their evidence by cross-examination, and the prosecution may re-examine them with a view to re-establishing it. Then counsel for the defence (or the defendant) makes a speech rebutting all this, and if he think fit calls witnesses.

Since 1898 a prisoner may be called as a witness, and so may the parties in a civil suit. Of course, counsel for the defence may not care to put the prisoner in the box lest he should do his case more harm than good under cross-examination. If he does not do so, the prosecution is not allowed to make insinuations, though the judge may call attention to the omission in his summing-up.

If there have been witnesses for the defence, counsel for the prosecution makes the closing speech ; if not, the Defence has the last word. Then if there is a jury the judge sums up, stating the issue in plain terms, estimating the weight that ought to be given to various parts of the evidence, and explaining the law. Or, if there is no jury, he proceeds at once to give judgment, expounding his reasons for it.

In civil cases, whether in County or High Court, judgements are often given for the payment of money. Should the defendant fail to pay, the plaintiff may in the last resort enforce the judgement by 'execution.' That is to say, the court bailiff will take the defendant's goods up to the value of the sum in default.

If the defendant has not sufficient goods to meet the claim, the plaintiff may not be able to enforce the judgment at all, and may be saddled with the law-costs for both sides. Formerly a defaulting debtor (see *Pickwick* and *Little Dorrit*) could be committed to prison until he paid, but the *Debtors Act* (1869) expressed the modern view that people cannot be imprisoned for debt unless their default is wilful.

The general supervision of Assizes is one of the traditional duties of the High Sheriff of the County. This is an unpaid and indeed expensive, post—a survival from medieval times. The sheriff has formal responsibility for the reception of the judges (including fanfares to greet their arrival at the courthouse, and an Assize Sermon at the parish church) ; he summons jurors ; clad in levee dress, with knee-breeches and lace cravat, he may sit for part of the time on the bench beside the judge ; he has to see judgments carried out, including the disposal of persons sentenced to imprisonment and the hanging of those sentenced to death.   But in practice most of the details are left to a paid Under-Sheriff—generally a local solicitor.

Costs.—As we have already noted, we have good reason to be proud of our legal system ; but it also has drawbacks, and the chief of these is its expensiveness.   True, our courts make no actual distinction between rich and poor, but the cost of their services may put them beyond the reach of any but the well-to-do.   (' The Law is open to all—like the Ritz Hotel,' as a facetious judge once remarked.)   Court costs have trebled or quadrupled in the course of this century, and the maintenance of the highly paid personnel falls mainly on litigants.

It is sometimes argued that if it were not for their costliness the courts would be snowed under with litigation ; but that has not been the experience of the USSR, where the service of the courts is free, and the best advocates do not earn much more than a skilled mechanic.

Normally ' costs go by the event '—that is to say, the loser pays all.   But even so, the ' taxing-master ' attached to the court may pronounce the counsel's costs unreasonably high, and in that case he will have to make up the difference out of his own pocket.   Some provision is made for really poor people.   Under the *Poor Prisoners' Defence Act* (1930) magistrates can grant ' Legal Aid Certificates ' to persons charged before them, while prisoners committed for trial can obtain ' Defence Certificates.'   And in the last resort a prisoner can give a ' Dock-side Brief '—that is to say he can, with the permission of the judge, call upon any disengaged counsel in the court to undertake his defence for the sum of £1 3s. 4d. This is payable by the court, but a defence conducted at such short notice is not likely to be heard to advantage.   And in civil cases the position is even less satisfactory.   A poor person can get help from a ' Poor Persons' Committee ' (if he happens to be within reach of one—they do not as yet form a regular public service), provided he can prove to it that his income is not more than £2 (in some cases £4) a week.   His case will then be taken by a solicitor and (if necessary) counsel who volunteer such services from philanthropic motives.   But the means-test disqualifies many in dire need of assistance.

Some big towns also have ' Poor Man's Lawyers ' from whom legal advice can be obtained ; but these rarely have funds from which to provide for action in the courts.   Nor can the Citizens'

Advice Bureaux to be found in most towns go beyond legal ' first aid.'

There is a wholesome tendency towards simplifying legal processes. For example, when all divorce suits had to be heard in London, divorce was a luxury for the rich ; undefended cases and Poor Persons' cases can now be heard at Assizes, with a great saving of time and money. But ' Poor Persons ' procedure applies only to the High Court. Most of these cases which concern working-class people come before the County Courts (*e.g.* under the complicated Rent Restriction Acts) in which no legal aid is available at all.

Thus we must look to the future for reforms that will put the stately edifice of our law at the service of us all on really equal terms.

CHAPTER XI

THE EMPIRE

ITS ORIGIN AND STRUCTURE

THE Empire is as much an embodiment of the British spirit as the Constitution, and came into existence in the same haphazard way. Little of it was built up by design, none of it pays tribute, and the trade-advantages which it confers are negligible. But changing conditions and ideas create imperial problems which can only be solved by understanding and good will, and we all bear a share of responsibility in the matter.

THE FIRST BRITISH EMPIRE.—What sent our forbears questing overseas was the search for new markets and the search for new homes. The one drew them mainly to Asia, the other to America. Both trade and colonisation were promoted by Companies authorised by Royal Charter. The adventurers clashed with Dutch, French, Spanish and Portuguese rivals; but by the end of the seventeenth century the East India Company, though driven from the East Indies by the Dutch, had established a number of fortified depots on the mainland of India; while twelve British colonies had grown up along the Atlantic coast of North America, and the Leeward Isles were producing valuable crops of sugar with negro slaves.

Overseas trade needed the protection of the Navy, which reciprocally was maintained by the wealth it brought. That combination enabled Britain to outstrip her rivals. By the end of the Spanish Succession War (1713) the naval and economic energies of Spain, Portugal and the Dutch Republic were already in decline; France was worsted in the Seven Years' War through the genius of the elder Pitt; and the Peace of Paris (1763) raised Britain's First Empire to its zenith.

Twenty years later it had ceased to exist. Pitt had driven France from North America regardless of expense, and his successors tried to put part of the burden on those who benefited most—the colonists. Nobody likes paying taxes, and to the Americans it was an unpleasant novelty. They took up arms in defence of that palladium of British constitutional liberty, 'No Taxation without Representation.' All that concerns us here about the American Revolution is that it taught Britain to avoid the conditions which led to it—the attempt to rule colonists and regulate their trade from London. Looking backward in the light of experience we see that such people, being of British blood with British history behind them, had instincts for self-government which it was dangerous to thwart. Even Burke, the champion of American freedom, was as fixed as King George himself that 'there can be no gradations of sovereignty.' We know better nowadays, and two Americans of that age had glimpses of what we have since learnt by trial-and-error. Benjamin Franklin argued that Americans could be subjects of the Crown without being subject to the British Parliament ; and Stephen Hopkins had a vision of 'a new imperial state consisting of many separate governments in which no single part, though greater than any other, is by that superiority entitled to make laws for or tax any other.' A hundred and fifty years later these conceptions were embodied in the Statute of Westminster.

'ALL FURTHER EXPANSION WOULD BE INEXPEDIENT.'—The Peace of Versailles (1783) left Britain humiliated, almost bankrupt, and very sceptical about the value of colonies. It seemed that Turgot had been right when he said that they were like fruit that falls from the tree as soon as it is ripe. Of course, commercial interests in the West Indies (preserved by Rodney by his victory off The Saints in the last year of the war) were worth while. So were those of the East India Company, which under Clive and Hastings had undertaken the administration of the provinces round its 'factories,' and made treaties with neighbouring princes. The Government recognised this situation by an *India Act* (1784) which gave it ultimate control over the Company's political activities ; but there was a cordial understanding that further commitments were to be eschewed. The Company wanted dividends, not dominions ; the Government wanted votes in Parliament (where the Company's interests were already powerful) not Asiatic wars. How this resolution broke down under the pressure of circumstance we shall see in a later chapter ; but of Pitt's sincerity in making it there can be no doubt.

Yet in these years of disillusionment between 1783 and 1860

the Government unconsciously laid four foundation-stones of a Second Empire far greater than the First.

(1) Something had to be done for the United Empire Loyalists—the Americans who had stood by the King in the late war and were persecuted beyond endurance by the victorious rebels ; so they were given lands in unoccupied New Brunswick and Ontario ; and these settlements (along with the old-established French ones centred on Quebec) formed the nucleus of the future DOMINION OF CANADA.

(2) Now that persons sentenced to transportation could no longer be sent to forced labour in America, a new dumping-ground was found for them at Botany Bay ; and the discovery of grazing-lands led to the creation of the wool-trade which is still the economic basis of the AUSTRALIAN COMMONWEALTH.

(3) The lands at the back of the Cape of Good Hope were bought from the Dutch Government, as half-way house on the long voyage to India ; and this was the starting-point of what is now the UNION OF SOUTH AFRICA.

(4) Missionaries who went out to NEW ZEALAND to save the souls of the Maori besought the Government to protect their converts from the lawless whalers and convicts escaped from Australia ; and the Government's hand was eventually forced by a private Company which planted a colony and got into conflict with the Maori over land-purchase.

Thus in none of the future Dominions did the Government set out with aggressive intent. The first people to make colonisation an ideal were a little group of ' Radical Imperialists ' led by Edward Gibbon Wakefield and Lord Durham. They saw a vision of Britains overseas, complementary to the homeland, drawing off its surplus population, providing its industries with raw material and foodstuffs, and taking its manufactures. They formed a New Zealand Company and a South Australian Company ; but to extend the authority of the British Government was the last thing they wanted. They showed this by their epoch-making ' Report on Canada ' (1839). Durham, with Wakefield as his chief-of-staff, had been sent to inquire into the cause and cure of disturbances in Canada. The Report set forth the principles which ultimately produced the British Commonwealth of to-day. The only way to keep colonies was to let them govern themselves ; Governors should still be sent out to represent the Crown but the administration should be in the hands of ministers responsible to an elected assembly.

This advice was quite in accord with the ' Little England ' spirit of the British Government. Within twenty years it had thrown off as much as it could of responsibility for ' these colonial dead-weights which we do not want and cannot govern.' Three self-governing colonies were set up in Australia (New South Wales, Victoria and South Australia) ; another in New Zealand ; and the *British North America Act* (1867) created the Dominion of Canada by federating the colonies which had already grown up there, with power to add to their number.

The development of South Africa was complicated by the presence of another European race in greater numbers, and by the Government's fitful sense of responsibility for the African races. The Dutch and Huguenot ancestors of the Boers had gone to the Cape to get free from governmental constraints. They farmed with slave-labour, and they strongly resented interference by a distant alien government. The abolition of slavery in British possessions (1833) drove many of them to make the Great Trek into the unknown North, where they could live their patriarchal lives free from pestering humanitarianism. They set up two primitive little republics, one just beyond the Orange River, the other further on, across the Vaal ; and after some hesitation the British Government recognised their independence (1852–54). But that was far from being the end of the story.

The abolition of slavery had equally disturbing effects in the West Indies, for the freed negroes were not disposed to undertake more than the slight labour needed in that genial climate to provide the necessaries of life. The ruin of the sugar-planters, begun by the development of sugar-beet in Europe during the Napoleonic Wars and hastened by the lack of labour, was completed by the Free Trade policy which under Peel and Gladstone deprived them of their preferential market.

BRITAIN BECOMES ' EMPIRE-CONSCIOUS.'—When in the middle of the nineteenth century the Industrial Revolution reached continental Europe, it led to economic nationalism and the quest for overseas possessions. The British Government took only a belated and reluctant part in the ' scramble for Africa,' but came out of it with the lion's share. Cecil Rhodes and

Joseph Chamberlain were types (contrasted and opposing types) of the forces at work. Rhodes created Rhodesia by his own initiative and resources, and wanted to build up a United States of South Africa free from the control of the Colonial Office. Chamberlain, the first minister of front rank to take charge of that Office, brought the enterprising vigour of a successful business man to the development of colonial resources.

Among other activities he started agricultural research at Kew, and a School of Tropical Medicine at Liverpool.

'Imperialism' became a popular creed. People began to glory in ' the Empire on which the sun never sets,' and plumed themselves that 'Trade follows the Flag'; while Rudyard Kipling exhorted young Britain to 'take up the White Man's Burden' of ruling black men, and exhorted the nation to remember Who it was that had given it 'dominion over palm and pine.'

This spirit led to the South African War (1899–1902). After unexpected set-backs we conquered the Boers; but the reverses, and the outburst of anglophobia which they called forth from every quarter of the globe, gave a wholesome shock to our national pride. Imperialism of the flag-waving sort died away, giving place to a sober realisation of the problems and duties involved.

'DOMINION STATUS.'—It was in this mood that the Government in 1906 gave back to the Boer Republics the right of internal self-government, and three years later they joined with the two British colonies (Cape Colony and Natal) to form the 'Union of South Africa.' The Australian colonies, now five in number, had joined to form a 'Commonwealth' in 1900.

The four Dominions were all created by federating provinces which had already acquired self-government on their own account. In this respect they resemble the U.S.A., but, unlike the U.S.A., they all adopted the British system of ministers responsible to an elected parliament. And in all of them the central Government has more power, compared with the provinces, than has the Federal Government of the United States. All of them have checked the immigration of cheap labour and have adopted protective tariffs behind which to build up industries.

The situation in South Africa has several peculiarities. There are more Dutch than British in the Union, and a knowledge of Afrikaans (a local form of Dutch) is required for all public appointments. (All the occupants of the house outside Cape Town which Rhodes bequeathed for the use of Prime Ministers of the Union, have been ex-Boer generals—Botha, Hertzog and Smuts.) There is a strong colour-bar. Africans, who form a large majority of the population, are not allowed to take part in public life, or to own land outside special areas, or to rise above the lower levels of labour. And much bitterness has been caused by the use of the bar against Indian settlers, of whom there are 150,000, descended mostly from coolies imported 50 or 60 years ago to work on tea and sugar plantations. South Africans, British as well as Dutch, are determined to keep the Union ' white,' but the rising national spirit of India is sorely affronted at these humiliations. It was by organising protest against them that Gandhi first became famous.

It was long the fervent hope of Imperialists that the Dominions might join the Mother Country in a federation ; but the Dominions have never been willing to surrender any of their sovereign and separate independence. The Conference of Prime Ministers which met at the time of Queen Victoria's Diamond Jubilee (1897) under the chairmanship of Chamberlain, politely declined his plan for a ' Great Council of Empire.' Nor was he more successful with a proposal of ' Free Trade within the Empire ' at the Conference which met for the coronation of Edward VII (1902). None of the Dominions would lower its tariff walls to British manufactures, and Britain with its Free Trade was already wide open to their exports. Chamberlain became convinced that the future of the Empire lay in co-operation rather than centralisation, and he committed political suicide by trying to induce Britain to give up Free Trade and bind the Empire together with ' preferences ' (i.e. lower import duties) for imperial as against foreign produce. But the Dominions continued to hold aloof ; and when Britain went into the first Great War in 1914 they were not committed to support her. The fact that they all did so, independently and voluntarily, proved that an Empire can be held together by ties other than those of legal obligation.

In a speech made during that war Smuts said of the Dominions ' We are not an Empire—we are a Commonwealth of Nations.' That was the first recorded use of the expression. It describes the character of the association better than the word ' Empire,' for ' Empire ' implies rule, and Britain certainly does not rule the Dominions. The Treaty of Versailles (1919) made this clearer than ever, for they signed it separately, and became separate member-states of the League of Nations. In 1920 the British Government expressly recognised their right to secede. In 1922 the refusal of Canada and South Africa to join in turning the Turks out of Asia Minor had decisive effects on British policy, and in 1923 some of the Dominions began to keep Ministers of their own at foreign capitals.

These developments were given form and substance at the Imperial Conference of 1926. This gathering decided that Governors-General should be appointed by the King in Council with the Dominion concerned, and not with the British Government. Relations between the Home Government and those of the Dominions were no longer to be conducted through the Colonial Office but through a new Department with a Secretary of State of its own. The Conference agreed that ' nothing would be gained by trying to define the Empire,' but accepted a formula devised by Lord Balfour which has become famous :

' Great Britain and the Dominions are autonomous communities within the British Empire, equal in status, in no way subordinate one to another in any aspect of their domestic or external affairs, though united by a common allegiance to the Crown and freely associated as members of the British Commonwealth of Nations. . . . But the principles of equality appropriate to status do not universally extend to function. . . . In the sphere of defence the major share of the responsibility rests now and must for some time continue to rest with His Majesty's Government in Great Britain.'

Certainly ' nothing would be gained ' by trying to extract any precise meaning from this definition ; but the Dominions had no reason to question the proviso that the British taxpayer should continue to bear almost the whole cost of the Royal Navy which was their main defence. After the next Conference the implications of the formula were embodied in the *Statute of Westminster* (1931), which expressly swept away the right (long atrophied through disuse) of the British Parliament to interfere with Dominion legislation.

COLONIAL PROBLEMS.—The parts of the Empire still controlled, directly or indirectly by the Colonial Office (and therefore ultimately by the British electorate) have been likened to pilgrims moving at different stages and at different speeds towards Dominion Status. Southern Rhodesia and Ceylon are in sight of the goal, the West Indies well on the way, Nigeria only just starting ; and one or two have had temporary set-backs.

E.g. Newfoundland, which actually reached Dominion Status, but slipped back when she had to apply for financial help and submit to control by a Commission from the Home Government (1934) ; and Malta, which had to forgo responsible Government when it led to ferocious quarrels over the use of the Italian language and the political influence of the Roman Catholic Church (1936).

But the simile of a pilgrimage towards self-government over-simplifies the situation. Some of these possessions (*e.g.* Gibraltar) are little more than strategic outposts to enable the Navy to give security to all (not only the British) who pass upon the seas. Others (*e.g.* Jamaica) have Governors appointed by the Home Government and Assemblies partly elected and partly nominated, whose acts are subject to approval by Whitehall. Others again (*e.g.* West Africa) are under indirect rule ' through and by ' native chiefs.

This system of Indirect Rule was developed by Lord Lugard, Governor of Nigeria 1900–14, on the principle that the interests of the mass of the population must not be subordinated to those of a minority, whether of Europeans or of educated natives. Lugard was also the author of the doctrine of the ' Dual Mandate '—that Europeans can rightfully claim access to the products of tropical lands provided that they help the natives to cope with the forces to which they are exposed by this intercourse with White civilisation. This means in effect seeing to it that economic conditions allow of their being fed, clothed and housed, that they are provided with necessary health-services, and have opportunities for education which will in time enable them to govern themselves.

Then there are the Mandated Territories. Mandates were a form of trusteeship under the League of Nations, adopted after the first World War for dealing with the Arab provinces of Turkey and the African colonies of Germany. They were divided into classes according to the character of the inhabitants. Where these were very backward the territories were practically annexed by the mandatory Power (*e.g.* South-west Africa by the Union of South Africa). Where the inhabitants were politically more advanced they were given guidance and support for the minimum time required to set them going as independent states (*e.g.* Iraq., which quickly became a parliamentary monarchy in which Britain retains merely the right to ' advise ' on foreign policy).

Britain's main concern in that area is to see that the Mosul oil-field (one of the main sources of fuel for the Navy) does not fall into the hands of a hostile Power.

The mandate for Palestine has proved very troublesome. In the course of the first World War Colonel Lawrence made promises to the Arabs which proved incompatible with an undertaking given by Lord Balfour that Palestine should be once more the national home of the Jews ; and the Colonial Office has ever since been vainly trying to induce the two races to tolerate each other's existence.

Anglo-Egyptian relations go back much further, of course. They really turn on our need to prevent the Suez Canal (a bottle-neck of Empire routes) from ever being closed to our shipping. This is now ensured by a treaty of Alliance which gives Britain the right to station troops in the Canal zone.

It should be noted that Britain claims no exclusive rights over the Canal—merely to keep it open on equal terms to all nations. It was her observance of this limitation that enabled Mussolini to attack Abyssinia.

One of the most pressing problems of Empire is exemplified in Kenya. There in a comparatively small upland area we have 10,000 British settlers mostly engaged in coffee-planting with native labour, while in the coastal regions there are 25,000 Indians mostly engaged in trade. And—an almost forgotten ingredient in the population—there are about half a million native Africans. What progress towards democratic rule can be made in such conditions ? The British settlers demand as a natural right an electoral system that will give them control, and want the Indians segregated in particular districts ; while the Indians want a ' common roll ' of non-African voters, and the right to buy land and sell goods anywhere. The British Government is most anxious not to offend India by setting up a colour-bar in Kenya like that which the Union has imposed in South Africa ; and it has traditions of trusteeship for backward races. It has therefore reminded European and Asiatic settlers alike that ' Primarily Kenya is an African territory in which the interests of the natives must prevail over those of immigrants,' and that ' racial discrimination is contrary to British tradition.' This made the ' immigrants' very angry. Naturally it is hard for the Kenya British to change from the Imperialism of Cecil Rhodes to that of Lord Lugard—much harder than for officials in Whitehall to do so. But the Colonial Office cannot repudiate its responsibilities and leave British, Indians and Africans to fight out the issue among themselves in the name of democracy. Certainly neither Indians nor British would welcome such a course.

Another aspect of the same problem is seen in Rhodesia. Rhodesia wants freedom from Colonial Office control largely because that Office asserts the paramountcy of Native interests. And similarly the Home Government, despite its desire to placate the Dominions, hesitates to hand over the colony of Basutoland and the protectorates of Bechuanaland and Swaziland to the Union of South Africa largely because it does not feel justified in letting these territories be used, like the Native Reserves in the Union, as reservoirs of cheap labour for white factory-owners and mine-owners and farmers. Nor does it approve of Governments putting poll-taxes on natives to force them to leave their villages to earn the money.

Critics of ' British imperialism '[1] sometimes suggest that we ' exploit ' our overseas possessions for our own benefit. The truth is very different. To be sure, British capital draws dividends from Colonial and Dominion investments, but the stock-markets are open to all. As to commerce, the Dominions and India control their own tariffs, and use them to exclude many British manufactures ; whereas until 1932 Britain gave free access to her home and colonial markets ; and even now ' Imperial Preference ' does not affect more than 3 per cent. of its trade with the colonies.

No. Our colonial policy has its faults, of course, but they are mostly negative, arising from the unfortunate fact that the Government and nation are not very interested. The subject is seldom mentioned in Parliament except on the one day in the year when the Colonial Office vote is taken, and even then only a handful of members take the trouble to be present. For that Office is the Cinderella of the Departments. The

---

[1] Nowadays this word is falling from the dignity implied by a capital letter. In fact it is regarded, especially by Americans, as an expression of abuse.

' National Government ' had a new Colonial Secretary almost every year of its existence—a sure sign of a lack of settled policy, and a sore discouragement to Colonial Governors. But the root of the trouble goes even further back : members would take the trouble to be present at Colonial debates if they felt that their constituents cared deeply about the issues.

In the years between the wars the only really prosperous area was Malaya with its exports of rubber and tin—the latter almost entirely in the hands of Chinese. We have been slow to realise that most of the Empire is poor because its peoples are backward, and vice versa. The average family income in British West Africa, for instance, is about £7 a year. This is more ' real ' income than has ever before been enjoyed in that region, but it does not leave much taxable wealth out of which to provide medical care and technical education !

Until recently the British Government regarded it as axiomatic that dependencies should in normal circumstances be self-supporting. Not until 1940 did we put through the *Colonial Development and Welfare Act* by which we undertook to spend £5,500,000 a year for the next ten years on research, agriculture, education, health and housing. As the country was at the time spending twice that amount every day on the war, this did not seem extravagant provision for the welfare of sixty million people. Still it was a beginning. And the scale of war-time expenditure had its effect even on colonial affairs, for five years later (with the war still on) an amending Act was passed increasing the amount to £120 millions and extending the operative period to twenty years.

THE DOMINIONS AND FOREIGN AFFAIRS.—The *Statute of Westminster* removed the last chance of political federation ; and a few years later a short-lived attempt at economic co-operation broke down. The Great Slump of 1929–31, by impelling Britain to abandon Free Trade, seemed to offer an opportunity to encourage commerce between different parts of the Empire by means of preferential duties. In 1932 deputations from the Dominion, Indian and Home Governments met at Ottawa for the purpose. They soon found that their interests diverged too widely for anything so sweeping as ' Empire Free Trade.' The best they could do was to arrange a number of separate tariff-agreements between pairs of members, Great Britain doing what she could on behalf of the Colonies. But even this measure of agreement was soon whittled away. The Dominions found that they could not prosper on the limited sales to other Dominions, while Britain, anxious to increase food production at home, had to protect her own farmers against outside competition, even when it came from countries that quartered the Union Jack on their flags. So many of the tariff-bargains were dropped. Canada made another 'most-favoured nation' agreement with the United States, India and Australia came to terms with Japan, and the Imperial Conference of 1937 urged that ' every effort

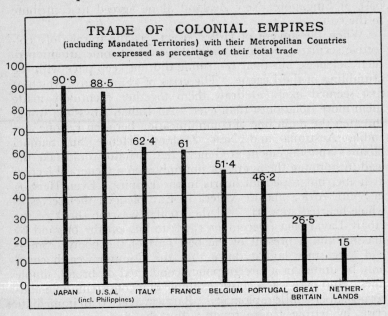

TRADE OF COLONIAL EMPIRES
(including Mandated Territories) with their Metropolitan Countries expressed as percentage of their total trade

TRADE OF COLONIAL EMPIRES

should be made to promote commerce with European countries as an essential step towards political appeasement.'

By a ' most-favoured-nation ' agreement a Government promises a commercial ally to let it share the most favourable tariff-terms which it grants to any other Power.

The only other field of co-operation open to the Dominions was defence, and it might have been expected that they would at least have attempted some approach to the pooling of resources and the unity that is strength. But they did not.

They, like Britain herself, began the post-war period full of faith in the League of Nations, which seemed to make the Commonwealth a union within a union enjoying security within security. They went even further than Britain in disarming, for they rejected Admiral Jellicoe's proposal for an Imperial Navy, and urged the mother-country to drop the alliance with Japan. And when Britain at the Imperial Conference of 1923 announced the intention (as a natural consequence of the lapsing of that alliance) to build a great naval base at Singapore, New Zealand alone agreed to contribute to the cost.

When the advent of Hitler (1933–34) the mirage of 'collective security' began to fade, they turned some attention to their defences, but their re-arming did not keep pace with the crumbling of the League. The crisis of 'Sanctions' which at first seemed likely to draw them together eventually made them more isolationist than ever. An Italian Abyssinia would threaten the main line of communication between Europe and India, Australia and New Zealand. Hence Sir Samuel Hoare's announcement at Geneva that Britain would take the lead in stopping the aggressor not only won a General Election at home, but raised all hearts in the Empire. Even Hertzog in South Africa and de Valera in Eire pledged themselves to whole-hearted support. All the greater was the shock of the Hoare-Laval pact (December 1935) to buy off the brigand by making him a present of the best part of the booty. Smuts had long since laid it down that the Commonwealth could only be united in a foreign policy conducted on broad, simple lines ; and here was a classic example of inconsistent, hole-and-corner super-subtle diplomacy. Baldwin averted an immediate crisis by letting Hoare resign ; but the damage was done, and was aggravated by the subsequent withdrawal of Sanctions and the return of Hoare to the Government in another office. Australia and New Zealand were shaken by Britain's apparent readiness to surrender control of the Mediterranean, which they pointed out was nearly as much their Sea as Italy's. In the South African Parliament the leader of the Opposition, Dr. Malan, advocated an immediate announcement that the Union would remain neutral in any future European War, and demanded the immediate return of Germany's former colonies (except South-west Africa, which was 'a special case ').

Canada seemed a nation divided against itself, for 20 per cent. of its population were recent immigrants who felt no loyalty to Britain (and not much to the Dominion itself), while there was a strong party in Quebec which wanted to start an independent French Republic. In 1937 the Imperial Conference was unanimous in encouraging Neville Chamberlain to pursue appeasement. No wonder Hitler thought that the British Empire would henceforth be a negligible factor in world-affairs. And no wonder Chamberlain made his great surrender at Munich !

But Hitler's seizure of Czechoslovakia (March 1939) in defiance of his pledges caused as great a revulsion of feeling in the Dominions as in Britain—no one could any longer pretend to believe that he was bent merely on righting the wrongs of the German people. What Chamberlain had gained at Munich was not, as some maintain, a year in which to re-arm (for in that year Germany acquired the war-material of the Czechs—at least double the amount of serviceable material produced by Britain) but the unanimous support of the Empire. The Home Government had shown itself ready to go to an extreme of humiliation to avoid war, and when war came after all it was over a plain issue on which people of British blood and traditions could not but be unanimous. Australia and New Zealand assumed that they were at war when Britain was—and their Parliaments merely registered the fact. In Canada there was something less than unanimity, but the vote was decisive when it came. In the South African Parliament the Prime Minister, Hertzog, brought in a declaration of neutrality, but Smuts defeated him on it by a small majority and took office with the support of all the British and perhaps two-fifths of the Africander members.

He also has the moral support of the natives, who are strongly pro-British. The war gave them an opportunity to serve along-side Whites in the forces and factories, to enjoy equal pay and con-ditions, and to acquire some of the technical skill which was for-bidden them in peace-time. It is to be hoped that comradeship in war may help to solve ' the Native Question ' in peace.

Thus the war drew the Commonwealth together by making it conscious that collectively it stood for a range of ideas in-compatible with, and in danger from, the totalitarianism of Germany, Italy and Japan.

CHAPTER XII

WHAT IS WRONG IN IRELAND

THAT IT SHOULD BE DIVIDED OVER A STRUGGLE AGAINST FASCIST SUPPRESSION OF RELIGIOUS AND POLITICAL LIBERTY ?

A HANDBOOK for British citizens cannot ignore the problem of Ireland. J. S. Mill said ' No civilised nation is so far apart from Ireland in the character of its history as England, and there is none therefore which if it applies to Ireland the modes of thinking and maxims of government that have grown up within itself is so certain to go wrong.' And that is just what happened, with results unfortunate for Britain, tragic for Ireland, and in 1940–42 perilous to civilisation. ' The Irish know too much history and the English too little ' ; and Anglo-Irish relations cannot improve unless Englishmen recall the ancient tale of wrong which forms so much of the mental background of Irish nationalists.

JOHN BULL'S OTHER ISLAND.—The first important fact in Irish history is that Rome, the great unifying force of Western culture, never crossed the Irish Sea. And when Anglo-French nobles in Plantagenet times obtained Irish fiefs they brought the feudal notion that land belongs to the king among folk imbued with the tribal notion that it belongs to the people. Hence seven centuries of friction. It was redoubled when at the Reformation the ruling class (of Ireland as of England) became Protestant while the ' mere Irish ' remained Catholic, and England's struggle with Spain identified Catholicism with disaffection to the English Government. To suppress this latent opposition Irish land was confiscated for British immigrants—a fresh cause of bitterness. The most remarkable of these schemes, and the most fateful for Ireland, was James I's Plantation of the north-east with Presbyterian Scotsmen-ultra-Protestants to whom Papists were as vermin.

In the eighteenth century the Government treated the Irish as people without natural rights. Catholics (four-fifths of the population) had no votes, and could not buy land, or get their children educated. Even worse were trade-regulations designed to prevent the Irish (Protestant and Catholic alike) from competing with the British in home or colonial or foreign markets. Pitt tried to introduce free trade between the islands, but found vested interests in Parliament too strong. So in 1800 he put through an Act of Union. In lieu of the Dublin Parliament (in which only members of the Protestant Church of Ireland could sit) Ireland was to send a hundred members to Westminster. He hoped that this would not only break down tariff-walls but make it possible for Catholic Ireland to be represented by Catholic Members of Parliament, since there would be no fear of 'Papist domination' in a Parliament representing the whole of the British Isles. If this promise had been kept the whole course of Anglo-Irish relations would have been changed. When George III's conscience prevented it Pitt resigned, but that did not undo the damage. The Irish were more than ever convinced that the 'Saxon' was tyrannical and faithless. Dan O'Connell (the first political leader of Catholic Ireland) won Catholic Emancipation in 1829, but it was too late ; and when he went on to agitate for repeal of the Union he failed because he hesitated to start a shooting war.

Then came the Great Divide of Irish history, the famine of 1845–48. Potato disease destroyed the sole sustenance of the Irish peasantry. The land was over-populated, for there is no crop which in normal times can keep so many people per acre just above starvation-level ; but within a few years one-third of the people died or emigrated—mostly to the United States, but many to Canada and Australia. Emigration became a main factor in Irish national life—it was said the Connemara babies were born with their faces to the West. And wherever the Irish went they formed compact communities united by hatred of England.

Even to-day the population of Ireland is less than it was in 1840, and there are more Irishmen in exile than in Ireland.

Out of the grief and anger of the famine years grew a determination to 'repeal the conquest'—to eliminate from Ireland the alien, heretic and landlord power to which all its ills were ascribed.

Hunger for land (in a country where it was the sole source of life) made peasants compete for holdings by offering impossible rents. This put them at the mercy of landlords (mostly English) and their agents (mostly Scotch). The unimaginable degradation and squalor that resulted are depicted, half-unconsciously, in Maria Edgeworth's *Castle Rackrent* and Lever's *Tom Burke*. A special grievance was the turning of tracts of the best land into game-preserves, over which landlords living in England came to shoot expensively-reared pheasants once a year.

The peasantry could not hope for redress from laws made in a distant Parliament and administered by officials and judges of ' the middle nation.' So their protests took the form of sabotage and assassination ; and as no Irish jury would convict the perpetrators, the Government had to replace the law of the land by Coercion Acts giving arbitrary powers to the Courts. Thus began a sporadic civil war, of which the ' Young Ireland ' rebellion of 1848 and the ' Fenian ' rebellion of 1867 were the high lights.

Gladstone devoted the last twenty years of his life to trying to ' pacify Ireland.' He dealt with its religious grievances by disestablishing the Protestant Irish Church, and its agrarian grievances by Land Laws that gave tenants security of tenure at fair rents. Then he tried to meet the demands of the Irish Parliamentary Party, led by Charles Stuart Parnell, for a subordinate Parliament at Dublin to deal with Irish internal affairs. But in this he was overborne by the Imperialism of the age. Home Rule was rejected by Parliament in 1886 and again in 1893 as the thin end of a wedge which would shatter the Empire. The Liberals who disagreed with his policy crossed the floor of the House and ultimately became merged with the Conservative Party—which, indeed made resistance to Home Rule the main plank in its platform by changing its name to ' Unionist.' Its alternative was the firm repression of disorder coupled with loans to help Irish farmers to purchase and stock their holdings.

' ULSTER WILL FIGHT.'—The defeat of Home Rule turned Irish patriots towards ' direct action.' The very year after the Unionist Government tried to ' kill Home Rule by kindness ' with the Wyndham Land Act (1903), there was founded a society called Sinn Fein (' ourselves alone ') which aimed at turning the British Isles into a sort of dual monarchy like Austria-Hungary.

Sinn Fein began as a group of intelligentsia like the Gaelic League which had been founded ten years earlier to revive interest in the ancient speech and culture of the race. But the recurrent refrain of this sad tale is 'Too late.' Gladstone reforms, Home Rule, Wyndham Acts—any of these might have saved the situation if it had come before delays had given time for passions to rise and push demands a stage further. The 'dual monarchy' notion, which seemed like asking for the moon in 1904, would have been welcomed by all but the hard core of Unionists twenty years later.

Liberals were still pledged to Home Rule, but even after their triumph in 1906 they left the dangerous topic alone as long as they could. Only when the elections of 1910 made them dependent on the Irish vote did they bring in the third Home Rule Bill. Their fears were speedily justified. This Bill offered Ireland much less independence than either of its predecessors, for it reserved control of Irish Trade, Finance and Police, as well as Defence and Foreign Affairs to the Imperial Government. But it caused one of the most fearful convulsions in our political history.

As far back as 1886 Lord Randolph Churchill in his vendetta against Gladstone had seen that 'the Orange card'[1] was the ace of trumps with which Home Rule could be defeated. Ireland had once been united in resistance to England —the heroes of Irish nationalism in the eighteenth century had all been Protestants and most of them Ulstermen. But Lord Randolph raised the watchwords 'Ulster will fight and Ulster will be right!' and 'Home Rule means Rome Rule,' and now in 1911 that spirit was revived by the Unionist Party with great effect. That Party had just chosen as its leader Bonar Law, by descent a Presbyterian Ulsterman, and the Orange cause found a contentious protagonist in Sir Edward Carson. They did not merely aim at saving Ulster from Dublin rule—Protestant liberties were amply guaranteed in the Bill—but at preventing Home Rule for the rest of the country. This was thwarting the will of the majority in Ireland, in Parliament and in the Empire (for the Prime Ministers of all the Dominions approved of the Bill). But Bonar Law declared that he would not shrink from the consequences though they shook the

[1] The Protestantism of North-East Ireland regards William III as its hero, and still keeps the anniversary of the Battle of the Boyne (July 1, 1689) which re-established the 'Protestant Ascendancy.' This spirit was, and still is, focused in 'Orange Lodges.'

foundations of the Commonwealth, and Carson armed and trained Ulster Volunteers to resist the King's Government.

Thus political extremes may meet, and loyalty become so fervid as to be scarcely distinguishable from treason. There has been another example of this in our own time, when Kenya settlers talked of joining the South African Union in an All-White Republic rather than be compelled by the British Government to give full political rights to Indians.

This appeal to violence by the Party that had always been the mainstay of Law and Order and the Constitution, was an example which the Irish nationalists were only too ready to follow. The issue was hung up at the outbreak of the first World War, when the Home Rule Bill was put on the statute book with the understanding that it would be revised before coming into force. But the Nationalists felt that it was a mere invoice from a firm that could not deliver the goods, especially when the Liberal Government was replaced by a coalition with Bonar Law and Carson in the Cabinet; and they were dismayed to see their countrymen crowding to fight for a Power which professed to stand for the rights of small nations but denied those rights to Ireland. Republicanism, which had lingered in obscure corners since the days of Young Ireland began to take possession of Sinn Fein, and a group of desperadoes planned an armed rebellion for Easter Sunday 1916. They could not hope that the few hundred active members of the 'Irish Republican Army' would defeat the thousands of British regular troops stationed in Ireland, but they wanted their cause to be stimulated by blood-letting. The rising was mismanaged; it was confined to Dublin; and it was suppressed within a few days. It was extremely unpopular with the people as a whole until the Government began shooting prisoners for treason after military courts-martial. Of those condemned to death one was an old Fenian, two were boys under seventeen, two were poets of distinction, one was a cripple. Hundreds were sentenced to terms of imprisonment —among them a young half-Spanish schoolmaster named De Valera, who was saved from death by the fact that he was technically an American. The incident called forth protests from the civilised world which were very embarrassing for the Government; it made America's entry into the War less likely than ever, since President Wilson, seeking a second term of

office, could not afford to ignore the Irish vote. Most of the
prisoners were soon released, but the damage was done. In
Ireland the executions caused such a revulsion of feeling that
Home Rule and the old Nationalist Party which had sponsored
it at Westminster faded out. Sinn Fein swung over to Republicanism, and the people of Ireland swung over to Sinn
Fein. At the General Election of December 1918 its candidates
won seventy-eight seats. Instead of going to London, they
(or rather the twenty-eight of them not in gaol) met in Dublin,
proclaimed themselves *Dáil Eiraan*, the parliament of an Irish
Republic, under the presidency of De Valera, and appealed for
support to the Peace Conference then assembling in Paris.
They hoped that President Wilson, who had coined such high-
sounding phrases about self-determination and the rights of
small nations, would uphold their claims as he upheld those
of Czechs, Poles and Serbs. But he could not afford to make
difficulties with Britain, and he refused even to receive their
deputation.

THE IRISH REVOLUTION.—The question now was, What was
the Lloyd George Coalition (in which Unionists predominated)
going to do about it ? Of course the pre-War Home Rule Act
was quite out of date—a much completer degree of self-
government was inevitable. But this involved a baffling
problem of practical politics ; how to safeguard a minority
without robbing the majority of its democratic rights. Self-
determination for Ireland as a whole would give a three-fourths
majority in favour of an independent government at Dublin—
which the other fourth would die rather than accept. But
Britain could scarcely be expected to thwart the determination
of the North-east to remain British !

The *Government of Ireland Act* (1920) cut the Gordian knot
by Partition. It set up two parliaments and ministries, one
for Southern and one for Northern Ireland, with members
from both at Westminster as well.

Note the expression ' Northern Ireland.' Orangemen always
professed to speak for ' Ulster,' but only 4 of its 9 counties had
Protestant majorities. In 3 counties Catholics were 75 per cent.
of the population, and in the other 2 (Fermanagh and Tyrone)
55 per cent. So the Unionists could not allow a plebiscite either
of Ulster as a whole or by counties ; and as 4 counties would have
been too small an area for self-government they insisted on adding

Fermanagh and Tyrone. Events proved the accuracy of their calculations, for they have ever since had a 66 per cent. majority in 'Northern Ireland.' It is frozen at that figure, for where political and religious passions run so high there is practically no ' floating vote.'

No part of the Act aroused more resentment among the Catholic Irish than this artificial frontier ; and on the other hand the Protestants of the old ' Ascendancy' in Southern Ireland felt bitterly aggrieved that the English Unionists should have left them to the mercy of their former subjects.

The North reluctantly acquiesced, but Sinn Fein was outraged at this ' dismemberment.' It certainly was a freakish phenomenon to have two separate states inhabited by people who all considered themselves equally Irish, shut up in one small island ; but circumstances, deeply rooted in history, seemed to make it the only way.

The British Government's next problem was to get the constitution working in Southern Ireland. The Dáil claimed authority over the whole country, derived from the sole source of democratic power, the will of the majority ; and a second election gave it authority to reject Partition. To those who took this view, the British were foreign interlopers, disturbing the peace of a legitimate government ; whereas the British Government claimed that until it had handed over its sovereignty it was still the only legal power in Ireland. De Valera's shadow cabinet gradually ousted the established authorities in tax-collecting, local government and the law-courts, for in these matters it is only the support of the populace that enables government to function. Collision was sooner or later inevitable. It came over the police. The Royal Irish Constabulary had always been quite different from British policemen—they were armed and lived in barracks and were under the orders of Resident Magistrates. The civilian ' soldiers' of the Irish Republican Army ambushed the constables and burned down their barracks until they were driven out of Connaught and Munster altogether. The British Government had to rule or abdicate. It sent over an auxiliary force who became known as ' Black-and-Tans' from their uniform of khaki trousers and black Royal Irish Constabulary tunics, and a horrible guerilla war began—a war of ambushes and gangs, of reprisals and counter-reprisals. ' A competition in 'crime' it was called by a courageous judge who defied the hostility of both sides.

The British Government found itself in a wretched position. Its failure to keep order was encouraging revolutionary movements in India and Egypt, and its methods were arousing hostility in the Dominions and the United States, with their strong Irish minorities. But on the other hand de Valera and his colleagues came to see that they could never expel British power by force of arms. So in the middle of 1921 an armistice was arranged, and after much preliminary fencing a deputation was sent over to London to discuss terms.

Compromise was made difficult by outside influences—Sir James Craig (Prime Minister of Northern Ireland) who feared that Lloyd George would barter away the rights of Ulster, and de Valera, who insisted on an All-Ireland Republic. It was only when the conference was on the point of break-down that the dread of a renewal of the 'war' drove the Irishmen to sign the Treaty.

The very word 'treaty' implied sovereignty more complete than that enjoyed by any of the Dominions. Much of the argument at the Conference had been about the exact wording of the oath to be taken by office-holders of the New State. The upshot was that they were to swear allegiance not to the King but to the Irish Free State. To the King they merely promised to be faithful 'in virtue of the common citizenship of and adherence to the group of nations forming the British Commonwealth.'

Note how carefully actual membership of the Commonwealth was evaded. The Treaty, which gave Ireland far more independence than any of the Home Rule bills had proposed, was the work of a Coalition Government predominantly Unionist ; and that Party, conscious that its name had become somewhat incongruous, changed it back to 'Conservative.' But malcontents in other parts of the Empire could not fail to mark that violence had been more effective than constitutional methods in winning concessions from Britain.

The Treaty split Sinn Fein. De Valera declared that the delegation had exceeded its powers, and that it should have held out for an all-Ireland republic 'associated with' but not 'adhering to' the Empire ; while Griffiths and Collins, the leaders of the delegation, maintained that having gained the substance of their aims it would have been criminal to renew the war for the sake of phraseology. After a fortnight of vehement debate the Dail accepted the Treaty by a majority of seven (January 1922) ; whereupon De Valera resigned the presidency, to be succeeded by Griffiths, with Collins as head of a provisional Government.

But the end was not yet. De Valera and his supporters maintained that the Republic proclaimed by the first Dáil was still in being, since the second one had no legal power to abolish it. The new Government, disregarding these protests, proceeded to build up a constitution with a Dáil elected by proportional representation, a Senate of distinguished Irishmen of all types, and a Governor-General appointed by the Crown on the nomination of the Free State Government. The Irish Republic Army resisted its authority, and there followed a civil war more frightful than the Anglo-Irish war which had just ended. Collins himself was killed in an ambush, and Griffiths died with suspicious suddenness. But William Cosgrave, who now became head of the Government, put the rebellion down with a ruthless hand, executing fifty and sending ten thousand to prison.

WHEN IS A REPUBLIC NOT A REPUBLIC ?—For the next ten years the Free State pursued a policy of fulfilment ; a sixth chair was set for Cosgrave at Imperial Conferences, and the overseas Irish seemed satisfied that England had at last given Ireland a fair deal. De Valera and his friends would not take the oath required to make them eligible for the Dáil, but for the time being it seemed that the bulk of the nation (including the clergy) had no use for pedantry. The Cosgrave Government was giving the country what it most needed after the Troubles—order and self-respect and budgets that were models of sound finance. Republicanism was self-condemned to gnash its teeth in outer darkness.

Yet as the years went on this unexciting efficiency seemed to pall on the Irish people. The craving for the forms as well as the substance of independence revived. In order to become the spokesman of this quasi-Republicanism de Valera had to sacrifice his principles so far as to take the hated Oath. In 1927 he and his new Fianna Fáil party, forty strong, entered the Dáil.

How far is a man justified in taking an oath to uphold a constitution which he means to wreck? Nobody doubts that de Valera is a man of high principles, but few can understand how he applies them. Out-and-out Republicans did not try—they treated him as a traitor to the sacred cause.

In 1932 Fianna Fáil (in coalition with Labour) obtained a majority, and de Valera became Prime Minister with a programme of removing the Oath and stopping payment of the Land Annuities.

These Annuities were the interest on loans raised from private subscribers in England to finance the purchase by Irish farmers of their farms. Other advances for this purpose, made out of the British Treasury, had been wiped off the slate after the settlement of 1922, and de Valera argued that if these Annuities were not included they ought to have been.

As to the Constitution of the Free State, he declared that the Treaty was null and void, having been imposed by threat of war, and that the Irish people had a natural right to decide what form of government they would live under.

J. H. Thomas, Dominions Secretary, pointed out that if treaties could be cancelled whenever one of the parties had a change of Government there would be an end of good faith between democracies ; and the Dominions besought the Free State ' to observe the conventions which regulate the conduct of Commonwealth members towards each other.' But de Valera cared for none of these things. The Dáil abolished the Oath and withheld the Annuities after a General Election which was in effect a referendum. The British Government thought to bring de Valera to his senses (or to his downfall) through the dependence of Irish agriculture on the British market. Ostensibly to raise money to pay the annuitants, it laid duties up to 40 per cent. on Irish cattle and meat and dairy produce, and restricted their importation by drastic quotas. But de Valera, declaring that no threats would bend the will of the Irish people, retaliated with prohibitive tariffs on British iron, coal and hardware. He called on his people to tighten their belts and put up with hardship for the sake of beating Britain and attaining national self-sufficiency.

Like Gandhi in India, de Valera is an apostle of the simple life, though even his loyalest supporters quailed before his admonition that they should give up imported tea and coffee for 'milk and light Irish beer.'

The economic war hit the Free State a good deal harder than it hit Britain. What worried the British Government was the strategic danger of having a hostile island so close to its shores. But negotations for a settlement were crabbed by fresh demands from de Valera, including compensation for alleged over-taxation of Ireland in the nineteenth century.

Some interesting points arose over proposals for arbitration. Britain would not let the matter come before the Hague Tribunal on the ground that it would be a bad precedent to call in foreigners to settle a domestic dispute within the Commonwealth; while de Valera declined to bring it before a tribunal drawn from the Dominions as in this case 'the dice would be loaded against Ireland.'

In 1937 de Valera proceeded to the revision of the constitution which had been inevitable even since his coming into office. The name 'Eire' was adopted. On the critical question of the monarchy it announced (the wording was important—Ireland had been deluged with blood for the sake of verbal formulae) that

As long as Eire is associated with the other nations of the Commonwealth and as long as the King is recognised by those other nations as the symbol of their co-operation, he is authorised to act on behalf of Eire in its external affairs, as and when advised by the Executive Council.

Nobody to this day is quite clear what this implies, or exactly how the constitutional position of Eire differs from that of Canada or Australia. Perhaps so metaphysical a matter can best be illustrated by a diagram which de Valera is said to have drawn to make his meaning clear.

DE VALERA'S VISION

But the British Government was wise enough not to press for clarification. War-clouds were rolling up. Its only practical concern with Eire was the fear that it might serve as the starting-point of an invasion, and the hope that it might serve as an outpost in defence. Appeasement was in the Whitehall air, and the Chamberlain Government determined to take a risk to remove the causes of friction. In April 1939 an agreement was made by which the trade war was ended, Eire paid £10 millions in final discharge of annuities amounting to £2 millions a year, and received back the fortified naval bases at Berehaven, Cork and Lough Swilly (which had been left in British hands by the Treaty of 1922) in return for an undertaking that Irish soil should never be used as a base for enemy operations against Great Britain. The agreement did not mention the subject nearest to de Valera's heart, for Northern Ireland intimated that nothing short of armed coercion would make it submit to a Dublin Government, and Chamberlain could not go so far as that even in pursuit of appeasement. In fact only sharp use of Party Whips wrung approval for the agreement from a House of Commons a good deal less trustful than the Prime Minister.

NEUTRALITY.—When war came, five months later, their doubts were justified. Eire declared for neutrality, and categorically refused to return, or even to lease, the naval stations from which the U-boat menace could have been thrust back 300 miles farther from the Channel Approaches. For the first three years of the war Eire was a standing menace to the human race. The whole civilised world now had reason to be thankful for the intransigence of Northern Ireland ; for if its ports had been controlled from Dublin Britain might well have succumbed to the blockade, and with Britain out of the war in 1941 nothing could have stopped the triumph of the Axis. And although Eire undertook to defend herself from invasion, her forces were ludicrously inadequate. What saved her from the fate of Norway and Holland and Belgium was the Royal Navy.

The most remarkable thing about Eire's neutrality was that the nation was unanimous in support of it. Only for one moment was this unanimity shaken—when America became involved in the war ; for it was to America that Irish nationalism had always looked for moral and financial support in the struggle against England. But it was only for a moment ; soon de Valera was protesting, with general backing, against American troops being landed in Northern Ireland. That a people so full of idealism, of courage and of pugnacity should have taken this line is the most unaccountable phenomenon of modern history. A larger proportion of volunteers came from southern than from northern Ireland, yet those volunteers, who as individuals rushed to act as Good Samaritans to afflicted Europe, mostly upheld their country in passing by on the other side. De Valera declared that it was all owing to Partition ; end that, and then . . . *all Ireland would be neutral*. The argument does not seem persuasive to British minds. No doubt the subconscious purpose of neutrality is to register at all costs the fact of independence. Arthur Griffiths once said that to decide the foreign policy of the Free State he would only have to inquire about England and do the opposite. For such immaturity of outlook British misgovernment in the past has been largely to blame.

But Eire's neutrality had one good effect : it enabled us to show that we respect agreements even when they work to our dire peril. Anglophobes in Ireland and elsewhere had prophesied that Britain would violate Irish neutrality in time of war ; and her abstention from this easy but evil course impressed the world, especially the parts of it where a good standing is most precious to her—the Dominions and the United States.

On the other hand the policy of neutrality has postponed the re-union of Ireland to the Greek Kalends, and has pushed Eire into a political and moral backwater. And Britain, the Commonwealth and the United Nations are the poorer for the lack of her support and comradeship in the tasks before them.

CHAPTER XIII

WHAT IS WRONG IN INDIA

AND CAN BRITISH DEMOCRACY BE ADAPTED TO SOCIAL AND POLITICAL CONDITIONS THERE ?

WHEN Britain went to war in 1939, the Dominions joined her of their own will ; India, on the other hand, was drawn in without being consulted. Yet its peoples form four-fifths of the population of the Empire, and represent civilisations older than Britain's own. Indians are aggrieved that their land should be treated as the chattel of a far-off alien country ; and we British would gladly end this state of affairs, if only we knew how. It is damaging to our self-esteem and to our reputation, and contrary to our political common-sense. This generation has to find a solution of the problems involved, and to do so it must take the trouble to understand them and how they arose.

THIS INDIA.—Let us avoid inapplicable terms about India. It is not a ' country ' and its peoples are not a ' nation ' in the European sense. India is a sub-continent nearly as big as Europe ; its inhabitants differ in race, speech, colour and religion far more than Europeans do. Almost all Europeans are of the white Caucasian race and speak languages of Aryan root and are of the Christian tradition. But Indians are of several distinct racial stocks, speak tongues as unalike as English and Russian ; and of their many religions Islam differs from Hinduism far more than it differs from Christianity.

Hinduism takes varied forms, from mystic other-worldliness to crude idolatry and superstition. It has no organised Church. Its social characteristic is Caste, by which people are born into social-cum-religious water-tight compartments. Mohammedanism, on the other hand, has no subtleties : it is a faith for action. It teaches one God, worshipped without images, before whom all men are equal, and one moral code set forth in the Koran ; and, unlike Hinduism, it is a world-religion.

The mixture of races which is a main factor in the Indian problem began 3,000 years ago when (as part of the migration of peoples which brought our own ancestors to Europe) Ayran Hindus, pressing in through the Himalayan passes, pushed the Dravidian aboriginies down into the peninsula. Then, 2,000 years later, Moslem invaders (in the expansion which elsewhere provoked the Crusades) began to impose their rule on the Hindus. They eventually set up the Mogul Empire centred at Delhi, and it was the decay of this Empire that created the conditions in which the East India Company became the Paramount Power. We have seen how the Company took over the government of some provinces and made subsidiary treaties with the rulers of others, and how the British Government had willy-nilly to take indirect control.[1] In the first half of the nineteenth century this supremacy was extended to almost the whole of India.

But the Indian Mutiny (1857) was not a revolt against foreign rule—' foreign ' was a word that as yet had little meaning for Indians. In the main it was a military rising provoked by disregard of religious taboos. After it was suppressed the Government took direct control. The Company was wound up. Its Court of Governors in London gave place to a Council of India, its Chairman to a Secretary of State, its Governor-General to a Viceroy ; its officials were replaced by a special branch of the Civil Service, recruited by competitive examination ; its troops were made a special branch of the British Army, and the Government took over the treaties by which Resident Officers ' advised ' the Indian Princes. And twenty years later Queen Victoria simplified the position by taking the title of Empress.

Looking back over the century between Plassey and the Mutiny it is difficult to see when or how the British could have checked the process by which they became masters of India. And to have withdrawn after the Mutiny would have left a pandemonium of warring races and rulers, besides involving the loss of millions sterling invested by the British public in railways, canals, roads and harbours. The payment of interest and dividends on these was a strain on India's resources, especially as her coal and iron were kept undeveloped, and Lancashire machine-made cotton goods were poured into what had, for a thousand years, been the greatest

[1] See p. 145.

cotton-exporting land in the world. But few Indians deny the advantages which India has gained from British public works, even if these were constructed mainly for British purposes.

THE BIRTH OF INDIAN NATIONALISM.—The fifty years after the Mutiny were the golden age of ' Service India,' with the Government in the hands of an intelligent, upright and devoted bureaucracy, drawn from the younger sons of the British ruling classes. But among the more doubtful blessings which the British brought to India was the idea of Nationalism. Though the passions engendered by it were already plaguing Europe, they could never have arisen in India but for roads and railways made with British capital, and the use of English as a common language by the educated classes.

Indian nationalism was from the first associated with the ' Indian National Congress.' This was founded in 1885 by an English civil servant, with the approval of the Viceroy of the day, as a safety-valve for criticism of the Government. Its name does not imply that it is a representative body like the American Congress. It is a political party, open to anyone on payment of four annas a year, and with even this low subscription it has never mustered much more than 1 per cent. of the population.

National sentiment was greatly stimulated when, in making the Anglo-Japanese alliance (1902), Britain for the first time treated Asiatics as equals, and when the result of the Russo-Japanese War (1904–5) seemed to show that European domination in Asia was passing away. By this time the Boer War had killed red-on-the-map imperialism in Britain, and Lord Morley, Secretary for India in the Liberal Government of 1905, made reforms which placed some Indian notables on the Legislative Councils of the Governors of the Provinces. But Morley, Radical as he was, saw that majority-rule was inapplicable to people so divided and so lacking in the traditions of democracy. He declared that if he thought his reforms would lead to a parliamentary system he would drop them. And the mere possibility threw up a fresh obstacle to Indian unity. Moslems, with the proud traditions of a conquering race, dreaded the idea of being swamped in a democracy by the numerical superiority of the Hindus ; and an influential group of them, headed by the Aga Khan, formed a Moslem League which petitioned the Viceroy that in any Electoral system that might be set up they should have separate representation. Thus began ‘ Communalism ’—the demand of minorities such as Moslems, Sikhs, Indian Christians and Untouchables not to be subjected to the rule of the Caste Hindus who form two-thirds of the population.

There are about 80 million Moslems in a population of about 400 millions. The Sikhs, numbering about 3 millions, are a Puritan sect of Hindus. The Untouchables (nowadays called, more politely, ‘ The Scheduled Classes ’) are below the lowest castes of Hinduism, condemned by their birth to squalor and degradation, presumably on account of misdeeds in a former existence. There are some 65 millions of them. It is among them, naturally enough, that the Christian missionaries have made most of their converts, to the number of 3 millions or so.

The first World War made Britain anxious to expand not only the Indian Army but Indian industry ; and a war to make the world safe for democracy could not leave India in permanent subjection. In 1917 Secretary-of-State E. S. Montagu made a momentous speech in Parliament, in which he promised India ‘ the greatest possible development of self-governing institutions as an integral part of the British Empire.’ ‘ But,’ he went on,

‘ the British Government, on whom the responsibility lies for the welfare of the Indian peoples, must be judges of the measure of each advance, and they must be guided by the co-operation they receive from those on whom new opportunities of service will be conferred.

Our conception of the eventual future of India is a sisterhood of states, self-governing in matters of local or provincial interest, over which there will be a central government, increasingly representative of and responsible to the people of all of them, dealing with matters, both internal and external, that concern India as a whole, and representing the interests of India on equal terms with the self-governing units of the British Empire. In this picture there is a place for the Native States.

Thus the British Government reversed the judgment uttered by Morley only ten years earlier. It now saddled itself with the tremendous task of turning India into a democratic member of the British Commonwealth ; and efforts to carry out that undertaking have been the main theme of Indian politics ever since.

The first stage was the ' Montagu-Chelmsford Act ' of 1919. This set up a central parliament at Delhi and local parliaments in each of the eleven provinces, elected by a system by which a fixed proportion of the seats was allotted to each of a dozen ' Communities.' In the Central Government the ministers (Indian and British) were still to be nominated by the Viceroy, but in the Provinces a ' dyarchy ' was set up ; some departments (*e.g.* Education and Health Services) were ' transferred ' to ministers responsible to the legislature, while others (*e.g.* Finance and the Police) were ' reserved ' to ministers responsible to the Governor. Finally, a Chamber of Princes was created to confer with the Viceroy on the concerns of the Native States.

GANDHI.—But the Nationalist leaders, dissatisfied with the prospect of Home Rule by instalments at the discretion of Whitehall, set themselves to wreck the scheme. There now appeared on the forefront of the scene one of the most remarkable figures in the history of the present century. Mohandas Karamchand Gandhi, returning in 1914 from upholding the rights of Indians against the Government of South Africa (see p. 149), began to devote himself to a spiritual regeneration of India based on the simple life, quietism, and universal brotherhood. Such ideals were incompatible with British imperialism and the Western way of life generally, so he sought to combat these influences by every means short of actual violence.

He and his followers wear *khaddar*—homespun cotton cloth which they spin (in theory at any rate) on portable spinning-wheels, to symbolise the revival of Indian village crafts and the revolt against the ' dark Satanic mills ' of European civilisation.

Unfortunately just as the new Constitution was coming into force Anglo-Indian relations were embittered by the Amritsar massacre (April 1919), when a British general ordered Gurkha troops to fire on a crowd of excited but unarmed persons who had assembled in defiance of a decree. Opinion was divided as to whether the action was justified, but it stirred India from end to end, sweeping into the nationalist movement many who had hitherto kept aloof ; and it convinced Gandhi that British rule must be rooted out. *Swaraj* (self-rule) was his aim, and *satyagraha* (soul-force) his method, and the fact that these words would bear different interpretations according to circumstances made them the more useful. *Satyagraha* usually took the form of ' non-co-operation ' : if enough people defied the salt-tax regulations or stopped traffic by lying down in the roadway, Government could be brought very nearly to a stand-still. Gandhi's teaching, personality and asceticism made an immense appeal to the masses, and before long his influence was supreme.

Owing to that influence Congress boycotted the first elections under the new Constitution : but this left the field clear for those who were willing to give it a trial, and in the next few years they carried through some valuable reforms. The British Government raised no difficulties when they adopted customs-duties to keep out British goods, and threw the Civil Service open to Indians on conditions that were equal in fact as well as in form.

India is no longer ruled by a British bureaucracy or drained by British tribute. More than half the 1,200 members of the I.C.S. are Indians, and of the half-million persons in the service of the Provincial Governments practically none are British. The interest on Indian debt amounted in 1938 to £13 millions—less than half that paid by Australia ; and the second World War has put the boot on the other foot—Britain is now in debt to India. As to the ' burden of defence ' : before the War India, with a population comparable to that of Europe, had 200,000 soldiers, three-fourths of whom were Indians. The whole cost of modernising its equipment was borne by the British tax-payer, as well as most of the cost of naval and air defences.

Meanwhile a change was coming over Congress. Rich Indian capitalists saw in it a means of putting pressure on the Government in the interests of Big Business, and landowners wanted to get control of it to prevent its extremists from opposing the payment of rent. The lavish subscriptions of these classes enabled it to become a powerful political party, able to send speakers primed with propaganda into towns and villages all over India, and to buy up vernacular newspapers.

The constitution of Congress, as revised by Gandhi in 1921, is an ingenious combination of democratic and autocratic elements. The four-anna members vote in the Provinces for delegates who attend the annual session of Congress which meets, about 2,000 strong, in a different city each year. At home these delegates form Provincial Congress Committees, which elect one-eighth of their number to the All-India Congress Committee. They also decide whom to support for the Presidency at the forthcoming session of Congress. The President, elected for one year, chooses 14 members of the A.I.C.C. as his 'Working Committee,' much as an American President chooses his Cabinet; and it is this inner Sanhedrin which really settles the policy and directs the actions of Congress.

Congress has a few Moslem and Untouchable members, but Hindus of the professional classes form the prevailing element. One of the great troubles in India is the superfluity of graduates of Provincial universities who, unable to find employment in the Law or Civil Service, have leisure to blame the Government for their position. And the ' Failed B.A.' often returns to his native village and reads anti-British newspapers to ' gazing rustics ranged around.'

Gandhi was torn between his ideals and the need for the wherewithal to propagate them, and he was painfully sur-prised to find ordinary mortals unable to rise to his own high plane of spiritual life. At the Congress of 1922 he carried a resolution in favour of holding up the new system of govern-ment by non-violent non-co-operation. But his followers soon got out of hand. When ' civil disobedience ' led to riots in which hundreds were killed, he was so shocked that he called off the campaign, declaring that his disciples were not yet ripe for *satyagraha*, and underwent a prolonged fast to expiate their sin. This retreat weakened for a time his hold over Congress. The Working Committee decided to contest the next elections and do their wrecking from within instead of from without ; and being the only organised party they won majorities in several of the Provinces. Some of the ministers whom they nominated, belonging to classes with traditional capacity for administration, were successful almost in spite of themselves ; but they aroused suspicion and resentment in Minorities which had always acquiesced in impartial British rule, and alarming riots broke out.

THE CONSTITUTION OF 1935.—It had been laid down in 1919 that the Constitution was to be re-considered after ten years, and in 1927 a Statutory Commission under the chair-manship of Sir John Simon was sent out to investigate condi-tions and advise the British Government. The omission of Indians from it gave great offence, and Congress boycotted it. Its report, published in 1930, recommended immediate responsible government for the Provinces and a Central

N

Government that could be made responsible by easy stages in the future. Two vital problems remained to be solved : the safeguarding of Minorities and the share of the Princes in the All-India Government. So a Round Table Conference of all parties and interests was held in London. (Congress refused

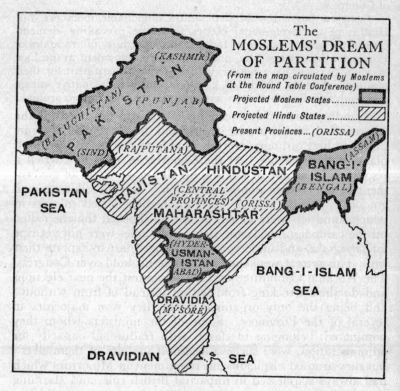

The
MOSLEMS' DREAM
OF PARTITION
(From the map circulated by Moslems at the Round Table Conference)

Projected Moslem States..........

Projected Hindu States ....

Present Provinces...(ORISSA)

(KASHMIR)

PAKISTAN

(BALUCHISTAN)

(PUNJAB)

(SIND)

(RAJPUTANA)

RAJISTAN   HINDUSTAN

BANG-I-
ISLAM
(BENGAL)

(ASSAM)

PAKISTAN
SEA

(CENTRAL
PROVINCES) (ORISSA)

MAHARASHTAR

(HYDER
USMAN-
ISTAN
(BAD)

BANG-I-ISLAM
SEA

DRAVIDIA
(MYSORE)

DRAVIDIAN   SEA

MAP OF INDIA

to take part in the first session, and sent only Gandhi to the second.) The upshot of it was that the Central Government should be federal, and that the Communities should be separately represented in the various parliaments.

But fresh obstacles kept rising. The Moslems now demanded that the predominantly Moslem Provinces should form 'Pakistan,' a sort of Indian Ulster. Congress, on the other hand, claimed that the only power that could create a government for India was the Indian people, through a constituent assembly elected by universal suffrage throughout the whole country, including the Indian States. Utterly repudiating both federalism and communalism, it insisted on the essential unity of India. The difference between Congress and British or American political parties was emphasised by this totalitarian claim to speak for the whole of the people. India was already represented at Imperial Conferences, and enjoyed fiscal autonomy and many other practical assets of Dominion status, and the British Government had renewed its assurance that this status was the goal towards which it was working. But Congress was affronted that India's 'national rights' should be promised as a reward for good behaviour.

Congress was dominated sometimes by the right wing which financed the Party machine, sometimes by left-wing socialists like Jawarharlal Nehru (of Harrow and Trinity). Sometimes Gandhi was pushed forward to spellbind the masses, sometimes he was allowed to slip into obscurity. His words were often enigmatic even to devout disciples, as when he announced that *Swaraj* did not mean Home Rule for India but self-control for the individual, just after Congress had passed a resolution declaring that it implied political independence. In 1934 he retired from active membership, saying that he could work for its ideals more effectively outside.

Another complication was the formation of the Mahasabha, an organisation of conservative Hindus to oppose both the separatism of the Moslem League and the radicalism of Congress, and to seek salvation in a revival of the legendary Golden Age of Hinduism.

The British Government held to its purpose of finding the greatest common measure of agreement among these conflicting factions. The conclusions of the Round Table Conference, presented to Parliament in a White Paper, were sifted by a Joint Committee of Both Houses, which co-opted a number of the Indian delegates to the recent Conference.

The Committee sat for 18 months, held 159 meetings, and examined 120 witnesses. Sir Samuel Hoare, Secretary for India and himself a member of the Committee, was asked 7,000 questions.

The result was a new *Government of India* Bill. Part I set up a Federal Government of All India, uniting representatives of the eleven Provinces with those of such princely States as chose to accede, in a legislature of two Houses. The Executive was for the time being to remain dyarchic, with certain ministers responsible not to the Legislature but to the Governor-General, who also had a veto on legislation and the power to enact laws of his own, should need arise. Part II set up Provincial Government in which all ministers were to be responsible to legislatures in which a certain number of seats were allocated to each of the chief Communities. But even here the Governor could intervene if the ministry seemed likely to endanger religious liberty, or law and order, or financial stability.

The Bill was fiercely resisted by a section of the Conservative Party, led by Winston Churchill, who declared that it would wreck the work of generations of Englishmen in India. But Baldwin and MacDonald (now practically joint Prime Ministers) forced it through.

THE CONSTITUTION CRIPPLED.—The Act of 1935 was the outcome of seven years of careful inquiry and earnest discussion, but it met with a very chilly reception in India. Congress rejected it with contempt as a characteristic piece of British humbug, designed to perpetuate imperialism behind a democratic façade. They argued that the powers retained by 'official' ministers nullified all the machinery of responsible government; that the Princes had been brought into the scheme to counteract Congress; and that the Communal basis of voting was designed to foment religious feuds which enabled Britain to 'divide and rule.' To this the British Government's reply was that, much as it wanted to see Indians ruling themselves, its first duty to them was to keep government going until they could come to terms with each other. The reserved powers were held merely to safeguard this work from people who avowed their intention to wreck it.

But the final blow to Part I of the Act came not from Congress, nor from the Moslems (who complained the 'Pakistan' was ignored), nor from the Mahasabha (who resented the strong representation given to Moslems and Untouchables), but from the Princes. They had at first welcomed federalism as the only way for them to join in an All-India government without losing their sovereignty; but it now looked as if the new Constitution would in some degree subject them to 'babu' Government controlled by Congress; and some of the greater among them resented the prospect of having to give up their own stamps and coinage, and the customs duties on which they depend for revenue. So they held aloof, and the federal part of the scheme never came into operation.

Part II narrowly escaped the same fate. Congress, with its monopoly of electioneering technique, obtained majorities in eight of the eleven Provinces. Pandit Nehru proposed that the Committee should forbid members to take office. That, he argued, would shatter the Constitution at a blow, whereas if Congressmen formed ministries they would settle down to collaborate with the British, and would give people a local pride that would break up the unitarianism of the Congress creed. But many influential members of the Party wanted to make a start on the social reforms promised at the election ; and Gandhi supported this course, on the understanding that if a Governor could not accept the advice of a ministry he would not simply supersede it, but would dissolve the Assembly and appeal to the electorate.

So Congress ministries were set up in eight Provinces. But Nehru and his friends found that they could keep the situation under control after all : for it was the Working Committee that allocated offices and decided on the policy to be pursued in each Province. Nehru justified this by the argument that it was for Congress policy, not for individual candidates, that the electors had voted.

This was a form of government new to political science. Something of the sort is seen in Australia, where the Labour Party Caucus, outside the State Assemblies, controls the ministries. But that Party does not impose a totalitarian dictatorship—it does not, like Congress, fly its Party flag on public buildings and substitute its Party song for the national anthem. Nor does it stigmatise as traitors anyone who seeks the good of Australia by any other means than those which it prescribes.

The ministries were in office for less than three years, but like those of 1923 they enjoyed their work and did it well. The Governors used their emergency powers scarcely at all. There was some shortage of revenue owing to Prohibition (insisted on by Gandhi), but this was a matter in which experience could be left to teach its own lessons. New land-laws gave security of tenure at reasonable rents, and the greed of moneylenders (one of the banes of Indian social life) was

checked.   A system of vocational training—another particular
interest of Gandhi's—was established : self-respect was given
to Untouchables (*Harijans*, ' Children of God,' Gandhi called
them) by allowing them to worship in Hindu temples and by
stopping grants to schools in which their children were not
allowed ' to sit in front of the teacher and the blackboard.'
All these reforms had been attempted before, but only now could
they be put into effective operation—a fact which seemed to
justify the Congress contention that self-government was a
necessary condition for dealing with Indian backwardness.

But there was another side to the picture.   The totalitarian leanings of Congress provoked fierce opposition from
interests which felt endangered by it.   The Moslem League
(now under the vigorous leadership of M. A. Jinnah) had
always argued that where people are not agreed on the funda-
mentals of religious and social life, majority tyranny can be
the most oppressive in the world.   It insisted that Moslems
were a separate people, whose religion affected their whole
lives and modes of thought.   Congress professed to be non-
sectarian, but it was dominated by Gandhi, whose mind was
impregnated with Hindu ideas, and by Nehru, an agnostic.
They objected to Congress-controlled schools, in which their
children were expected to bow down before the Gandhi-shrine,
and to the attempt to make Hindi a *lingua franca* when most
Moslems spoke forms of Urdu.   It was a cruel injustice that
Britain, having ousted Moslems from supremacy in the eighteenth
century, should use the power thus gained to put them under
the rule of Hindus in the name of democracy.   Rather than
submit they would disrupt India by creating ' Pakistan ' by
force.

Congress rule brought fears and grievances to the Indian
States, too.   These had not shared the steps towards democracy
that had been taken in British India ever since Morley-Minto
days ;   the Government's contacts had always been with the
Princes, not with their peoples, and as recently as 1929 a
Royal Commission had laid down the principle that if (apart
from gross misgovernment) attempts were made from within
a state ' to substitute some other forms of government . . . the
Paramount Power would feel bound to maintain the rights and
privileges of the Prince.'   Congress hotly resented this attitude.
A united, democratic India would be impossible so long as

these strongholds of decrepit autocracy were bolstered up by Britain. Why did she make so much of these outworn Indian treaties when she condoned Hitler's contemptuous breach of much more recent ones in Europe. Was it because she *feared* Indian unity? Congress, at any rate, had no obligations towards the Princes, and it encouraged its partisans in their territories to agitate for full responsible government by civil disobedience. Some of the Princes made concessions by allowing their Councils to become partly elective ; but the situation in the two largest States was very difficult. In Hyderabad the Nizam and his ruling class are Moslems, with a population 80 per cent. Hindu ; in Kashmir the Maharaja and his ruling class are Hindus, with a population 80 per cent. Moslem. These were particularly striking cases ; but there were others in which a change to democracy would cause a similar upheaval. The mere possibility led to communal disturbances such as had never before been known to the India of the Princes. They would have been even worse but for the restraining influence of Gandhi, who intervened more than once to moderate the indiscreet ardour of local Congress Committees.

THE IMPACT OF WAR.—September 1939 brought home to all how unfortunate it was that the federal part of the Act of 1935 had been still-born. The general feeling was strongly for resistance to Hitlerism, but there was no constitutional power that could speak for India as a whole, and Indians bitterly resented being brought into the conflict on the same terms as Aden or Basutoland. The Governor-General reiterated the promise of Dominion status, and besought the parties to sink their differences and co-operate in a coalition Government for the duration of the war. But Gandhi declared that, as Congress spoke for all India and demanded unadulterated independence, it could not join forces with those who denied these claims ; while the Moslem League demanded an equal share in any Provisional Government, which would otherwise be ' a packed body managed by a Congress caucus.' In October (1939) Congress enforced its side of the argument by calling on its eight Provincial Ministries to resign and so make constitutional government impossible in them : whereupon Jinnah proclaimed a Moslem feast-day to celebrate deliverance from ' an era of oppression which must never be allowed to return.'

But the martial instincts of many Indians brought them to recruiting-stations faster than they could be equipped or trained, and there was a mushroom-growth of war-industries. To check this Gandhi ordered ' disciplined individual *satyagraha*,' by which Congressmen nominated for duty by the Committee got themselves arrested by denouncing Britain's ' imperialist war.' The dark days of 1940 wrung from him an admission that there would be no more liberty for anyone if Britain and France went under ; but the reconstruction of the British Government in May, which gave new confidence to the democratic world, brought no such feeling to India—Churchill was too closely identified with ' White Man's Burden ' views.

These doubts were confirmed when a year later Churchill explained that Clause III of the Atlantic Charter, which recognised ' the right of all peoples to choose the form of government under which they will live,' did not apply to India. Even Indians who had hitherto taken no part in politics asked ' Why not ? '

The New Indian Secretary, L. S. Amery, renewed and emphasised the promise that immediately after the war Indians should take part in amending the Constitution of 1935. ' If Congress could in fact speak, as it professes to speak, for all the main elements in Indian life, however advanced their demands, our problems would be far easier. . . . Why cannot all parties lay aside their strife for the time being, and say : " India first " ? '

To Western minds these words seem trite truism, but they touched Congress on the raw. Gandhi raised his terms to unconditional surrender.

' Mr. Amery has insulted Indian intelligence by reiterating that Indian political parties have but to agree among themselves and Great Britain will register their united will. But it is British statesmen who are responsible for the divisions in India's ranks. . . . I admit that there is unfortunately an unbridgeable gulf between Congress and the Moslem League. But let the British withdraw and I promise that Congress and the League and all other parties will find it to their interest to come together and devise a home-made solution for the government of India. . . . It may be that before we reach that happy state of affairs we shall have to fight among ourselves.'

But with a world war threatening every day to spread to Asia the moment hardly seemed propitious for leaving India

to be the battleground for an armed conflict between its own
peoples, or to let the direction of affairs fall into the hands of
an uncompromising, if inconsistent, pacifist.

THE CRIPPS MISSION.—But when early in 1942 the Japanese
invasion of Malaya brought the enemy within striking distance
of India a fresh effort was made to enable India to throw
herself unitedly into defence. The British Government sent
out Sir Stafford Cripps, a member of the War Cabinet and a
left-wing Socialist who had always sympathised with Indian
Nationalism, with a new plan which they hoped would bring
all parties together. They proposed that at the end of the war
a constituent body representing Provinces and Princes should
frame a new constitution, and pledged themselves to carry its
decisions into effect. The All-India Government thus created
would have full Dominion status (which by the Treaty of
Westminster includes the right of secession), and they would
transfer sovereignty to it by a treaty similar to that made in
1922 with the Irish Free State. But in order to enable Britain
to fulfil her obligations to the Princes there was one reservation
—that any Province or State which did not want to come into
the new federation could remain outside.

These were great concessions from a Churchill Government ; but they were rejected both by the Congress and by
the League. Congress objected that the right to stay out of
the federation would shatter Indian unity, and that for the
States to be represented in the constituent assembly by
nominees of the Princes would rob ninety million Indians of
their rights. And would Britain ever be able to carry the
scheme into effect ? Gandhi sarcastically called it a post-
dated cheque drawn on a bank that was obviously failing. As
for the Moslems, nothing would reconcile them to the majority-
rule of Hindus.

Still, the parties might have agreed to postpone these questions until after the war. The immediate reason for the
failure of the Mission was that the British Government insisted
on keeping control of military operations and the supply services for the duration of the war, whereas Congress demanded
that the Party leaders should be brought together at once to
frame a Provisional Government with complete sovereign
power. Cripps pointed out that this would involve a tremendous upheaval, and the dictatorship of an irresponsible

autocracy which would arouse fierce opposition from the Minorities, at a time of deadly peril. And he might have added that there was not the least sign of the party leaders coming together. He had flown thousands of miles to meet them, but they would not move a yard to meet each other.

Thus the dispute was not over independence—independence was guaranteed. It arose because Britain felt that with the Japanese battering at the gates sovereignty could not be handed over to ' India ' until Indians had made an ' India ' to take delivery ; while Congress said that an ' India ' could be created only when Britain had ceased to support Princes and Minorities.

As so often before, the offer of a step towards independence made the Nationalists raise their demands still higher. They now announced that, though British forces might be permitted to remain to fight off the Japanese, the British Government must ' Quit India ' forthwith. Otherwise they would launch a campaign of mass-disobedience, which as Gandhi admitted, would be nothing less than ' open rebellion.' When they carried this threat into effect (August 8, 1942), the Viceroy's Council (which now consisted of eleven Indians and four British members) unanimously decided to ban Congress and arrest its leaders. Gandhi from prison called on his followers to ' do or die,' and for some weeks the defence of India was hampered by the burning down of railway-stations, the destruction of stores and the murder of policemen. But the perpetrators were not all genuine Congressmen—many of them were mere hooligans ; and the other political parties, and the more moderate elements of Congress itself, condemned the riots. By the end of September all was quiet again.

And meanwhile the dangerous corner was gradually and painfully turned by the blood and sweat of non-political Indians struggling to save India from the fate of China.

CHAPTER XIV

OTHER DEMOCRACIES : I. THE U.S.A.

HOW BRITISH DEMOCRACY TOOK A DIFFERENT FORM WHEN SET UP IN THE NEW WORLD

THE statesmen who framed the American Constitution were men of British blood who sought to give a fresh lease of life to British liberties in a new land where they could be preserved from the evils that had befallen them in the Old Country. The Democracy which they created grew into one of the greatest and richest states the world has ever seen. Some acquaintance with the structure and working of its political institutions is necessary for us British. For the Anglo-American collaboration will be greatly hampered unless each of the peoples knows how the other governs itself.

CAUSE AND EFFECT. Owing partly to geographical conditions and partly to anxiety not to saddle themselves with a new despotism, the Fathers of the American Union (chiefly Jefferson, Washington, Madison, Hamilton) devised a constitution as unlike the British as it could well be. The United States is a federation—Britain is strongly unified ; its Constitution is rigid and written—ours is fluid and unwritten ; that Constitution separates the Legislative from the Executive which in Britain are interlocked, and provides for review of legislation by a law-court, whereas the British Parliament is sovereign and supreme.

For each of these innovations there was a definite reason.

(1) Why did the Americans set up a federation ? Because there were thirteen colonies of varied origin and character very jealous to preserve their identity. They had been forced to make common cause against King George, but the moment the struggle ended they had fallen apart again, and six years of conflict within and peril without were needed to convince them that they must renew their league. They restricted the federal power to foreign relations, foreign and inter-state trade, defence, indirect taxation, currency and the post office. All

the other functions of government the States kept in their own hands ; and, lest the Constitution should not have made the position clear enough, one of the earliest amendments to it expressly declared that ' the powers not delegated to the United States by the Constitution are reserved to the States.'

This contrasts with the Constitution of Canada, in which all residual powers not expressly permitted to the Provinces belong to the Dominion Government.

The division of powers between State and Federal Governments split the ' Founding Fathers ' into the factions from which the modern political parties are descended. Thomas Jefferson of Virginia (chief author of the Declaration of Independence) stood for State Rights—he said in effect : Let us be *free*. Alexander Hamilton of New York, on the other hand, stood for a firmly-knit federation—he said, ' Let us be *strong*.'

(2) Why is the American Constitution rigid ? Because the States had to define their rights and duties towards the federal government which they were creating, in a document to which reference could be made whenever a dispute arose. Such an instrument would be useless if it was subject to the whims of the federal legislature ; altering it was therefore made a very cumbersome process. Amendments have to be passed by a two-thirds majority in each House of Congress and then ratified by the legislatures of three-fourths of the States.

Only twenty-one have been passed since the enactment of the Constitution in 1789. Of these the first ten came in 1791, when the first Congress bethought itself that no State ought to be free to abrogate the Rights of Man as guaranteed by Magna Carta, the Petition of Right, the Bill of Rights, and Habeas Corpus. Of the others, the most important may be briefly summarised as follows.

Four were passed in connection with the Civil War (1861–65). The Thirteenth abolished slavery, the Fourteenth disfranchised all who had fought for the South, the Fifteenth (1870) declared that ' the right of citizens of the United States to vote shall not be denied by any State on account of race, color, or previous condition of servitude.' (But many of the Southern States found means to evade giving negroes the vote.)

The Sixteenth (1913) gave Congress power to collect a federal income-tax. (Hitherto direct taxation had been reserved for the States.)

The Seventeenth (1913) provided that Senators were to be elected, not as theretofore by the State Legislatures, but by the direct votes of the citizens.

The Eighteenth (1919) was the famous ' Dry ' Amendment, which forbade the manufacture and sale of intoxicating liquor.

The Nineteenth (1920) compelled all States to give votes to women.

The Twentieth (1933) ordained that President and Congress take office early in the New Year after the November in which they are elected, instead of in the following March. This will prevent such anomalies as occurred in 1932–33 when the retiring President, Hoover, and the incoming President, Roosevelt, had diametrically opposed ideas of how to deal with the great slump but could neither of them move hand or foot for four critical months.

The Twenty-first (1933) rescinded the Eighteenth, which had caused an orgy of smuggling and gangsterism—first-class material for sensational films but ruinous to public morals. This new Amendment merely removed the compulsion from the States. Any that chose to remain ' dry ' could do so ; and some (*e.g.* Wisconsin and Vermont) did so.

(3) Why does the Constitution keep the Legislative, Executive and Judicial powers separate ? Because the Fathers were imbued with the eighteenth-century idea that the union of them led to despotism. This had happened in France, and they thought it was coming to pass in England, too. They felt that they must at all costs prevent such a monopoly of power from arising in their new Republic. So they contrived a scheme of checks and balances. Whereas, in Britain the Prime Minister and Cabinet MUST be Members of Parliament, in America the President and his Cabinet must NOT be Members of Congress.

(4) Why is Congress not a sovereign body like Parliament ? That follows from the separation of powers and the rigidity of the Constitution. At Westminster, if a conflict arises between Ministry and Parliament, either the Ministry resigns or the electorate is called on to elect a new House of Commons —the Government cannot be carried on without parliamentary approval ; and there is no law, constitutional or other, which Parliament cannot pass or repeal by its normal legislative routine. At Washington the powers of the President and of Congress are defined in a document which requires to be applied to particular cases by expert legal knowledge and

experience. This function belongs to the Federal Supreme Court, which thus completes the trinity of powers.

THE FRAMEWORK OF GOVERNMENT.—The relationship of State and Federal Government is, of course, very different from that of county and central Government in Britain. Each of the forty-eight United States is an autonomous entity which has delegated some of its sovereign powers to a federal authority of which it is a component ; whereas in Britain the solely sovereign central power merely allows County Councils to be the vehicle for some part of its authority. Half an American's political relations are with his State, and most of the rest with his city or county. He is rarely conscious of being ' American ' except when he reads about foreign affairs in his newspaper.

Each State has its own Constitution, enacted by its own citizens. Each has its own Legislature, mostly of two Houses, the lower and more numerous being generally elected for a shorter term than the upper. Each has a Governor, elected separately, and administratve officials, also mostly elective. Each has its own laws, covering all matters not expressly reserved to Congress, and its own courts and judges and police to enforce them.

These State courts and judges and police are quite separate from those of the U.S. which enforce federal laws.

Among the matters in which the States are autonomous is the franchise—apart from the Amendments which compel them to grant votes to negroes and to women. Another is the Marriage Laws. Another is Education. Speaking generally, the spheres of government controlled by the States are those that in this country are conducted by the Home Office, the Ministries of Health and of Education, and the Board of Trade.

The Federal institutions were modelled on those of the already-existing States. Congress consists of a House of Representatives (' the House ' for short, like our House of Commons) and a Senate. It meets at Washington, in the district of Columbia which was specially created as the seat of the United States Government. The members of both Houses are paid $10,000 a year. The lower House is elected every two years by districts of approximately equal population ; there are at present 435 members. The Senate has two members from each State, irrespective of its size or population, elected for six years, one-third retiring every two years.

Thus Nevada, with 100,000 inhabitants and only one member of the House, has the same number of Senators as the State of New York, with its 15 million people and its 45 seats in the House. This difference between the Houses was a concession which the Federalists had to make to the States-Rights party when the Constitution was founded. The latter feared lest their sparsely-populated southern States should be swamped by the expanding business and industrial interests of the north-east, and hoped that equal standing in the Senate would enable them to hold off legislation that might injure them.

The head of the Executive is the President. Together with the Vice-President he is elected for a term of four years by an Electoral College, chosen for the purpose by the voters in each State. This College meets and votes not as one body but in the various State capitals. The voting is a mere formality, however, for by an inviolable tradition the delegates vote for the candidate favoured by a majority of their State electorate. Each State has as many votes in the College as it has members in Congress. Thus a small majority of the millions of voters in New York State is enough to give a presidential candidate the whole of its forty-seven votes.

This shows how constitution-planning can go astray in practice. The Founders thought that the College would consist of the wisest and best men in each State bringing calm wisdom to bear on the choosing of a President ; but this design was frustrated by party passions.

The President is the most powerful personage in the world. His functions combine those of our King and of our Prime Minister, and a great deal besides. He personifies the nation on all formal and ceremonial occasions. He is commander-in-chief of the Armed Forces. He appoints the Cabinet, and dominates their departments far more than a British Prime Minister dominates Whitehall. He appoints ambassadors and receives those of foreign Powers. He nominates hundreds —thousands—of officials, judges and dignitaries of all kinds. He has a veto on legislation, and although this can be over-ridden by a two-thirds majority in both Houses, he constantly exercises it.

The Cabinet consists of the heads of administrative departments whom the President is in the habit of consulting—the Secretary of

State (= Foreign Minister [1]), the Secretary of the Treasury, the Attorney-General, and so on. It usually meets once a week, but it has no collective policy and does not pool ideas to anything like the same extent as our Cabinet. And nobody save the President can call any member of it to account for his conduct of his office.

The Constitution is silent about presidential re-election. Most Presidents have been re-elected once, but until 1940 they followed the example set by Washington, who declined a third term on the ground that this would make the United States too much like a monarchy. But in 1940 the position of world-affairs made the American people feel the need to retain the services of an experienced statesman ; and in 1944 those conditions had still not passed away. This is not likely to be taken as a precedent, however ; for very few men have either the appetite or the stamina for more than eight years of such strain.

As to the Judicature, the result of the Founders' anxiety to make it independent of the other branches of Government resulted in the Federal Supreme Court, which wields almost sovereign power. It consists of nine judges appointed for life by the President, subject to Senate approval. Its prime function is to interpret the Constitution, and prevent its being violated by either President or Congress, or by any of the States. By a bare majority it can nullify any Act of Congress or of the State Legislatures ; and against its decision there is no appeal.

PARTY MACHINES.—Thus one notable contribution of the United States to democratic mechanism is in the development of federal government ; another is in the elaborate organisation of political Parties.

The most remarkable thing about the American Parties is that, despite the strength of the ties they create, it is very difficult to define the difference in principle between them. The Democratic Party can be traced back to Jefferson's stand for State-rights. Its stronghold was, and is, the South, where cotton and tobacco are grown for export. The Republican Party, on the other hand, is descended from Hamiltonian Whiggism, which stood for firm central government and high tariffs to preserve the home market for the rising industries of

---

[1] It may be recalled that at the date when the United States was founded the British Secretary of State was primarily a Foreign Minister. (See p. 46.)

the north and east. The modern Democrats have a liberal wing which prides itself on enlightenment and sympathises with the ' forgotten folk ' of the working-classes (though not with the claims of the negro to political and social equality) ; whereas present-day Republicanism holds by individual enterprise and big business and high finance, and asserts that the interests of Labour are best served by conditions that ensure high profits for Capital.

(Attempts to run an independent Labour Party have never come to much. For one thing, the old Parties have too strong a hold ; and, for another, American workers are not very ' class-conscious '—their leading spirits mostly have hopes of reaching the ' capitalist class ' themselves, some day.

There are two Trade Union organisations, the old-fashioned craft Unions of the American Federation of Labour under William Green, and the Committee for Industrial Organisation which some years back branched off under John L. Lewis, to pursue a more vigorous policy by enlisting all those engaged in each industry in the same organisation.

But many Republicans are as liberal in sentiment as any Democrat, while many Democrats (especially in the ' deep South ') are as conservative as any Republican. So it is not safe to push any characterisation of the Parties very far.

For instance, some Republicans were active supporters of President Roosevelt's ' New Deal ' (for the rationalisation of industry and the development of social services), while many Democrats were bitterly opposed to it as interference with individual liberty. And it is noteworthy that in this case it was a Democratic President who was calling for federal control and the Republican opposition that was upholding State Rights.

Party allegiance was greatly intensified by the system of ' The Spoils to the Victors ' which began (as a system) with the Presidency of Andrew Jackson in 1828. It became the custom for an incoming President to turn out all holders of Government jobs who did not belong to his Party. Thus, tens of thousands of people came to have a keen personal interest in the success of their Party at the polls, and subscription to its campaign-fund became an investment which might bring handsome returns. And the fact that (until 1912) Federal Senators were chosen by State Legislatures impelled the Parties to fight hard for the control of these too. Immensely wealthy and powerful 'Party Machines' were built up, with an elaborate hierarchy of committees, from Ward Primaries in cities to the National Convention which selects the Party's candidate for the Presidency.

There is a definite tendency to take posts in the public service 'out of politics' by making them permanent, and dependent on examination, like the British Civil Service. But Congress is reluctant to forgo its 'patronage,' and there is a strong tradition of 'senatorial courtesy' by which Senators are supported in nominating their Party friends to Federal offices within their own State.

Three circumstances made political parties root themselves deeply in American life. One was the rapid development of the States, as they spread westwards across the continent all through the middle of the nineteenth century. For this provided endless opportunities for the Party in power to keep itself there, by giving adherents posts in the public service and contracts for 'public utilities'—roads, drains, gas, water, electricity, civic buildings of all kinds. Another was the crowding in of European immigrants who, as strangers in a strange land, were delighted to find Party officials ready to welcome them, to smooth over their difficulties, to find them jobs, to keep them on the right side of the police, and get them enrolled as citizens —all in return for a mere promise to vote the Party ticket at election-times.

Since 1920 the United States has restricted immigration by quotas which regulate the racial elements poured into the melting-pot each year. A larger proportion is admitted from northern and western Europe than from southern and eastern. Except for a quota of Chinese the yellow races are no longer admitted at all.

The third stimulus to the Party spirit was that State and City constitution-makers, in the cult of 'pure democracy,' made many posts elective which in Britain are filled by higher powers. Judges, Magistrates, Mayors, State and District Attorneys, Treasurers, Surveyors and Police officials are mostly appointed by popular vote for terms short enough to keep the holders always in mind of their responsibility to the electorate. This not only provides more openings for jobbery than are available elsewhere, but so increases the number of offices to be voted for annually that the average voter cannot possibly weigh the merits of the candidates, and relieves himself from bewilderment by voting for the Party list *en bloc*. The handling of large Party funds, the dispensing of patronage to the best Party advantage, and the control of a hierarchy of Party officials, calls for very special aptitudes, and a local Party ' boss ' often has more power and prestige than the Mayor of a city or the Governor of a State—who may indeed, owe their positions to him.

In those States where one Party is in permanent control, the power to nominate its candidates is practically the power to choose the officials. So most States now hold Party ' Primary ' Elections, at which *candidates* are chosen, either by the electorate at large (' open Primaries ') or by registered Party members (' closed Primaries '). And this is certainly a more democratic way to select candidates than the common practice in this country of adopting candidates sent down by the Party machines in London.

Great Party festivals come in the summer of every fourth year, when delegates to the number of a thousand or more meet in National Convention to choose the Party's candidate for the Presidential election due in the following November. The delegates come charged with instructions from their State Convention to support some particular candidate, with alternatives in case the early ballots show that their first choice has no chance. Each Party holds its Convention in some great city, often in a building specially erected for the purpose. The proceedings, which take place in the presence of crowds of spectators, sometimes degenerate into a pandemonium of perspiring oratory, bannered processions, brass-bands blaring theme-tunes, loud-speakers shouting slogans, amid organised cheering and catcalls from the public galleries. But it often happens that the issue is eventually settled by bargains struck by the leaders behind the scenes ; and when two strong candidates have about equal support, an outsider may slip into the nomination.

The Convention is sometimes swayed less by a candidate's suitability for the great office of President than by his ' availability '—*i.e.* acceptability ; for the delegates have a strong interest in finding a candidate who will capture the greatest possible proportion of the floating vote which decides all popular elections. He must have 'personality,' but must be free from 'fads' or peculiar views, for these estrange more voters than they attract. And as the vote of a doubtful State may go in favour of its own sons, no candidate is likely to be chosen from a State which is permanently in the pocket of either Party, or from one which counts for little in the Electoral College.

Thus, neither Party is likely to choose one from Alabama : the Democrats know they can rely on Alabama to support any candidate they put up, while the Republicans know that no candidate of theirs would have any chance of its vote. And that vote is too small to be worth bothering about, anyway.

Thus candidates generally come from one of three or four big States of doubtful allegiance. Of the last ten Presidents four have come from Ohio and two from New York.

This may seem rather an odd way to choose candidates for the greatest elective post in the world ; but it is based on a deep-down democratic feeling that one sound American is as likely as another to make good in Governmental office, provided he has honesty and common sense. And it works. It brings to the White House as high an average of ability as the British system brings to Number 10 Downing Street.

To take the present century alone, T. R. Roosevelt, Taft, Woodrow Wilson, Harding, Coolidge, Hoover, F. D. Roosevelt and Truman compare satisfactorily as a group with Balfour, Campbell-Bannerman, Asquith, Lloyd George, Bonar Law, MacDonald, Baldwin, Chamberlain, Churchill and Atlee. And it will be noted that each democracy found a leader of distinction when it really needed one.

The American distrust of experts in office is shown by the fact that half the United States ambassadors are men who are not diplomatists by vocation.

The other tasks of the Party Convention are to choose a candidate for the Vice-Presidency, and to approve the election address to be laid before the nation. But the Vice-President, though he presides over the Senate, has practically a sinecure, unless the President dies during his term of office ; and the nomination often goes to some section of the Party which has given way over the nomination for the Presidency. As for the 'Platform' : with no broad differences of principle dividing the Parties, the ingenuity of the drafter is displayed mainly in avoiding definite commitments which might offend some section of the electorate.

As the negro railroad-car attendant pointed out to the politician who wanted to travel on the end platform—'a platform is not made to stand on, but to get in on.'

But we must not lose sight of the fact that this elaboration of party organisation is no part of the American Constitution. It is just the form which conditions in the United States have caused democracy to take there. And there is something in the blood of Americans, or in the air they breathe, that makes them do things thoroughly and go all out to win, whether in politics or business or sport, to a much greater extent than we British do.

CONGRESS AND PARLIAMENT.—How does the position of Congress differ from that of Parliament?

One notable difference we have already noticed—that Congress does not, like Parliament, rub shoulders with 'the Government.' Indeed, either or both of the Houses of Congress may be opposed to the President in Party or in policy.

Such a situation is not likely to arise during a President's first two years of office, for the same political wave that has sent him to the White House will probably have given his Party a majority in the House of Representatives which is elected at the same time, and have had some effect on the Senate (though only a third of it will have been elected then). But two years later another House, and another third of the Senate, will be elected, and this gives the nation a chance to express disapproval of the administration by sending to Washington members pledged to thwart it.

The President can make a formal address to Congress, and can bring to bear upon it public opinion which he has worked up by radio talks or press conferences but he cannot ensure that any Bill which he induced some supporter to bring in will take the shape that he desires ; nor can his Cabinet Ministers steer through measures affecting their Departments. Hence a divided responsibility. If an Act turns out badly the President can say : ' This is not the Act I asked for,' while Congress can say : ' The Act is all right, but you bungled the application.'

Then again, whereas Parliament can make laws about *anything*, Congress is restricted to those fields of legislation which the Constitution expressly assigns to it ; the others belong to the States.   And even within its own field the measures which it carries, sometimes after months of toil, may be summarily nullified by the Supreme Court.

This was forcibly exemplified in 1935–37.   President Roosevelt had been elected in 1932 with a mandate to pull the country out of the economic slough which had brought business to a standstill, closed hundreds of banks, and brought millions to destitution. His measures, improvising social services and taking control of business, were passed by substantial majorities in both Houses of Congress ; and at the election of 1936 the nation endorsed his policy by re-electing him by a record majority.   (He carried 46 of the 48 States.)   But the Supreme Court pronounced most of his ' National Recovery ' measures unconstitutional, by majorities of 5 to 4 or 6 to 3.   Yet when he tried to circumvent this veto upon the nation's will by enlarging the Court to 16 (which would have enabled him to get a majority of ' New Dealers ' on it), public opinion turned against him so strongly that he had to drop the idea. For the American people reverence the Supreme Court as a sort of priesthood dedicated to the preservation of the palladium of American liberties.

Fortunately for the New Deal, two Justices died, and two more retired at the age-limit of 75, and thus F.D.R. was able to obtain a friendly majority on the Court without altering its constitution.

Another difference between the two legislatures is that members of Congress have to belong to the State which they represent, and Representatives must by an unwritten law be citizens of their electoral district.   Thus a man, however able and ambitious, may find himself shut out of Congress altogether if he happens to belong to a State in which his Party is in a permanent minority—no Vermont Democrat has the smallest chance of ever getting into Congress.   And it is nearly as fatal to belong to a State where one's Party abounds in able men—there are ten thousand able Republicans in Pennysylvania for every available seat in Congress.   More-over, the fact that if a member loses his seat he cannot find another, puts him under the thumb of the Party Managers in his constituency.

The legislative process is much the same in both systems, but more of it falls to Standing Committees at Washington than at Westminster.   This means that the average Congressman gets less chance to shine in public, but more chance to exert influence on Committees. The House of Representatives regards itself not as a talking body but as a deciding body, and it relies on its Committees to appraise the merits of the Bills that come before it.

The House has about fifty Standing Committees—one for every conceivable subject of every conceivable degree of importance : Ways and Means, Appropriations, Commerce, Rivers and Harbours, Postal Affairs, Naval Affairs, Invalid Pensions, and so on. It is the Speaker who nominates the House Committees, and being more of a Party man than his opposite number at Westminster, he sees to it that his Party has a controlling majority, including the chairmanship, of all important ones. There is more summoning of witnesses and hearing of outside views for and against a measure than there is in our system. Cabinet ministers may be sent for, or may ask to be heard.

In Parliament nine-tenths of the legislation is sponsored by the Government, which controls the time-table ; and no private member can make any proposal which would involve the spending of public money. In Congress there are no such restrictions ; and one result of this is the gathering round the ' Pork Barrel '—the promotion by Members of Bills to benefit their constituents out of Federal coffers, by establishing a naval shipyard, or by an irrigation scheme, or a canal or an airfield or something of the sort. Such Bills are sometimes pushed through by ' log-rolling '—by members making bargains to back each other's Bills. And ' lobbying ' is much more developed than at Westminster. Some ' interests ' maintain permanent offices at Washington, and employ full-time lobbyists to approach Members, persuade them, argue with them, arrange ' trades ' with them, organise the mass despatch of postcards and telegrams to them from their con-stituents. Some ' lobbies ' are supported by philanthropic institutions, such as the Anti-Saloon League, but others work for personal or business interests.

For instance, a combined lobby run by the Railways held up for years the compulsory use of safety devices.

The President's veto stops many of these private bills—in fact, Congressmen sometimes promote them rather to advertise themselves to their constituents than with any expectation that they will actually be enacted. But millions of dollars are squandered annually on the projects that do get through.

Bills to grant *ex gratia* pensions to individual ' veterans ' of the Civil War and their widows were still costing the country an average of $100,000,000 a year at the beginning of this century.

The Senate of the United States is the only second chamber in the world whose powers tend to increase rather than diminish. It is now far more powerful than our House of Lords. For the Lords cannot touch the money-bills which occupy nearly half the time of the Commons ; and though they do useful work in re-examining bills that the time-pressed Commons have had to rush through, their share in legislation is negligible. But the Senate stands on a level with the House of Representatives in all respects, save that it does not *initiate* money-bills. Its Standing Committees are at least as important as those of the House ; some of them—*e.g.* the Foreign Affairs Committee —far more important. And special Senate Committees of inquiry are more effective than such Committees of the House can be, inasmuch as they are more stable in membership.

Parliament sometimes sets up such committees, too, but it has less occasion for them since the Departments are under constant fire at Question Time. One recent Senate Committee which might well have had a counterpart over here was the Nye Committee on the private manufacture of arms. This was designed by its promoter and chairman, Senator Nye of North Dakota, as isolationist propaganda ; but it revealed evils which are not peculiar to America. It called for papers and accounts and witnesses (some of them very reluctant) from business houses, banking-firms and Government Departments ; and its report revealed that some firms had pushed the sale of munitions to potential enemies of the United States ; had employed secret agents to obstruct an international conference for naval disarmament ; and had bribed officials to give secret information which enabled them to make enormous profits out of the United States War and Navy Departments.

The Founders of the Constitution made one important exception to the Separation of Powers : they gave the Senate a hold over the President's conduct of Foreign Affairs. For the great point of the Separation was to prevent despotism, and it did not seem safe to leave one man in sole control of the nation's foreign policy for four years. So the President's appointments to foreign embassies are subject to the approval of the Senate, and all treaties have to be endorsed by a two-thirds majority there.

The most famous modern example of a treaty failing to be ratified was the Treaty of Versailles, which included the League of Nations. There was a majority of 49–35 in favour of it, but as this was less than two-thirds the Treaty was rejected and the United States remained outside the League. And, as we all know, the League, thus weakened at the outset, fell into a decay which involved the world, including the United States, in another Great War. But it may be argued that this rejection was in accordance with the general feeling of the nation, just as the House of Lords represented the feelings of the British nation in rejecting the Home Rule Bill in 1893.

Senators loom larger in the American firmament than Peers do in ours. Nobody takes special notice of what the average Peer thinks about things, whereas a Senator's views always have ' news-value.' And most Congressmen would like to become Senators, whereas for Members of Parliament a Peerage marks retirement from the arena of active politics.

BRITAIN AND AMERICA.—American foreign policy has always been based on Washington's famous warning against ' the insidious wiles of foreign influence ' and ' political connection with foreign nations.' His figure looms rather more than life-size in American traditions, and his words have been treated as oracles of unfading wisdom, as applicable to the twentieth as to the eighteenth century. Moreover Americans have been fully occupied at home, with vast territories to develop and no potential enemy within striking distance, thousands of miles away from European affairs. And their prevailing isolationism was intensified when, after a brief departure from it, they felt that their Government had been tricked into going to war and in making peace. They refused to join the League, and cited the evil results of this action as proofs of the wisdom of this refusal.

When the Fascist dictators began to stir up trouble in Europe, influential groups in Congress played up the general desire to keep out of it, to put through the Neutrality Acts. They argued that America had been drawn into the last war by the fact that her business men had supplied war-material to the Allies on credit, and feared to lose their money ; and by the indignation aroused when U-boats, to prevent these supplies from reaching Europe, sank American shipping. So these Acts forbade the supply of war-material (which in these

days of total war comprises almost everything) to all bel-
ligerents.   President Roosevelt tried to insert a clause enabling
him to discriminate against an ' aggressor,' but the isolationists
would have none of it.   America was to make no distinction
between the thieves and the man who fell among them, but
was to pass resolutely by on the other side.

The White House and the State Department in Washington
are separated from the Capitol, the home of Congress, only by the
length of Pennsylvania Avenue, but that street may be spiritually
a thousand miles long.   For the President and the Secretary of
State are daily receiving messages from all over the world, whereas the mail of members of Congress comes mainly from their
constituents, whose outlook is, to put it mildly, rather more
restricted.

It would be an impertinence for us to blame this attitude,
but we may seek reasons for it.   Broadly speaking, there are
two.   In the first place, a large proportion of Americans are
only a generation or two from immigrants who left Europe
to get away from the conditions that prevailed there, and do not
want to hear anything more about them.   In the second place,
Americans felt secure, assured that the misfortunes of Europe
could never affect them if they held aloof and left Europeans
to wallow in the results of their perverse quarrelsomeness.

And we may well ask ourselves if the British attitude was
not very similar, as long as Hitler allowed it to be.   Some of
our newspapers ran a ' crusade ' adjuring us to mind our
imperial business and quit the League—and such newspapers
only give their readers what those readers want.   The famous
Oxford Union resolution was as typical of the sceptical (or
should we call it cynical ?) attitude of the young people of
this country as of the United States during the twenty years'
truce between the wars.   Our own rulers were as insistent
upon non-discrimination between right and wrong in Abyssinia
and Spain as Senators Vandenberg and Nye ; and it was a
British Prime Minister who excused indifference to the murder
of a small nation by pointing out that they were ' far-off people
of whom we know very little.'

To be sure, we were a little quicker than the United States
to see that this policy was unsafe—but then we were geo-
graphically much closer to the dangers it entailed.   And long

before December 7, 1941, America had realised that the world had shrunk since 1795. She had already modified, then repealed, the Neutrality Act, and had inaugurated Lend-Lease, which in its first stages was, as our Prime Minister said, the most generous deed ever done by one nation to another.

And now, to quote Churchill again, let us go forward together.

CHAPTER XV

OTHER DEMOCRACIES : II. THE U.S.S.R.

HOW COMMUNISM BECAME EMBODIED IN A NOVEL FORM OF DEMOCRACY

PREACHERS of revolution seldom foresee where their doctrines will lead. Marx and Lasalle expected the overthrow of Capitalism to begin in the countries where it was most developed, and therefore, by their theory, nearest to decay ; whereas it came in Russia, industrially one of the most backward countries in Europe, and has not so far spread elsewhere. Moreover, the Russian Communist state was given an unexpected form by the remarkable men to whom the opportunity came of putting the gospel into practice. And since then it has developed on lines that would have greatly surprised them.

RED OCTOBER.—At the beginning of 1917 the Tsarist regime collapsed of its own rottenness. It had long been fantastically out of date. Traces of serfdom, abolished only sixty years earlier, were still visible in the social, economic and spiritual condition of the people. The autocratic government refused to share its powers with an effective parliament ; it fettered the people by repressive laws and secret police ; it scarcely tapped the vast resources of the country ; it kept the people illiterate ; it was corrupt and inefficient beyond relief. When these evils led to the military disasters of the Japanese War (1904) Tsarism was threatened with overthrow. Revolutionary movements had long been spreading among the educated classes, but the political police kept them underground and drove the leaders into exile ; and in 1906 the Government once more succeeded in suppressing the symptoms of revolt.

But the far greater strain of the war of 1914 broke down the governmental machine altogether. The nation was subjected to terrible losses and sufferings. The troops lacked arms and munitions and clothing ; there were three million casualties in two years ; the civil population died like flies of starvation. By taking personal command of the army the Tsar made himself responsible for its defeats. In February 1917 a conspiracy of high officers and nobles forced him to abdicate in favour of a provisional government under one of themselves. But this was coincident with a bread-riot in Petersburg (later re-named Leningrad) which gave the Socialists a chance to come into the open and set up a ' soviet ' or work-men's council. With authority thus divided, confusion para-lysed the government ; and soon a new element was thrown into the seething pot.

In 1905 a conference of exiled Russian Socialists, which opened in Brussels but was transferred after trouble with the Belgian police to London, had split into factions. The majority (*bolshevik*) party followed the Marxian thesis that capitalism must be overthrown by violence, while the minority (*menshevik*) aimed at reform rather than revolution. The leader of the *bolsheviks* was Lenin,[1] who lived in Switzerland develop-ing plans for putting Marxism into practice. He was little known outside the circles of international Socialism until in May 1917 the German High Command decided to repatriate him in the hope that his activities would compel Russia to get out of the war. At Petersburg he made contact with other returned revolutionaries including Leo Trotsky, who had been in Canada.

There is generally a leftward tendency in revolutions. The Liberal aristocrats who aimed at a constitutional monarchy were ousted in May by Kerensky, who wanted to set up a middle-class republic like that of France ; and in October he in turn was ousted by the revolutionary Communism with which Lenin and Trotsky had inoculated the Petersburg Soviet. The 'Bread and Peace ' which they offered were just what the people wanted. Every detail of the seizure of power was worked out with military precision by Trotsky. At the appointed moment the Government buildings were captured—it all went 'like a piece of music played from notes.' Kerensky fled, and a Congress of Soviets gave authority to a committee of Bolshevik Commissars with Lenin as its chairman.

The new Government entrenched itself by terror. The peasantry were incited to murder their landlords and seize the

---

[1] His original name was Vladimir Ulianov. The Bolsheviks often adopt " revolutionary names."

land, and the new Government set up a ' Supreme Commission to Combat Counter-revolution,' commonly called the ' Cheka, which (like the Committee of Public Safety in the French Revolution) kept reaction at bay by the summary trial and execution of persons suspected of hostility to the new government. The promised peace had to be purchased by the treaty of Brest-Litovsk, which cost Russia some of its most valuable territory.

The old regime fought back for nearly three years longer. At first it was supported by France, Britain and the United States, partly to prevent the spread of Communism, and partly from concern for money invested in Tsarist Russia. But the ' White ' forces were not under a single command, and Trotsky showed amazing genius in organising and inspiring ' Red ' armies. When early in 1920 the Allies withdrew their support, the White armies disintegrated, and the Revolution was safe—for the time being, at any rate.

THE SOVIET STATE.—In giving substance to the Marxist design for a Communist state, Lenin wove a number of existing institutions and familiar ideas into a new fabric. In July 1918 he issued the Fundamental Law of the Russian Socialist Federative Soviet Republic, beginning with a declaration of the Rights of the Labouring and Exploited Classes.

I. Russia is a republic of soviets of workers', soldiers' and peasants' deputies. All central and local authority is vested in these soviets.

II. The Russian Soviet Republic is established as a free federation of national soviet republics.

III. With the fundamental aim of suppressing all exploitation of man by man, of abolishing the division of society into classes, of . . . bringing about the socialist organisation of society, the All-Russian Congress of Soviets further decrees :

(a) Private ownership of land is abolished ; all land is declared national property and is handed over to the labouring masses, without compensation, giving the right of use only.

(b) All forests, underground mineral wealth, all live-stock and appurtenances . . . are proclaimed national property.

(c) As first step towards the complete transfer of factories, workshops, mines, railways and other means of production and distribution to the ownership of the Republic . . . the authority of the Supreme Economic Council is confirmed.

'A Republic of Soviets' was a novel form of democracy. It was in 1906 that the word 'soviet' began to be associated with meetings in village or factory for the election of committees to co-operate in promoting the revolutionary movement. These early soviets were suppressed, but the idea sprang to life again in 1917. Up to then the Bolsheviks had not proposed to set up anything more original than some very democratic form of parliament ; but during that fateful summer Lenin came to see that a system of soviets would be much better suited to a population of 150 millions, very varied in race and language, mostly illiterate, and wholly unused to political liberty. Mass-meetings of village or factory or regiment could by show of hands send delegates to county soviets, who could send delegates to the provincial soviets, who could send delegates to a national soviet, which could appoint a 'Council of People's Commissars' to carry on the actual work of government ; and the stream of power which gathered volume in passing upward through this pyramid would return down through it in the form of laws and 'directives.' There would be no distinction between legislative and executive, or between central and local functions—the soviets would exercise them all. And the economic control which the government assumed under the Fundamental Law could be administered by similar pyramids of Trade Unions, Collective Farms and Co-operative Stores, each with its apex in Moscow.

The classless society at which the Communists aim is only now beginning to be realised. Soviet Russia was long the most caste-ridden country in the world. Manual labourers formed its aristocracy. A Trade Union card entitled its holder to preferential treatment for everything from cheap travel to university education. Black-coated workers and professional men were disfranchised. As for the 'idle rich,' they were liquidated.

Marx had always foreseen that the ignorant and apathetic multitude would in early years of the Communist Republic require a leaven of instructed devotees to guide and inspire it, and after their October triumph the Bolsheviks transformed themselves into a 'Communist Party' for just this purpose. The word 'Party' must not mislead us. This is no political party contending with other political parties for the right to govern the country. It is more like a religious Order.

Membership—attained after a period of probation and lost by misconduct or slackness—calls for higher standard of Communist ethics than is expected from the common herd. Its members must take up and perform diligently any special duties assigned to them by higher authority ; and at all times it is their duty to stimulate, instruct, exhort, and set an example of zeal and devotion without pay or reward except a consciousness of moral influence and of service in a great cause. There are about five million members (*i.e.* about 3 per cent. of the population) including the Comsomols, the 'Young Communists League.'

Naturally, Party-members, being an *élite* of the most active and intelligent citizens, are often elected to paid posts under the Soviets and in the management of Trade Unions and Collective Farms ; but the great majority continue to work in factory or on the farm. Of course they get subsistence-pay when engaged on full-time work for the party, and free facilities for travel by rail, car or aeroplane. But no Government or Party job in Soviet Russia is much better paid than that of the skilled mechanic.

The Party is itself a pyramid, based on units of from two or three to a dozen or more in each workshop or mine or farm or regiment. At the top is a Central Committee at Moscow. Officially this Committee takes no part in the government of the Republic—it has no direct voice in the selection of the People's Commissars, or in the management of Trade Unions and Co-operatives. But its members are also the directors of policy in these other bodies ; for everybody who is anybody in the Republic is a Party-member, and all owe obedience to the decisions taken in its Central Committee. Its power is unseen—it is not even mentioned in the Fundamental Law of the Russian Socialist Federated Soviet Republic (1918) or the Constitution (1923) ; but that invisibility makes it the more irresistible. During the 1930's Kalinin as Chairman of the Presidium of the Supreme Soviet was the ceremonial head of the Republic, but far greater power was wielded by Stalin, who until 1941 was merely General Secretary to the Central Committee of the Party.

THE UNION.—No sooner had the Red Republic beaten off its external enemies than it had to cope with an economic crisis. A Supreme Economic Council had been set up to 'socialise' the production and distribution of goods ; but the members had to buy their experience, and their tasks, in a population of 150 millions spread across two continents with very poor communications, would have baffled the most practised of administrators. The result of their enthusiastic meddling and muddling was a spectacular chaos. The peasant farmers who formed three-fourths of the population had been eager to seize the land, but stoutly refused to communise the crops ; and they countered attempts at enforcement by producing only enough for their own use. Thus there was no surplus to feed the town workers, and industrial production fell far below the very low pre-war level. Trotsky tried to turn his armies into Labour Corps, but economic facts refused to be drilled. Revolts were followed by wholesale executions to enforce respect for the Government. During the winter of 1921-2 the worst famine in the history of Russia was followed by raging pestilence.

One of Lenin's greatest qualities was his readiness to admit mistakes. He saw that the new system was going too fast, and in 1922 he started the ' New Economic Policy ' (NEP for short). In the country the peasants were allowed to sell their produce for what it would fetch, after paying their taxes in kind ; in the towns private traders (' Nepmen ') were allowed to do business side by side with the Co-operative Stores.

A particularly striking innovation in the Russian Socialist Federated Soviet Republic was the reversal of the Tsarist attempt to Russify the non-Russian parts of the Empire. That is the meaning of Clause II of the Declaration of 1919. Marx had regarded patriotism as beneath the spirit of high-souled Communism, but Lenin accepted the facts of human nature and used national feeling to strengthen the Soviet Republic. He established a Commissariat of Nationalities and put in charge of it one of the ablest of his lieutenants—Joseph Stalin, himself a Georgian, who did not learn to speak Russian till he was grown up.[1] Under him the submerged peoples of Greater Russia and Siberia were encouraged to keep their own speech, manners and customs. Books were printed in fifty languages, for some of which alphabets had to be specially invented. And each of the nationalities was proud to elect a soviet like those established in the provinces of the Russian Socialist

---

[1] His personal name is Yossif Vissarionovich Djugashvilli.

Federated Soviet Republic, and to send a delegation to the Supreme Soviet at Moscow.

In 1923 the outlying European Provinces—the Ukraine, White Russia and Transcaucasia—had settled down after the civil war and had adopted soviet governments, and the time had come to federalise them into a Union of Socialist Soviet Republics. We need not examine it in detail, for it has since been superseded ; but its main feature was an All-Union Congress of Soviets, which met occasionally at Moscow to approve with tumultuous unanimity the reports of the People's Commissars, and to elect (under Party guidance) a Council of Union chosen on a population basis, and a Council of Nationalities, which consisted of ten deputies from each ' Union Republic ' and five from each of the satellite states which Stalin had set up in the Russian Socialist Federated Soviet Republic ; and these conjointly chose a Central Executive Committee, which wielded sovereign power in the name of the Supreme Soviet.

The four original Union Republics in Europe were later joined by five in Asia, and during the second Great War five more were added in Europe (Karelia, Estonia, Latvia, Lithuania and Bessarabia).

The smaller states (later graded into ' Autonomous Republics,' ' Autonomous Regions,' ' Regions,' ' Oblasts ' and ' Krais ') were given separate representation, nominally on the same basis as the Union Republics. But the Union of Socialist Soviet Republics is not a federation in the same sense as the United States of America. The Russian Socialist Federated Soviet Republic, which covers 6·3 million square miles of the 8·3 million square miles of the whole Union of Socialist Soviet Republics, is a very predominant partner. Moreover the central government housed in the Kremlin controls industrial, agricultural and commercial activities which in other countries are run by private firms ; above all it controls the political police, the OGPU, successor to the Cheka. And another centralising force is the fact that nearly half the Commissars of the various Republics are sent down from Moscow—presumably to see that the Councils do nothing contrary to the policy of the Union of Socialist Soviet Republics —*i.e.* of the Communist Party.

The Constitution expressly gave the Union Republics the right to secede ; but as such a suggestion has more than once been treated as ' counter-revolutionary activity,' this appears to be a fiction. (That, however, does not in itself weaken the claim of the USSR to be a federation, or we should have to exclude the U.S.A. from that category !)

Still, we British have something to learn from the Soviet method of raising up primitive peoples. Before the Revolution the races of Central Asia were nearly as backward as the African races of our Empire. But there is no prejudice about race or colour in the USSR ; nor, since no money can be made from ' investments,' is there any economic motive for exploiting backward races.

Lenin wore himself out in creating the Republic. In 1923 he was struck down by paralysis, and in the following year he died. His body lies embalmed in a great tomb in the Red Square, Moscow, and thousands of Russians make pilgrimages to it every year.

There followed a struggle for supremacy between Trotsky and Stalin. Trotsky was a clever cosmopolitan Jew, a brilliant orator with a wide experience of men and affairs. Stalin was a country-bred man with no pretensions to wit or eloquence, but he was a pertinacious worker behind the scenes and had all the strings of the Party in his hands. The personal rivalry focused on a vital question of future policy. Trotsky still held the view of the original Bolsheviks—that the Communist revolution must be spread as quickly as possible all over the world by Comintern.

Comintern was the abbreviated name of the Third Communist International, with its headquarters in Moscow. It was really little more than the propaganda department of the Soviet Republic, for the Communist parties in other countries mostly held aloof from it.

But events had shown that there was no immediate prospect of world revolution, and Stalin suddenly—some time after March 1924—decided to set the idea aside and concentrate on making the Union of Socialist Soviet Republics a shining example of a communistic state. Trotsky fought hard, but the forces at his rival's command were too strong for him. He was driven out of the Government, then out of the Party, and finally out of the country. And this turned out to be the most important event in the history of Soviet Russia.

'SCIENTIFIC HUMANISM.'—In this book our main concern is with politics, but a people's political institutions reflect its outlook on life. The philosophy of Soviet Russia is materialist. It accepts nothing as true, good and beautiful save what can be apprehended by the senses. It rejects belief in the supernatural as a soporific which deadens the will of the toiling and suffering masses to throw off their shackles. Hence the ruthless extermination of the Orthodox clergy (who were, moreover, associated with the Tsarist regime), and the teaching of atheism as part of the curriculum in schools.

Christianity was replaced by Scientific Humanism—the remaking of man by the development of his intellect and character, and the quest of his well-being by the increasing of his power over nature through his advancing knowledge of the universe.

It begins with the care of the young, which starts before they are born by the most elaborate provision for motherhood, and places the best available education within the reach of all. It is seen in the complete equality of the sexes. Public money is poured out for scientific research and development. Whereas before 1917 there were only thirty institutes for such work, and these mostly half-starved, there are now well over a thousand, and some—e.g. those for medical research, for the study of the brain, for Endocrinology and for Röntgenology—are the most lavishly equipped in the world. Education has a strong bias towards the practical—medicine, applied mathematics, chemistry and physics, electrical, mechanical and civil engineering.

But this does not mean that Communist 'Humanism' ignores things of the spirit. On the contrary, large subsidies are given to book-publishing (especially text-books), to museums and picture galleries, to drama, music and the ballet.

THE FIVE-YEAR PLANS.—In capitalist countries industrial expansion was brought about by private persons acting individually for their own interest ; but in the Socialist Republic it had to be set going by the State, and the State had to have a plan. In 1918 Lenin had set up a Planning Commission (GOSPLAN) which in the course of the next ten years grew to 150 members with a staff of over a thousand engineers and statisticians, and branches in each of the Republics. As soon as Stalin's supremacy was secure in 1928 he set this organisation to work on the greatest piece of economic planning ever conceived. It was designed to fulfil the ultimate purpose of the Revolution, the lifting of the workers out of their primordial poverty, by an Industrial Revolution carried through, not by capitalists competing for profits during a century or more, but by a few years of intense effort and self-denial for the common good. The old Russia had been extremely backward mechanically, and its few engineers and technicians had mostly shared the fate of other 'bourgeois' during the Revolution. A start had to be made with the basic industries—coal, steel, electricity and mineral oil. To lay down the plan for this entailed a capital expenditure of something like five thousand millions sterling. Other Governments might have raised loans at home or abroad, but in Russia nobody had anything to lend, and the Soviet State had destroyed its foreign credit by repudiating the Tsarist public debt. So the imported machine-tools had to be paid for by exports of timber and wheat while the Russian people went cold and hungry.

On the agricultural side, production could only be secured by large-scale farming with tractors, which entailed turning village-lands (in many parts still under strip-culture) into great collective farms (*kolkhoses*). The better-off peasants (*kulaks*) who resisted this process were condemned as un-social persons and carried off by the OGPU to work—usually to die—in the timber-camps of the frozen North, or to dig the White Sea ship-canal.

The *kulaks* seem to have made themselves very unpopular with their poorer neighbours, but their elimination was quite as cruel as anything that happened under the Tsars. On the other hand, we shall do well to consider whether the short and sharp upheaval of the Five-Year Plan caused as much suffering to as many people as our own long-drawn-out process of enclosures and industrialisation.

Early in 1932 it was announced that the First Five-Year Plan was completed ; but the net result was admittedly disappointing : quantity had been gained at the expense of quality, and the new machines were constantly breaking down under inexperienced handling. The Planners seemed to have suffered from a kind of megalomania, based on the idea that the bigger the undertakings the more likely to be successful. The average size of the original *kolkhoses* was about a quarter of a million acres ! And the Great Slump, which nobody

could have foreseen, completely nullified those parts of the
Plan that depended on external trade. However, the Second
Five-Year Plan, now set going, made use of the experience so
painfully gained. A certain amount of consumption-goods
could now be made, and the workers began to enjoy some return
for their labours and privations, until the rise of Nazism compelled the Soviet Government to build up its defences.

The growth of industry gave increased importance to
Trade Unions. But since production was not for private
profit, their whole method and purpose differ from those of
Unions in capitalist countries. The prosperity of the worker
depends in Soviet Russia not on the proportion of the produce
that can be squeezed out of the proprietor, but on the aggregate
production of the industry. Nobody but the worker (by
hand or brain) had any right to a share in its profits, so the
interest of all is to increase productivity. The Unions are
neither ' Craft ' nor ' Industrial ' ; they are ' Employment '
Unions. All the employees of an establishment constitute a
branch of the Union that caters for that particular industry.
There is a factory committee with a whole-time secretary
(generally but not necessarily a Party-man) which is in constant touch with the management (which also may include
Party-men) respecting conditions of labour—sanitation, ventilation, canteens, transportation, club and educational facilities,
crêches (a large proportion of the workers are women) and so
on. Above this base there is a pyramid of committees like
those of the Soviets and of the Party, each selected by the one
below and transmitting the orders of the one above, up to an
All-Union Congress of Trade Unions which meets every two
years to elect an All-Union Central Committee (AUCCTU) in
permanent session in Moscow. This deals with the disputes
(of which there are plenty) between the Unions, and super-
vises their bargains with the various Commissariats about the
proportion of the produce of each industry to be spent on wages,
on expansion of the plant, in payment of the Turnover Tax
(the chief source of revenue in the Union of Soviet Socialist
Republics) and on the Social Services. The AUCCTU also
works out with the Executive Committees of the various Unions
—there are about 150 of them, all with offices in Moscow—
the grades of payment in each industry.

Stalin soon educated the workers out of the idea that all men ought to get equal wages, whatever their work. Special skill has great ' rarity-value ' in the USSR, and young workers are given every opportunity and encouragement to acquire it. In some industries there are eight grades.

There are two further distinctive features of Soviet Trade Unionism. Since in these factories and farms increased production does not rob comrades of jobs and does not enrich shareholders, workers are ready to vie with each other for the general good. This is known as ' Socialist Competition.' In some of the great industrial towns there are ' Shock Brigades ' (*udariniki*) with specially high standards, who are given great privileges by their Unions, the Government and the Party, with publicity in Press and on Radio, the insignia of the ' Order of Red Labour ' and special accommodation in trams and trains and living accommodation and communal restaurants.

A Donbas miner named Stekanov became a national hero because he raised the output of his gang from the customary 20 or 25 tons per shift to 50 or 60, and on one memorable occasion sent 105 tons to the pithead in 7 hours. ' Stekhanovism ' has since spread to other industries.

Secondly, it is the Trade Unions that work the elaborate social services, which include full employment-pay and sick pay, comprehensive medical services, maternity and funeral benefits, old-age pensions and holiday homes.

The maintenance of the working-man, his wife and children, in good times and bad, is the first charge on the annual production of the whole community. Of course, the more that is spent on the ' socialist wage ' of these services, the less dividend there will be for his ' personal wage '—but the fewer calls there will be on it. This is a frequent subject for disputation at Trade Union meetings —the Russians love arguing.

THE STALIN REPUBLIC.—Under Stalin the Union has grown into something that would have astonished—perhaps unpleasantly—the men of October. Lenin is still revered as its founder, but most of his old comrades have disappeared, and Trotsky called his book on the revised Republic *The Revolution Betrayed*. There is no sign of the Marxist ' withering away of the State.' With the whole of the country's agriculture and industry and communication under ' People's Commissars directed by the Party Executive, the Kremlin has a tighter grip on the daily lives of its subjects than any other Government in the world. And the Constitution of 1936, initiated and devised by Stalin, has eliminated many characteristic features of the original Soviet State. In some ways it seemed to point out to the rest of the world that there is nothing alarming about Soviet Democracy after all. It abolished the Soviet pyramid in favour of direct election ; it substituted the civilised ballot for the crude show-of-hands ; it gave the vote to the 'deprived classes'—the clergy, the bourgeois and former proprietors (what was left of them).

To be sure, these concessions to western ideas did not go quite so far as they seemed. ' Direct Election by Universal Suffrage ' does not amount to much when only one candidate is nominated, and that one candidate is selected in ' primaries ' controlled by the Party. Nor is the ballot of any great significance when it is used only in the ' voting ' for the single candidate.

The Stalin Constitution mentions the Communist Party by name—the first time this has occurred in any State Paper. Article 125, after setting forth the right of citizens to unite in trade unions, co-operatives, organisations for sport and defence, and for cultural, technical and scientific interests, declares that ' the most active and politically-conscious citizens . . . unite in the All-Union Communist Party (of Bolsheviks) which is the vanguard of the working people in their struggle to strengthen and develop the socialist system.' The vital point of the clause is the omission from the list of permitted societies of any other political organisation.

The framework of the Constitution of the USSR, as laid down in 1936, consists of a Supreme Soviet of two chambers, elected by universal direct suffrage. (About four-fifths of the members belong to the Party.) This Supreme Soviet only meets occasionally. Between-whiles it commits its Sovereign power to an executive ' Presidium,' which controls the Council of People's Commissars (SOVNARKOM). This has now about forty members, of whom more than half are concerned with economic production, distribution and transport. Its Chairman was formerly Molotov, who was also Commissar for Foreign Affairs ; but the position was taken over in May 1941 by the Secretary of the Communist Party, Stalin.

Each of the constituent Union Republics, and the other local states has similar organs of government for its own affairs.

As to the Party, Lenin would scarcely recognise it. Most of the survivors of Red October have been expelled, or more forcibly removed, as hostile to the Stalin regime, and their names are either ignored or vilified in the official histories of the Revolution. Nowadays 90 per cent. of the Party Officials are under forty years of age ; the lower age-limit for admission has been reduced to eighteen, and the probation period to three months ; and young people can qualify for membership by prowess in war or industry.

But country-folk still seem to be suspected of disaffection. Though only a quarter of the population are town-dwellers, three-quarters of the Party are in that category—22 per cent. from Moscow and Leningrad, which have only 2½ per cent. of the population.

And Comintern, after struggling along in semi-obscurity for years, has now been dissolved—a tacit announcement that the Union of Socialist Soviet Republics has given up the idea of quickly converting the world to Communism.

The Red Army, too, developed under the threats of Fascist Powers into something very different from the informal militia which was Lenin's ideal. Nowadays officers are saluted, and have batmen, and wear rank-badges on shoulder straps, and belong to exclusive officers' clubs. But Stalin has taken advantage of having the young men of the Republic under arms to educate them in Communist theory and culture, so that when they return to civil life they spread the gospel in their villages and factories.

Then again Stalin had begun to discourage the militant atheism of the early days even before the sufferings of the War had revived the religious instincts of what is by tradition the most devout people in Europe. Even Party-members are no longer required to be 100 per cent. Godless.

Some of these changes are really aspects of a great revival of Russian patriotism. This does not mean that Stalin would ever go back to the policy of general Russification ; but whereas in the early documents of the regime the word ' Russia ' is carefully omitted, Russians are nowadays encouraged to remember the rock from which they are hewn. In 1937 a new textbook of history was produced for the schools, acclaiming the military glories of the monarchy—how Alexander Nevsky destroyed the German invaders at Novgorod, how Peter the Great made Russia a European Power, how it was ' 1812 ' that marked the beginning of the end for Napoleon, and even how in the first Great War Brussilov invaded Austria-Hungary. The centenary of the death of Pushkin in 1937 gave the Union of Socialist Soviet Republics the opportunity to show the world how a national poet should be honoured. The names of Kutuzov and Suvarov were given to military Orders of Honour. And in 1943 the Communist 'Internationale' was replaced as a National Anthem by a song extolling 'Russia the Great.'

INDEX